CW01512687

The Sensuous Cinema
of Wong Kar-wai

The Sensuous Cinema of Wong Kar-wai

Film Poetics and the Aesthetic of Disturbance

Gary Bettinson

HKU PRESS
香港大學出版社

Hong Kong University Press
The University of Hong Kong
Pokfulam Road
Hong Kong
www.hkupress.org

© Hong Kong University Press 2015

ISBN 978-988-8139-29-3 (*Hardback*)

British Library Cataloguing-in-Publication Data

A catalogue record for this book is available from the British Library.

10 9 8 7 6 5 4 3 2 1

Printed and bound by Paramount Printing Co., Ltd. in Hong Kong, China

For my parents

Contents

Acknowledgments

I am indebted to a number of people for their help in bringing this book to fruition. In particular, I must thank Murray Smith, as unerring a mentor as one could wish for, and David Bordwell, for his steadfast generosity and enduring inspiration. I owe a special thanks to my colleagues at Lancaster University, especially Richard Rushton. Thanks also to Catherine Grant for astute comments on early draft portions of this book. I am likewise grateful to the anonymous readers for their careful comments and criticisms and to Christy Leung, Clara Ho, Carrie Watterson, and the editorial team at Hong Kong University Press for their encouragement and diligence.

In recent years I have presented my research on Wong Kar-wai at various conferences and symposia, and I am grateful to audiences at the University of California, Los Angeles; the University of Glasgow; Queen Mary University of London; Queens University, East Sussex; Coventry University; Beijing Normal University; the University of Shanghai; National Central University in Taiwan; Assumption University in Thailand; and the University of Pecs in Hungary. In 2010 I undertook research on this book as scholar-in-residence in the David C. Lam Institute for East-West Studies at Hong Kong Baptist University, where I would particularly like to thank Emilie Yueh-yu Yeh. Since 2007 I have taught a course on Hong Kong cinema, and I am grateful to my students for many spirited discussions of Wong Kar-wai and Hong Kong movies.

Additional thanks go to Michael Grant, Debbie Andrews, Nigel Mather, Yiping Lin, Timmy Chen, Kristof Van Den Troost, Wing-Ho Lin, Yvonne Teh, Tim Youngs, Law Kar, Shan Ding, Bey Logan, David Chiang Da-wei, and Peter Chan.

Sarah Sardar, Russell Sardar, Nicola Tapsell, Rob Greens, and Peter Masters have my love and friendship always. Last but not least, I thank my family— Shirley, Robert, Paul, Tracy, and Lucie—for more than words can express.

1 | Wong Kar-wai and the Poetics of Hong Kong Cinema

In May 2004 Wong Kar-wai arrived at the Cannes Film Festival, exhausted. His new film *2046* was a competing entry, but Wong delivered the print twelve hours late. Festival organizers hurriedly arranged a last-minute screening. Official selections had to be rescheduled. Disgruntled delegates carped about Wong's tardiness. Worse, the film was not finished. Crucial computer-generated (CGI) sequences had yet to be added; the sound track was defective; whole scenes remained to be shot. Wong had started production in December 1999, but *2046* had become a behemoth, impossible to finish. His crew had been working twenty-four-hour shifts. Now Wong was fatigued and facing censure from critics and festival delegates. The film would win nothing at Cannes, and industry experts forecast retribution against Wong. Commentators debated the long-term effects on Wong's career: Would Cannes ever accept him back again?

The Cannes debacle has become part of Wong's legend. To Wong's detractors, this episode highlights the faults of a self-indulgent filmmaker. By their account, Wong is a notorious wastrel, adopting a shooting ratio so high that entire plotlines are excised from the final cut. His productions balloon over schedule and over budget. He is disorganized; the shooting commences without a script, and he may shoot forty takes of a scene, looking for something ineffable. His method can be "taxing on the actors," Tony Leung wearily notes (Yoke 2000: 30). However, Wong is feted as one of the world's finest directors. As a personality he is iconic, the omnipresent sunglasses an indelible trademark. As a beacon of Hong Kong cinema, he has kept that industry in the public spotlight, even when its fortunes were flagging. Critics hail him as a master of film technique and a romantic artist of the first order. His critics might decry his purported profligacy and self-indulgence, but without his unique production methods—the relentlessly varied takes and rough cuts, the protracted shooting schedules—Wong's films would lose the distinctive aesthetic that makes them so singularly exhilarating and elusive. Put simply, Wong makes splendid films.

Two years after the Cannes fiasco, he was invited back to the festival . . . as president of the jury.

This book treats Wong's films from the perspective of a poetics of cinema. It is concerned with his films as artworks and as aesthetic objects. It seeks to illuminate their narrative and stylistic systems and to account for how they affect spectators. The book places his cinema in context, tracing patterns of influence to pertinent cinematic traditions. More polemically, the book theorizes a poetics of Wong's cinema to fruitfully provide a greater appreciation of the director's artistic achievement. This broad conceptual approach—what David Bordwell calls a poetics of cinema—has so far been marginal to studies of Hong Kong films and filmmakers. Since the early 1990s the reigning approach to Hong Kong film has been culturalism, which posits broad correlations between films and social phenomena. Throughout this book, I aim to show that a poetics can shed light on aspects of Wong's cinema typically neglected by culturalist criticism. Another task of this monograph is to explicate and critique the dominant theories applied to Wong's films. These theoretical stakes frame the book's practical criticism, its formal analyses of Wong's films. These analyses, in turn, provide the marrow of the book. It is only by closely attending to Wong's films that their artistic richness and complexity can be appreciated.

A Biographical Sketch

Wong Kar-wai was born in July 1958 in Shanghai. At age five he immigrated to Hong Kong with his parents; two older siblings remained behind, stranded in Shanghai's French Quarter as the Cultural Revolution gathered force. Raised in effect as an only child, Wong grew up in the teeming Tsim Sha Tsui District, his isolation compounded by the region's alien dialects. (Wong would not become fluent in Cantonese and English until his teens.) His father managed a trendy nightclub; his mother adored movies, ushering the child to matinee shows. The local theaters served up a diverse menu—Hollywood epics and westerns, British Hammer studio films, Japanese ghost movies, French *policiers*, Mandarin and Cantonese films. In his late teens Wong began studying graphic design. He earned a diploma in the subject, graduating from the Hong Kong Polytechnic in 1980. Shortly after, he enrolled in the training program of local terrestrial station TVB. A stint writing serials and soap operas led to permanent employment at Cinema City, an independent film studio specializing in comedies with a local flavor. Though Wong chafed at the studio's house style, he spent much of the 1980s dutifully hammering out scripts. The finished films were occasionally diverting and mostly disposable—*The Haunted Cop Shop of Horrors* (1987), *Just for Fun* (1983), and *Rosa* (1988) are typical titles. More important was Wong's introduction to colleagues such as Jeff Lau, Patrick

Tam, and Frankie Chan, later to become long-term collaborators. After two years spent writing Tam's high-end effort *Final Victory* (1987), Wong became a partner in a new independent company, In-Gear, for which he would sign his first feature.

As Tears Go By (1988) piggybacked on the local triad-gangster trend, a genre revivified by John Woo's hugely popular *A Better Tomorrow* (1986). Wong's maiden film was shrewdly packaged as a commercial enterprise—the film's star, Andy Lau, had proven form in the triad genre; a Cantopop tune was chosen to accompany a crowd-pleasing MTV-style sequence; and gangster-film tropes ensured periodic stretches of kinetic spectacle. Ultimately, though, *As Tears Go By* was distinguished by its visual flair. Its moody palette was de rigueur for late 1980s triad films, but its step-printing technique brought fresh energy to the genre's chase-and-fight sequences. This technique, as deployed in *As Tears Go By*, liquefies hard blocks of primary color into iridescent streaks of light; its unfamiliar rhythms, moreover, wield a potent affective charge. The film's visual aesthetic, engineered by Andrew Lau and Patrick Tam, augured what many critics think of as Wong's signature style. At the same time, several of the film's shots possess a geometric precision atypical of Wong's later work.

Local critics championed Wong's distinctive aesthetic. He was quickly earmarked as an exciting new director, one of several pioneering a "second new wave" of Hong Kong filmmakers.[1] *As Tears Go By* found popularity and critical acclaim, empowering Wong to venture into more ambitious filmmaking. The film that followed, *Days of Being Wild* (1990), seemed indifferent to current fads. Relegating scenes of physical action, the film swerves from Hong Kong's action genre. As romance drama, it avoids the genre's cuteness and levity. *Days of Being Wild* seems intent on defying mass taste: its plotting is as enervated and languorous as its male protagonist, it solicits sympathy for a scoundrel, its portentous images bear the gravity of thematic significance, and its non sequitur ending risks anticlimax. Some critics found the film ponderous, others profound. Ultimately, mass taste prevailed, the expensive production culminating in a conspicuous commercial failure. Nevertheless the film accumulated honors. In the years that followed, critical appreciation deepened; by 2012, *Days of Being Wild* would be ranked the fifth-greatest Hong Kong film ever made.[2]

1. This second wave of directors emerged in the mid-1980s and included Stanley Kwan, Peter Chan, Gordon Chan, Ching Siu-tung, Mabel Cheung, Alex Law, Clara Law, Jacob Cheung, and others. The first new-wave directors, most of them graduating from local television in the late 1970s, comprised socially conscious and artistically adventurous filmmakers such as Ann Hui, Patrick Tam, Tsui Hark, Yim Ho, Allen Fong, and Alex Cheung.
2. In March 2012, *Time Out Hong Kong* published a critics' poll of the "100 greatest" Hong Kong films. Five of Wong's films appeared on the list: *Happy Together* (#79), *Ashes of Time* (#53), *Chungking Express* (#25), *Days of Being Wild* (#5), and *In the Mood for Love* (#1). See

In a way, the film's local failure was beside the point. With *Days of Being Wild*, Wong targeted an altogether different market—not the local audience nor even the pan-Asian market but the international audience for foreign art cinema, accessible via the festival circuit. One index of Wong's market strategy is his use of Asian stars. At the local level, relying on stars brings fiscal rewards, enticing financiers and audiences. But Wong's casting also reveals an astute sensitivity to the international art cinema market. His star players—Leslie Cheung, Maggie Cheung, Andy Lau, Tony Leung Chiu-wai, Gong Li, Brigitte Lin, Zhang Ziyi—were renowned on the international film circuit before Wong worked with them. Moreover, they were perceived to be affiliated with artistically significant filmmakers and projects of high cultural value.[3] From this angle, Wong's casting strategy—relying on actors with strong international profiles—betrays the director's transnational ambitions. Since *Days of Being Wild*, his films have been intended less for the local market than for international festival distribution. Wong's success on this network brands him not only as a "Hong Kong" director but as an international purveyor of film art—a reputation consolidated by his subsequent output, including such "prestigious" portmanteau films as *Eros* (2004) and *Chacun son cinéma* (2007).

By the mid-1990s Wong had assembled a cadre of trusted associates. At the production level, his entire oeuvre is unified by favorite colleagues. Production designer and editor William Chang and cinematographer Christopher Doyle proved crucial in shaping Wong's aesthetic. Composers Frankie Chan and Roel A. García lent a percussive energy to Wong's mid-1990s work. And to the aforementioned list of players can be added Chang Chen, Jacky Cheung, Takeshi Kaneshiro, Carina Lau, and Faye Wong. With one long-term associate, writer-director Jeff Lau, Wong founded Jet Tone Films, an independent production company formed in 1992, largely by necessity. *Days of Being Wild* was a financial disaster. Investors balked at its inflated budget, cost overruns, and meager returns. They shied away, too, from Wong's practice of shooting without a full-fledged script. "Nobody wanted to produce my films," Wong

Time Out Hong Kong (March 14–27, 2012), 21–34. I surmise that the high position of *Days of Being Wild*, and its rising stock in the past decade, is partly attributable to public affection for Leslie Cheung, whose death in 2003 is annually commemorated in Hong Kong.

3. Consider, for example, the following films, all of which achieved various kinds of international success and which preceded Wong's initial collaboration with the star in question. Leslie Cheung: *A Better Tomorrow* (1986), *A Chinese Ghost Story* (1987), *A Better Tomorrow II* (1987), *Rouge* (1988); Maggie Cheung: *Police Story* (1985), *Project A II* (1987), *Police Story Part II* (1988); Andy Lau: *Boat People* (1982), *Twinkle Twinkle Lucky Stars* (1985); Tony Leung Chiu-wai: *Love Unto Waste* (1986), *City of Sadness* (1989); Gong Li: *Red Sorghum* (1987), *Judou* (1990), *Raise the Red Lantern* (1991), *The Story of Qiu Ju* (1992), *Farewell My Concubine* (1993); Brigitte Lin: *Zu: Warriors from the Magic Mountain* (1983), *Police Story* (1985), *Peking Opera Blues* (1986), *Dragon Inn* (1992), *Swordsman 2* (1992); Zhang Ziyi: *The Road Home* (1999), *Crouching Tiger, Hidden Dragon* (2000), *Hero* (2002).

says, "so I had to start this company" (Forde 2000: 23). *Ashes of Time* (1994), the new firm's first production, was an investor's nightmare—with a budget of HK$47 million, Wong's sprawling *wuxia* epic took two years to complete, and it was eventually denied distribution in the West. (It would later be restored and repackaged as *Ashes of Time Redux* [2008] and released theatrically in world markets [Figure 1.1].) By now Wong had gained notoriety as a profligate director. As if to prove he could work cheaply and fast, Wong embarked on a "quickie," *Chungking Express* (1994), during a two-month hiatus from *Ashes of Time*.

These two films, released in 1994, were rich in contrasts. *Ashes of Time* is a historical costume epic, tonally somber and introspective; *Chungking Express* is urban, modern, and infused with a breezily wistful temperament. Whereas a distribution agent foiled the Western release of *Ashes of Time*, *Chungking Express* gained prominent Western exposure, distributed in the United States under the patronage of Quentin Tarantino and Miramax Films. Nevertheless, both films consolidated authorial themes salient in Wong's previous and subsequent films: the friction between social mores and romantic desire, the longing to surmount psychic inertia, the capricious forces that thwart or furnish personal encounters, the impregnability of time and memory, the burden of individual choice and responsibility. Again, though, the two films registered their material differently—if *Ashes of Time* seemed suffocated by the weight of its themes, *Chungking Express* wore its ideas lightly. The success of *Chungking Express* brought Wong international recognition.

If Wong's next film, *Fallen Angels* (1995), looked derivative of this popular hit, the two films differed sharply in visual style, affective tone, and plot structure. Still, *Fallen Angels* coaxed audiences to spot connections with *Chungking Express*. Wong elaborates the game of cross-referencing at a metatextual level too. A dense web of intertextual allusions recycles characters, locales, and music cues across the entire oeuvre. The apparent integrity of Wong's authorial universe tantalizes viewers into positing connections among his films' narrative agents and events. This is the sport of an *auteur* cinema—presupposing an intimate knowledge of his body of work, the filmmaker rewards the initiated viewer with intertextual referencing.

Critics dismissed *Fallen Angels* as superficial, but it remains a complex work, not only a brooding noir but a delicate, poignant meditation on father-son relationships. Unlike *Fallen Angels*, *Happy Together* (1997) bolstered Wong's critical cachet. A gay romance story shot largely in Argentina, the film ruminates on themes of exile and absent fathers—themes that found social resonance in the year of the handover. Another (transnational) context for *Happy Together* was the 1990s new queer cinema. Unlike many films of this trend, however, *Happy Together* avoids camp and caricature, wringing pathos from Tony Leung's soulful performance. The Cannes Film Festival feted Wong for *Happy Together*, awarding him the Best Director palm in 1997. Thereafter his career would be closely intertwined with Cannes. He chaired the jury in 2006; *My Blueberry Nights* (2007) opened the festival the following year. On the festival circuit more generally, Wong has won admirers and critics in equal measure. Though *Happy Together* and *In the Mood for Love* (2000) took major prizes, the *2046* affair hurt his reputation. Most critics, however, failed to note that Cannes frequently exhibits unfinished films (see Corless and Darke 2007: 179). Today, Wong regards the Cannes festival as both a production deadline (forcing him to terminate the editing phase) and a kind of high-profile test screening (which subsequently determines further revision and fine-tuning).

After the triumph of *Happy Together*, Wong announced his next project. *Summer in Beijing* was to be shot largely in Mainland China, but disputes with the Chinese censoring body (over filming in Tiananmen Square) persuaded Wong to abandon it. Instead he forged ahead with *In the Mood for Love*, his paean to period Chinese melodrama. Turning away from the zestful brio of his most recent work, Wong returned to the statelier rhythms of *Days of Being Wild*, prompting critics to compare Wong to Hou Hsiao-hsien. *In the Mood for Love* became a worldwide success and initiated a Chinese-language film renaissance in the West (e.g., *Crouching Tiger, Hidden Dragon* [2000], *Hero* [2002], *Infernal Affairs* [2002], *House of Flying Daggers* [2004], *Kung Fu Hustle* [2004], and others). This renaissance included Wong's *2046*, a production begun in 1999 and beset by difficulties. An ambitious science-fiction film, *2046* required elaborate CGI sequences that added months to the schedule. The severe acute respiratory syndrome (SARS) outbreak in 2003 caused further delays. By the time *2046* emerged, four years had passed since Wong's previous feature film. It would be another three years before *My Blueberry Nights*, Wong's first foray into English-language cinema. Filmed in the United States, this romance-drama employed Hollywood stars, embraced Hollywood genres (including the road movie), and reached down into American mythology. The film was perceived as a failure relative to Wong's previous work. Still, *My Blueberry Nights* confirmed a production strategy rarely pursued in Hong Kong. As his local contemporaries sought coproductions with Mainland Chinese partners, Wong looked increasingly to Europe for finance. His recent reliance on French capital, in particular, testifies to his renown in France as an auteur filmmaker. His ability to attract European and US funding, moreover, attests to the irreducibly transnational bent of his cinema.

As the first decade of the twenty-first century wore on, mooted projects fizzled out. A thriller entitled *The Lady from Shanghai* and a film about Hurricane Katrina came to naught. *The Grandmaster*, a kung fu drama centered on Bruce Lee's *sifu*, was characteristically beset by interruptions and delays. As obstacles postponed the film's completion by years, Wong stirred anticipation virally using teaser trailers and promotion art. (*The Grandmaster* would eventually open in Asia in 2013, becoming Wong's most successful film in Mainland China.) Amid these setbacks, however, Wong's stock showed no sign of waning. In *Sight & Sound*'s 2012 critics' poll, *In the Mood for Love* ranked 25th in the list of the greatest films of all time. In the same year, the film topped *Time Out*'s poll of the greatest Hong Kong films yet made. Wong's international esteem is unparalleled among Hong Kong's second-wave filmmakers. Today, Wong stands not only as the finest director in Hong Kong cinema but as one of the finest directors in the world.

Some Broad Assumptions

Wong's biographical legend can usefully illuminate aspects of his films. Noting Wong's cinephilia, for instance, cues us to spot intertextual allusions within the work or to consider the oeuvre in relation to other filmmaking traditions. However, Wong's legend also accrues fallacies that must be redressed. One premise holds that Wong's films are principally or wholly sensuous. On this view, the films are essentially superficial: they elevate style over substance; they disguise vacuity with visual pleasure. This premise casts Wong as an aesthete, preoccupied with sumptuous audiovisual style. A strong version of this position is epitomized by David Thomson, for whom Wong's oeuvre is ravishing yet vacuous (2010: 1053). A weaker version grants the films' "depth" but perceives them as primarily stylistic ventures. Buttressing these premises is the assumption that Wong's viewer is "seduced" by aesthetic beauty (Blake 2003: 343). Overwhelmingly, the viewer is characterized in passive terms—as "spellbound," "bewitched," "mesmerized." Then there is Wong the postmodern director, here again committed to surface impressions: his films serve up pastiche; they introduce radically new forms. Fragmentation governs their compositional strategies and characterizes the experience of the viewer, and the films are steeped in nostalgia. Still further, the legend presents the image of Wong the allegorist. Irrespective of explicit subject matter, the films are presumed to be "about" Hong Kong's 1997 handover to China, imperialism, globalization, postcolonialism, or some other sociohistorical phenomenon.

Wong as aesthete, postmodernist, allegorist—this book reconsiders these aspects of the popular legend. I certainly do not deny that Wong's films are highly sensuous, that they are innovative, or that they engage with social issues, but I do attempt a more nuanced account of these features than the constructed legend provides. I also contest the tacit and pervasive critical assumption that Wong's films are properly understood—*best* understood—as cultural allegory—more, that their cultural value and artistic merit stems precisely from their embedded social meanings. This assumption underlies what I call the culturalist approach to Wong's cinema. It is, I believe, the most widely adopted perspective in Wong scholarship. The remainder of this chapter provides an exegesis and critique of its broad premises and practices, before introducing an alternative—and to some extent, complementary—critical approach. I then go on to rehearse the book's main arguments.

Abbas's Culture of Disappearance

Ackbar Abbas's *Hong Kong: Culture and the Politics of Disappearance* (1997) offers a paradigmatic instance of the culturalist approach. Abbas draws his thesis from the historical circumstances of the moment. In the wake of the 1984 Joint Declaration, which formalized Hong Kong's return to China in 1997, the British colony faced potentially seismic cultural change. For Abbas, the countdown to the 1997 handover triggered a pervasive crisis of identity: "Now faced with the uncomfortable possibility of an alien identity about to be imposed on it from China, Hong Kong is experiencing a kind of last-minute collective search for a more definite identity" (1997b: 4). This search for a new identity, however, threatened the extinction of Hong Kong's distinctive heritage: its colonial identity, cultural traditions, and social values. Exacerbating this "space of disappearance" was the rise of globalization, further endangering local identity and tradition (3). "Disappearance" thus arises from the intermeshed forces of imperialism and globalization. These forces conspired to engender a collective sense of impermanence, a pervasive social anxiety. What would become of Hong Kong in the postcolonial era? Would its subjectivity and legacy simply vanish?

From the 1980s, Abbas argues, the new Hong Kong cinema began addressing this historical situation. A few films tackled the issue explicitly, but most evoked it indirectly by means of film technique. The local cinema's "new" images caught "the slipperiness, the elusiveness, the ambivalences" of Hong Kong's precarious cultural space (Abbas 1997b: 24). Disappearance was conjured in oblique ways, and visual style became a vessel for social meaning. Because it evoked the political situation indirectly, a film could be read for social comment "*regardless of subject matter*" (24; italics in original). Thus films as different as Stanley Kwan's *Center Stage* (1991) and Wong's *As Tears Go By* were assimilated to the "problematic of disappearance" (ibid.). According to Abbas, moreover, the new cinema did not merely evoke the historical situation; it critiqued it. *As Tears Go By*, for instance, problematizes visuality; a "general sense of visual overload" complicates the act of looking (36). Abbas takes this unorthodox visuality as a critique of the colonial gaze, that is, a gaze intended to produce social subjects, promoting a way of seeing that fosters acceptance of colonial space. As Abbas puts it, "Because Wong's film consistently gives us a form of visuality that problematizes the visible, it can be said to represent and critique such a space" (36). Ostensibly a formulaic gangster film, *As Tears Go By* thus becomes a political text by virtue of its "techniques of disappearance" (8).[4]

Abbas's analysis rests on a heuristic frequently employed in the culturalist approach. At an abstract level, Abbas starts with a general theory of culture and maps this conceptual scheme onto a group of artworks. Abbas's interest in these films is frankly illustrative, principally concerned with their propensity to prove the a priori theory. Abbas is explicit on this matter: "I will use [the cultural objects] to pursue a particular theme: the cultural self-invention of the Hong Kong subject in a cultural space that I will be calling a space of disappearance" (1997b: 1). Here a theory precedes film analysis and is applied to films in top-down fashion. Culturalist approaches, I shall demonstrate shortly, have often relied on such routines. That the new Hong Kong films respond to and represent (albeit obliquely) the 1997 situation, that they critique (rather than, say, celebrate) this situation, and that this critique is embedded in visual techniques—Abbas's thesis hinges on these contestable assumptions. The risk is that Abbas's interpretive moves create a causal link among several unsubstantiated assumptions, a problem that has often hindered the culturalist approach in general. Moreover, the critic often equivocates as to how far cultural critique is intended or recognized by the filmmaker. Are the film's meanings implicit or symptomatic? Can they be assigned to the filmmaker's explicit materials, or are they "leaked" by the text involuntarily as structured absences? Cultural readings have tended to fudge this issue. Culturalists often imply authorial intention, but problematically this intention is not always taken to be conscious on the part of the filmmaker. From a privileged position of omnipotence, the critic reveals intentions the filmmaker does not know he or she has.

Abbas's discussion spotlights another characteristic of culturalist readings. Reacting to what he sees as critics' homogenization of Hong Kong cinema, Abbas stresses the diversity of local filmmaking (1997b: 18–19). He exhorts critics to avoid "gross simplification," such as that which reduces all Hong Kong cinema to action spectacle. "There is," he writes, " . . . no easy homogeneity to Hong Kong cinema, in spite of appearances" (19). Yet in the same paragraph, Abbas goes on to say, "The films that are made cannot be reduced to 'a single metanarrative' but represent so many disparate attempts to evoke a problematic cultural space" (ibid.). To be sure, the new Hong Kong cinema

---

4. In a later work, Abbas claims that his thesis holds good for Hong Kong's postcolonial cinema too. Invoking Wong as an exemplary case, he writes of "the continuing relevance of . . . the cinematic—the production of images inside and outside cinema that respond to mutations in Hong Kong's geo-political, economic and cultural situation. The cinematic in this sense remains central to the project of cultural studies in Hong Kong" (Abbas 2001: 624).

cannot be reduced to the action genre. But neither can it be wholly assimilated to the critic's conceptual structure ("disappearance"). In disclaiming one generalization, Abbas imposes another. Though he cautions against homogenizing Hong Kong cinema, he falls prey precisely to this tendency. The catchall dimension of Abbas's heuristic seems to me a limitation of culturalist criticism, which invites a fairly damning criticism: in the culturalist approach, the a priori thesis is all, and all encompassing.

The Culturalist Approach

In the 1990s arguably no writer exerted greater influence on the field of Asian cinema studies than Abbas. But to take the measure of the culturalist approach, it is necessary to expand our discussion beyond his work. Scholars allied to the culturalist turn embraced Abbas's tropes of disappearance, as well as the broader symptomatic and implicit hermeneutics guiding his approach (already well-entrenched as a disciplinary practice). Surely no Hong Kong filmmaker received more culturalist analysis than Wong, and this scholarly attention yielded riches. Studies by Stephen Teo, Gina Marchetti, Rey Chow, and others have greatly enriched the field's understanding of Wong's films and Chinese cinema in general, often basing culturalist readings on careful scrutiny of the films' aesthetic features. The very best of this work displays the undoubted virtues of culturalist criticism. In its broadest compass, culturalism situates the film within and against pertinent contexts, including its immediate sociohistorical milieu. Culturalism can demystify anomalous features of the work that escape "internal" motivation. It can illuminate the film's implicit or symptomatic meanings. And it provides a welcome corrective to the perception that Hong Kong cinema and its filmmakers are politically disengaged. At an abstract level, however, the culturalist approach has harbored problematic practices and routines. Some of these problems stem from the weaknesses of Grand Theory, such as the critic's reliance on top-down interpretation, symptomatic criticism (allegorical readings, reflectionism), and recourse to punning maneuvers. Other problems arise from conceptual tropes pertaining to Hong Kong cinema and culture. It is worthwhile to examine these problems in detail.

A recurring tendency within socio-allegorical criticism involves thematizing the film's characters and personifying geographical regions. Teo provides a paradigmatic instance of this maneuver, mounting a symptomatic reading of *2046*: "On an allegorical level, the film denotes Hong Kong's affair with China through Chow's affairs with Mainland women: Zhang Ziyi, Faye Wong, Gong Li, and Dong Jie (playing Faye's younger sister who has a brief fling with Chow)" (2005: 149). (Note Teo's reliance on a pun—"affair/s"—to open up the associative link he wishes to pursue.) Under this personification heuristic, the critic's interpretations soon become repetitive. If Teo's interpretive frame can be mapped onto the characters in *Days of Being Wild*, the film allegorizes Hong Kong's impending reunification with the motherland. We might consider Hong Kong to be personified by Yuddy (Leslie Cheung); Britain to be represented by Yuddy's foster mother, Rebecca (Rebecca Pan); and China to be embodied by Yuddy's biological mother (Tita Muñoz), depicted in the film as an austere and implacable matriarch. Interpreted this way, Hong Kong's prospects under Chinese sovereignty look decidedly bleak—unable to reconcile with his true parent and estranged from his adopted home, Yuddy's fate is doomed. The fable that Yuddy recites, about a bird without legs, could be read along similar lines. Evoking themes of rootlessness, the fable correlates Yuddy (Hong Kong) with the aimless bird, which is destined to perish when it lands (in China). That the bird in the fable was "dead all along" might be construed as a critique of prehandover Hong Kong, the British colonizers having divested the city of its authentic and unique cultural identity.

With a little finessing, this reading would be passable as an example of the personification heuristic. Yet the account contains obvious infelicities. Reading the bird fable this way obliges us to execute two interpretive moves—first, to perceive the bird as a personification of Yuddy (as most commentators do) and, second, to perceive Yuddy (now aligned with the wayward bird) as a metaphor for Hong Kong. The accumulation of metaphors is not hermeneutically sophisticated. This approach also relies to a large extent on a partialized reading strategy, selecting certain characters (even minor ones, such as Yuddy's birth mother) and omitting others (including major protagonists such as Su Lizhen), depending upon which agents best fit the interpretive frame. Worse, this interpretive frame reveals nothing that the hypothetical critic had not surmised in advance of the analysis. The critic simply concludes that *Days of Being Wild* is "about" Hong Kong's relationship with China, much as *2046* is—thus reproducing the same interpretation in cookie-cutter fashion. Each film's distinctive features are minimized, flatly suppressed by a top-down heuristic. This heuristic might be endorsed for foregrounding the films' thematic affinities. But the affinities yielded by the personification heuristic risk being spurious and facile, imposed upon the work a priori rather than constructed from specific features within the work. At worst, the heuristic betrays the hypothetical critic's hermeneutic intransigence and reveals little about the shared traits and preoccupations of the films themselves.

Central to the culturalist enterprise are questions of identity and public "consciousness," notions beset by conceptual difficulties. If the notion of identity is often conceptually vague, the notion of a public consciousness is also problematic. For instance, the culturalist sometimes claims that the public "consciousness" operates at the level of the individual's or the society's *un*conscious—an impossible position to defend or discredit, for who is to say what dwells in the unconscious? In such cases, what is attributed to the populace as a collective sensibility can look more like hermeneutic categories imposed onto a society by cultural commentators.

Like Abbas, Teo (2000) considers identity a central trope of Hong Kong cinema. Both critics assume that, in prehandover Hong Kong, a drastic effort to define local identity consumed both the general populace and the region's cinema. "If I were to choose one word to characterize Hong Kong cinema," Teo writes, "I would choose Identity" (2000). He goes on:

> From Jackie Chan to Wong Kar-wai to Clara Law to Sammo Hung—from action pictures to art pictures—it is possible to see Hong Kong pictures as sharing one perennial theme, that of identity: the quest of, the assertion of, the affirmation of, identity. (Teo 2000)

Here again the specter of homogenization raises its head. In this case, though, a totalizing assertion homogenizes Hong Kong films as dissimilar as "action pictures" and "art pictures" (along with differences, one might suppose, within those broad categories). Teo's premise also invites top-down interpretations, obliging the critic to show how every Hong Kong film makes identity its major theme. The very notion of identity is conceptually (and conveniently) nebulous, the easier to summon evidence of it in a diverse range of films. Whether applied to Hong Kong films or Hong Kong society, the trope of identity is sufficiently vague to be applicable to all cases; but as a catchall, predetermined schema its utility and meaningfulness are limited.

Most generally, top-down culturalism bears a cluster of conceptual and methodological drawbacks. As Grand Theory, culturalism risks the pitfalls of simply "applying" theory. The routine of mapping a preexisting theory onto a given case is easily repeatable but essentially facile; at worst, it can distort both the film and the preexisting theory. Furthermore, if the culture offers up movies amenable to the critic's cultural thesis, it also furnishes numerous counterexamples. Not every Hong Kong film in the early 1990s featured bleak endings, a pessimistic mood, accelerated motion, and other purported repositories of 1997 allegory. Reducing films to political allegory, moreover, downplays their commitment to spectacle. For one symptomatic critic, the shopping mall climax in *Police Story* (1985) and the clock tower stunt in *Project A* (1983) evoke cultural disappearance (Collier 1999). But first and foremost these sequences set out to create a visceral impact, furnishing an affective, sensuous, physiological experience. Deriving allegory from such sequences is not (necessarily) wrongheaded, but *reducing* such sequences to allegory disregards the ways filmmakers utilize craft traditions to generate palpable effects and responses. By stressing *local* identity as central to a film's concerns, moreover, the culturalist may underplay the film's address to an international audience. This is especially pertinent to figures such as Wong Kar-wai, John Woo, and Jackie Chan, whose Hong Kong films harbored ambitions beyond pan-Asian markets. Lastly, the credence afforded allegorical accounts is often wholly reliant on the critic's rhetorical ingenuity; one must simply accept that x (i.e., a feature of the text) represents, say, a collective disquiet toward the 1997 handover, without the benefit of empirical evidence. As Noël Carroll puts it, "Given enough latitude, you can probably allegorize anything to say whatever you wish, but that won't establish causal connections where there are none" (1996: 42).

None of this is to deny that local filmmakers absorb materials from their social milieu. I do not, for instance, suggest ignoring the 1997 handover as a causal factor in, say, *Days of Being Wild*. But one must recognize that filmmakers assign these materials varying degrees of importance in any given film. Topical subject matter may permeate to the very marrow of the work, or it may assert a negligible influence upon the finished film. In any case, the basic material is inevitably deformed to some degree by the fiction-making process. For instance, the genesis of *2046*, we are told, stemmed from a historical circumstance within Wong's milieu (China's assurance that Hong Kong will remain a special administrative region for fifty years); but *2046* drastically deforms this referential material, not least by virtue of its overt science-fiction elements. The finished film makes no explicit reference to the actual historical situation. It is not that the film's political dimension—explicitly flagged in the title—is mere window dressing; rather, it provides a point of departure, a kernel or conceit enabling Wong's idées fixes fresh elaboration. As with any social allegory, moreover, the deformation of the work's materials produces a primary level of discourse—consisting of characters, settings, actions, and so on—that is sufficiently removed from allegorical meaning to warrant analysis in its own right.

Socio-allegorical hermeneutics also provides critics a useful tool in arguing for a filmmaker's significance. Allegorical readings provide an expedient way to boost a director's social relevance and critical esteem without obliging the critic to prove artistic ingenuity or innovation. Certainly there is no doubt that allegorical treatises by both Western and Asian critics contributed to Wong's burgeoning critical reputation during the 1990s. Still today, I argue, film studies scholars predominantly approach and appreciate Wong's films through culturalist lines of reasoning. For Teo, Wong's 1990s output "elucidate[s] the great issues of the decade," including the angst-inducing handover, civil rights for gays, and equal opportunities for women (2005: 161). Of *Happy Together*, Teo asserts, "Seen today, the power of the film resides in its sense of being a memorial to the pre-1997 anxiety of Hong Kong" (110). From the culturalist perspective, these films possess cultural value primarily because they speak to, and speak for, the culture. This is indeed one facet of their value. It is the purpose of this book, however, to show that the value of Wong's films resides at least as much in their artistry *as films*. Nonetheless, if allegorical readings inflate Wong's cultural cachet, I should also note Wong's own savvy in alluding to social reference points. Naming his film "2046," for instance, in part constitutes a shrewd marketing gambit, a "hook" attracting cultural commentators to a film whose political content is, arguably, negligible. For critic and filmmaker alike, then, symptomatic hermeneutics offers strong advantages, despite the array of conceptual and methodological pitfalls that addle the approach.

If Abbas's cultural theory of Hong Kong cinema inspired allegorical readings of Wong's films, it also informed a cognate culturalist tendency: reflectionism. Here the critic conceives the film not as embedding a "hidden" narrative but rather as reflecting the attitudes of the public it is perceived to be addressing. The reflectionist does not try to demonstrate causality but settles for a more or less tenuous linkage of film and social realm. Of *Chungking Express,* for instance, one critic claims that "collective anxiety about the handover is reflected in the situation of Brigitte Lin's blonde-wigged gangster" (Taubin 2008). Similarly, film scholar Janice Tong, evoking Abbas's culture of disappearance, finds the Hong Konger's experience of temporal flux "reflected in Wong's destabilising cinematographic self-image of Hong Kong" (2008: 65). Both writers require at least two leaps of faith—first, to accept that there *is* collective anxiety (Taubin) or temporal instability (Tong) among the local populace triggered by the impending handover and, second, that Wong's film reflects precisely this collective experience. As with allegorical readings, reflectionist criticism relies for its cogency upon the critic's rhetorical ability to persuade the reader—in lieu of causal explanations—of abstract notions immanent within both the film and its proximate milieu.

Sometimes the critic expands reflectionism beyond societal metaphor, so that the films are burdened with a freight of symptomatic meanings. One standard heuristic perceives the films as reflections of the biographical author. Teo (2005), for instance, construes Wong's films as essentially autobiographical, with the director's personal history discernible at several levels of narration. The narrative settings of *Days of Being Wild* and *In the Mood for Love* recreate Wong's childhood milieu (5), the visual strategies of *As Tears Go By* "attempt to translate [the filmmaker's] innermost feelings into images" (24), and characterization in *Days of Being Wild* "reflects the director's fundamentally shy nature" (43). That *In the Mood for Love* excises sequences set in the 1970s indicates that the decade does not hold personal resonance for Wong: "it was probably an uneventful period when [Wong] would have gone through primary and secondary schooling" (13). Even setting aside this recourse to speculation, the author-reflection heuristic becomes murky when Teo slides between the director as biographical individual and as authorial "personality." Teo appears to invoke the latter when claiming that Killer in *Fallen Angels* "reflects Wong Kar-wai, the author" (87). Whether this claim is persuasive (and I argue in Chapter 4 that Killer does not embody Wong's authorial world-view), the author-reflection schema is here clearly of a different order than that employed previously (e.g., when discussing Wong's shy nature). Likewise, Teo means to denote authorial personality, rather than biographical figure, when stating that voice-over in *Fallen Angels* "expos[es] [Wong] as perhaps danger-ously schizoid, split into several personalities. I am not suggesting that Wong himself is psychotic" (88). Wong's characters are assumed to reflect *both* the biographical individual with a personal history and the cinematic author who articulates a personal vision.

The author-reflection heuristic becomes murkier still when applied to con-trasting, even contradictory, cases. For Teo, "*Fallen Angels*, like all of Wong's films, is told from the multiple perspectives of its characters, and all of them reflect Wong, the writer and author" (2005: 88). Among the problems with this sweeping claim is that it irons out crucial differences among the film's characters, who are hardly of a piece and among whom Wong encourages us to weight judgments (see Chapter 4 of this book). It is not explained how the specific traits and trajectories of these various agents are unified into coherent form nor how they manifest an authorial worldview. Nor is it specified pre-cisely in what ways the characters of *Fallen Angels* dovetail with those of *Days of Being Wild*, in whom Teo also perceives Wong's reflection. Indeed, Teo's point might be precisely that the characters are not alike, that, moreover, they represent contradictory subjectivities. Each one possesses a distinct personality and they all reflect Wong, hence the view of Wong as "perhaps dangerously schizoid." By extension, Wong's authorial personality must be read as schizo-phrenic, fragmented, contradictory—an interpretation consistent with Teo's broadly postmodernist line of criticism. I will not digress here except to iterate that, as I attempt to argue in subsequent chapters, Wong's films exhibit a highly consistent and coherent worldview. My present point is that the author-reflec-tion model—potentially useful but beset by conceptual difficulties pertaining to the ontology of the "author"—becomes yet another mode of reflection theory imposed upon the work.

The accretion of reflectionist schemas puts a strain on both the film's levels of meaning and on the cogency of the critic's interpretation. Teo's study of Wong embraces social reflection as an explicatory schema. Even Wong's post-1997 Hong Kong work, he argues, "mirrors the pathology of Hong Kong society in the 1990s" (2005: 164). But Teo goes on to invoke still another reflectionist frame, asserting that "the downbeat mood of Wong's films reflects the mood of the [Hong Kong film] industry as it lingers on the downswing" (165). In sum, Teo saddles the films with a surfeit of associational baggage: the films reflect the author-as-biographical-person, the author-as-formal-component, the 1997 collective mood, and the waning Hong Kong film industry. Any film would buckle under so much symptomatic weight. Moreover, the critic's reflection-ist claims risk looking tenuous, even arbitrary. As Bordwell points out, "An ingenious critic can make virtually any film reflect anything" (2011: 23).[5] If a film's mood is broadly downbeat, how does one know that it is the 1997 zeitgeist, and not, say, the blue funk of the film's director, that is being reflected? And what should be made of those numerous moments in Wong's films that are decidedly not downbeat but euphoric? Why should the film's mood be assumed to be reflective of anything at all? Since interpretation here rests on loose associations, nothing prevents us from substituting 1997 anomie with any other somber affair culled from the historical milieu. At an abstract level, the reflectionist heuristic lacks the emphasis on concrete causal explanations promoted by a poetics of cinema.

If Hong Kong films are overburdened with symptomatic meanings, so too are they saddled with contradictory ones. For Natalia Chan Sui Hung, the postcolonial Hong Kong cinema—a period identified with the 1997 count-down—constitutes a nostalgia cinema, its films mounting a two-tiered system of meaning. On the one hand, they exhibit yearning for a bygone era in Hong Kong history; on the other hand, they are prompted to such nostalgia by con-temporary anxieties about the region's posthandover future. The nostalgic experience, Chan writes, "helps to manage the unpleasant present by celebrat-ing the past and transcending the future" (2000: 264). Citing as a characteristic case *Days of Being Wild*, Chan goes on to suggest that the film's cinematog-raphy "highlights not only the nostalgic feeling of love of the 1960s but the social insecurity of the 1990s" (267). Like Teo, Chan asks the film to bear the weight of multiple conceptual structures, but these structures are also mutually exclusive. A single feature of visual style becomes the locus both of affirmative feeling (nostalgic affection) and negative feeling (present insecurity).[6] In a sense Chan evokes both allegory (the film, though set in the 1960s, is also "about" 1990s Hong Kong) and social reflectionism (a feature of visual style reflects social disquiet). Precisely how cinematography embodies affective moods goes unanalyzed; indeed, the causal relation between Hong Kong's "nostalgia cinema" and larger social processes does not come into focus. The accepted

5. For Bordwell's astute critiques of reflectionist criticism, see *Planet Hong Kong* (2011: 23, 29) and *Poetics of Cinema* (2008b: 30–32).
6. The objection could be raised that it is one function of symptomatic readings to expose social contradictions, but Chan is not explicit about this. Further, it is not evident how a basically consistent cinematographic style can express incoherent attitudes.

routines of top-down criticism, at least on this occasion, absolve the culturalist critic from the burden of proof.

Chan's discussion exemplifies another broad tendency within culturalist theory—postmodernism. It has become critically orthodox to perceive Wong as a postmodern filmmaker; certainly some of Wong's most dedicated commentators characterize him thus (Brunette 2005; Teo 2005; Tsui 1995). In what sense is Wong's cinema postmodern? For some critics, the films are postmodern not only in their visual narration—the fragmented editing patterns, for example— but in their narrative elements, such as Ouyang Feng's role as archcapitalist in *Ashes of Time* (Tsui 1995: 106). The postmodern experience also manifests itself in the oeuvre's imputed "newness," its cultivation of an innovative film aesthetic. I certainly do not dispute Wong's innovativeness, but I will propose presently that it is more accurate to see Wong's films as recasting preexisting norms of Hong Kong's popular cinema rather than as inventing norms ab ovo. This is not to negate the postmodernist view but rather to qualify it—Wong's films, though innovative, are not wholly new insofar as they rely upon and rework some well-entrenched principles of local and transcultural storytelling. Finally, the postmodernist critic (and the culturalist generally) emphasizes what I call the *temporal salience* of 1980s and 1990s Hong Kong cinema. Films that are part of this trend foreground temporality as something complex, elusive, and transitory; the split time zones in *Rouge* (1988) or the juxtaposed rates of motion in *A Better Tomorrow* and *The Killer* (1989) are characteristic examples. Accordingly, postmodernists examining Wong's cinema pretune their attention to instances of temporal salience. Smudge motion, step printing, jump cuts, freeze frames, elliptical cutting, anachronistic music, period settings, tropes of memory and missed encounters—such features are magnified by the postmodernist applying implicit and symptomatic meanings (Figure 1.2). Inevitably, the films' temporal salience is treated as a direct result of social events. Consciously or unconsciously prompted by the Joint Declaration, local filmmakers (it is argued) began to thematize the notion of time ebbing away— hence what critics have called an "end-of-an-era sentiment," a "doomsday mentality," a "fin-de-siècle cinema," and a "crisis cinema." I will return to some of these arguments in later chapters, but suffice it to say that bending features of the film to fit a preconceived thesis repeats the interpretive errors assailing certain culturalist writings on Hong Kong cinema.

I have tried to suggest that, for all its virtues, top-down culturalism harbors significant shortcomings. By extension, there is a strong incentive to seek an alternative (yet potentially complementary) approach compensating for the flaws of meaning-centered criticism. This is not a repudiation of culture or interpretive practice. It is rather an appeal to not, as it were, put the cart before the horse. Tzvetan Todorov here refers to literary studies, but his comments hold just as good for film criticism:

> [I do not espouse] a denial of the relation between literature and other homogenous series, such as philosophy or social life. It is rather a question of establishing a hierarchy: literature must be understood in its specificity, as literature, before we seek to determine its relation with anything else. (1969: 71)

Often, culturalists move directly to the secondary level of the work, leaving the impression that the surface discourse is straightforwardly graspable. Yet as subsequent chapters will try to demonstrate, the surface level of Wong's films—however sensuous and beguiling—is typically fraught with perceptual and cognitive obstacles that render comprehension difficult. Before proceeding to "read" the film for allegory, the viewer must first master the film as a film, that is, grapple and come to terms with the film's often complex surface level. A good deal of how the film affects us springs from this primary level of discourse. Though Teo argues that the power of *Happy Together* springs from its social resonance, it seems to me that the film is no less powerful at its denotative level. Bordwell argues, "To treat these lovelorn films as abstract allegories of Hong Kong's historical situation risks losing sight of Wong's naked appeal to our feelings about young romance, its characteristic dilemmas, moods, and moves"—risks losing sight, in other words, of the films' delightful (and difficult) surfaces (2011: 178). To bypass the work's primary level is to neglect the complexities in Wong's cinema, its appeals to the emotions, and its sheer mastery of craft.

Bordwell's Transcultural Poetics

As doctrine-driven criticism dominated Asian film studies, Bordwell proposed an alternative approach to the study of Chinese film. Bordwell outlines the stakes of this approach in a 2001 essay published in *Post Script*, "Transcultural Spaces: Toward a Poetics of Chinese Film." Here Bordwell advances a bottom-up, comparative, and empirical historical poetics of Chinese-language cinema (restricted here to the cinemas of Hong Kong, Taiwan, and Mainland China). According to Bordwell, a poetics approach to Chinese film (and to films in general) focuses centrally on (1) *overarching form*, the relation of parts and wholes in the film's (or films') large-scale composition; (2) *stylistics*, the norms and conventions of audiovisual style; (3) *spectatorial activity*, the viewing effects created by the dynamics of form and style; and (4) *historical poetics*, how and why formal and stylistic patterns stabilize or mutate over time (2001: 9). As a conceptual framework, poetics pursues explanations to fine-grained questions about the film's composition and effects. Unlike Grand Theory, which takes as its point of departure an abstract theoretical proposition, Bordwell's poetics operates inductively from the bottom up. The poetician starts not from a broad theory of culture but from the film's particularities. From here he or she generates explanations for the film's distinctive patterns of form and style. In contrast to most culturalist approaches, poetics gives priority to a given film's integrity, to the film medium's specificities, and to the filmmaker's choice situation within historical and institutional constraints (10).

How does the transcultural figure in Bordwell's discussion? As conceived by Bordwell, the poetics approach is intrinsically comparative. It surveys a range of pertinent filmmaking traditions and practices, looking not only for divergence but for convergence. The transcultural perspective illuminates norms of composition and comprehension that operate across cultures. Here poetics runs counter to cultural essentialism, whose strongest version denies the possibility of cross-cultural translation. However, as Bordwell points out, "Chinese films, to put it bluntly, are Chinese; but they're also films" (2001: 11). As films, they constitute potent vehicles of transcultural expression. Moreover, they employ schemas pervasive in other national cinemas. If the culturalist program, stressing prehandover angst, is too narrowly parochial, Bordwell's transcultural poetics widens the playing field, relating Hong Kong cinema to norms and practices widely shared across filmmaking cultures. Focusing on transcultural conventions of film style, Bordwell demonstrates that Chinese filmmakers recast and elaborate these conventions in inventive ways. He charts the transcultural emergence of the planimetric shot in Mainland Chinese cinema (revived from the 1970s and 1980s European art cinema) and of the distant long take aesthetic in Taiwanese cinema (recasting the tableau tradition of early European cinema). As for Hong Kong cinema, its commercial film-makers adapted the stylistic norm of "intensified continuity" from Hollywood (itself a stylistic mutation of classical continuity).[7] Directors such as John Woo did not merely adopt the idiom of intensified continuity but revised it to their own ends. Intensifying intensified continuity, Woo, Tsui Hark, Johnnie To, and others reworked Hollywood style for greater pictorial precision, clarity, and kineticism (14).

Regrettably, Bordwell's poetics approach has had limited impact on the research field. Emilie Yeh's "Politics and Poetics of Hou Hsiao-hsien's Films," published in the same journal issue as Bordwell's essay, attempts to redress the dominance of culturalist hermeneutics in Hou Hsiao-hsien scholarship. Another Hou expert, James Udden, has brought a poetics perspective to the

---

7. Planimetric shots station the camera perpendicular to a background surface, encouraging lateral as well as depth staging. Intensified continuity is characterized by fast cutting, close framings, extreme lens lengths, and restless camera movement.

films of Hou and Wong (2000, 2006). These studies offer exemplary cases of inductive criticism and close analysis, building upon Bordwell's poetics of cinema. Bordwell himself exemplified the poetics approach in his *Planet Hong Kong: Popular Cinema and the Art of Entertainment* ([2000] 2011), as well as in several research essays.[8] Nevertheless, within the discipline at large, Grand Theory and top-down hermeneutics still prevail, while cultural studies has held sway since the 1980s. Despite a legacy including Rudolf Arnheim, André Bazin, Noël Burch, Sergei Eisenstein, and the Russian formalists, Bordwell's poetics and Kristin Thompson's neoformalism (see Thompson 1988) remain minority research programs. Yet there are compelling reasons for taking up the research project of poetics.

Because poetics is less centrally concerned with interpretive practice, it does not restrict our understanding to what films mean. As Bordwell has elaborated in other works (e.g., Bordwell 2008b, 1989), poetics does not exclude hermeneutics but extends its ambit to broader interests. Chiefly, poetics enhances our grasp of the work's composition. It does so not by applying a general interpretive scheme but by approaching the film inductively. Top-down analysis prioritizes the a priori theory; bottom-up analysis privileges the film. The latter approach enables the poetician to illuminate aspects of style and structure without producing endlessly repetitive readings. Because poetics focuses on the film's functions and effects, moreover, it can postulate causal relations between the film's qualities and the viewer's activity. As such, it is apt to spotlight the filmmaker's artistry—for instance, by positing correlations between the viewer's responses and the filmmaker's creative choices. By contrast, culturalist approaches pay relatively little heed to the filmmaker's craft knowledge. Poetics, then, can illuminate the way the film's components shape the viewer's activity; it can elucidate the role of the viewer, reconstructing the processes of inference making, hypothesis framing, and other perceptual and cognitive activities that guide the viewer's comprehension. Culturalists, in contrast, have tended to subsume effects to general theories of culture. A typical heuristic involves inferring the effect a filmic device has upon the viewer (e.g., handheld camera and rapid cutting produce disorientation) and then interpreting this effect as a symptom of the a priori theory (e.g., disorientation betokens cultural instability and disappearance; see, for example, Tong 2008: 65–66). If culturalism reduces the viewer's activity to a nebulous, univocal "condition" (e.g., cultural anxiety), poetics systematically reconstructs the viewer's moment-by-moment uptake.

Poetics often goes beyond the work to enrich knowledge of genres, institutions, and social contexts. By means of bottom-up analysis, the poetician can,

---

8. See, for example, the following essays in Bordwell's *Poetics of Cinema* (2008b): "Aesthetics in Action: Kung-Fu, Gunplay, and Cinematic Expression" (395–411) and "Richness through Imperfection: King Hu and the Glimpse" (413–30).

for instance, theorize generalized principles governing a body of films—say, the signature traits of an individual author or the reigning tendencies of a national cinema. In addition, poetics positions the film in history. Its emphasis on historical and transcultural norms enables a perception of the film's indebtedness to past and culturally diverse traditions. Hence poetics often has occasion to refine postmodernist critics' hyperbolic claims of "newness." This is not to say that poetics dismisses contemporary films as inescapably derivative. As an inherently comparative undertaking, poetics can highlight continuity as well as change, indebtedness as well as innovation. In all, the poetics approach circumvents many of the flaws of culturalism while opening profitable avenues of its own. The above cluster of virtues is by no means exhaustive. Even so, I think it summarizes some ways in which poetics offers a preferable alternative to top-down culturalist hermeneutics.

What of the "thorny" issue of culture and society? Does poetics not neglect cultural forces in favor of a blinkered emphasis on the aesthetic object? The very proposition of a transcultural cinema indicates this is not so. Bordwell simply weights his emphasis differently than many culturalist critics do. If culturalism often puts an accent on cultural difference, Bordwell attunes his analysis to the affinities between cultures. As he succinctly puts it, "Culture not only divides us; it unites us" (Bordwell 2001: 23). Moreover, if society impacts movies, as culturalism contends, this impact is not direct and unmediated. Several layers of mediation intercede between the film and its social milieu. The concrete forces of the filmmaker's working situation, mode of production, and institutional and historical circumstances impinge more proximately upon the film than a broad feature of society does. Bordwell proposes that the critic, as a default, starts from the film and moves outward—the better to achieve plausible causal links among the film, its proximate conditions of production, and wider social causes (2008b: 32). Thus Bordwell does not ignore society but reverses the culturalist's priorities. The poetics of cinema he advances does not oppose cultural hermeneutics, hermeneutics in general, or general theories of cinema in toto. It highlights the importance of fine-grained close film analysis, of the priority of the film above predetermined general theories, and of the critic's obligation to create causal correlations between the film and society that are concrete, plausible, and (at least potentially) empirically verifiable. Bordwell's poetics, then, does not discount social and cultural factors. But it does diminish the woolly assumptions of social-reflection theory, along with other Grand Theories of culture and society that seldom provide causal explanations of the sort a poetics strives for (31).

The chapters that follow pursue a poetics of Wong's cinema. In adopting this approach I am not trying to argue for replacing one method or perspective (cultural hermeneutics) with another (poetics or formalism). Film analysis should not reject cultural readings nor should it deny the value of interpretation tout court. I assume that the poetics approach can coincide with cultural hermeneutics as complementary practices. For the methodological reasons outlined in the previous section, however, the poetics approach and top-down heuristics do not always mesh well. Yet it is perfectly conceivable that a poetician could mount, say, a socio-allegorical reading of *2046* from the bottom up, moving from concrete features of the film to general conclusions concerning social factors. A poetics of cinema, therefore, does not preclude allegorical interpretation. Nevertheless, this book places primary emphasis on the films' denotative level, searching out patterns of composition and style; identifying textual motivations, functions, and effects; and reconstructing viewer responses (perceptual, cognitive, affective) cued by the work. This denotative level is not of concern only to the poetician interested in film art. Even allegorical critics should aim to know the film's surface intimately. I take it as given that allegorical content is always necessarily mediated by explicit textual features. One can only "access" embedded meaning by engaging with the film's primary level, its surface structure of style, story, and character. Studying this level of discourse, then, is not only essential to appreciating a filmmaker's mastery of craft. It is also *necessary* for the ascription of implicit or symptomatic meanings to the work.

Wong's Aesthetic of Disturbance

Central among this book's arguments is that Wong's cinema cultivates an aesthetic of disturbance. To explicate this idea, I need to set Wong's aesthetic against some key tendencies governing contemporary Hong Kong films. Bordwell identifies several of these features in his "Transcultural Spaces" essay and elsewhere (e.g., 2008b: 395–411). From the 1970s to the 1990s, he argues, Hong Kong directors adapted Hollywood's continuity practices to fresh effect. Close-ups, fast cutting, focus racking, and fluid camera movement were repurposed for a cinema based on expressive movement. Local directors harnessed these features to the principles of pictorial clarity and legibility, enabling the audacious movements of a swordsman or a kung-fu master to be crisply delineated. These pictorial principles are perhaps most visible in the action genre, though they govern other types of film too—romantic comedies, supernatural dramas, historical sagas. Even within Hong Kong's action cinema, however, directors adopted the legibility principle in different ways. Jackie Chan gives primacy to the profilmic event, stressing the spectacle's actuality; John Woo "constructs" action analytically, relying heavily on close-ups, rapid editing, camera movement, and the like. Both directors, despite their contrasting styles, prioritize the pictorial legibility of the spectacle. Against this context, Wong's films can look utterly opaque. Yet Wong repudiates neither the legibility principle nor the cluster of devices drawn from intensified continuity. Instead, he mounts an aesthetic of disturbance, rather than outright violation, of the norms of maximal pictorial clarity holding sway in the local cinema. Visual schemas of legibility are revised in the formalist sense of "roughened form," the play of devices within the work that complicates, retards, or thwarts the viewer's perception and understanding (see Thompson 1988: 36–37). Just as Bordwell's transcultural directors recast norms circulating within and between milieus, so Wong reworks the local cinema's legibility, pressing toward an aesthetic fostering perceptual and cognitive challenge.

Not that Wong's aesthetic of disturbance is solely or even chiefly visual. It is my contention that disturbance penetrates all parameters of his work. Again, this is partly a corollary of Wong's effort to flout the transparent devices of local cinema. Take, for example, narrative plotting. In the 1980s and 1990s, popular Hong Kong films made plot architecture maximally salient, explicitly parsing stories into discriminable episodes (Bordwell 2011: 114–26). From the outset, Wong also adopted the principle of episodic construction. At times, however, he roughens the schema in ways that obscure the plot's distinct phases. Tacit ellipses conceal progressions in the story, sending the viewer's comprehension into disarray. At a more abstract level, the plot's architectural design—explicitly episodic in most Hong Kong films—becomes harder to perceive; hence, critics tend to label Wong's plots "fragmentary" and "disjointed" rather than episodic. In addition, Hong Kong movies of this period incline toward *moral* perspicuity. Manichaeism is part and parcel of local films, as of popular cinema everywhere. Even the eponymous hero of *The Killer*, a paid assassin, comes forward as fundamentally virtuous. Wong, however, disturbs this norm of moral clarity, placing fairly malevolent and amoral protagonists at his films' center (think of *Days of Being Wild* and *Fallen Angels*). Popular Hong Kong films also furnish explicit emotional appeals. The emotions portrayed and elicited tend to be saturated, specific, and unambiguous; in other words, these films traffic in strong basic emotions. Wong's films are also emotional experiences, but they tend to depict and arouse more diffuse emotion states. His protagonists—many of them disinclined to emote openly—are prone to express the "higher emotions," that is, emotions that are complex, compound, or contradictory. At the level of effects, moreover, the films resist both the transparent emotions of popular cinema and the remote austerity of the art film. Drenched in mood, Wong's cinema elicits powerful yet diffuse emotional responses.

In these and other ways, Wong disturbs the principles of clarity and legibility intrinsic to Hong Kong's popular cinema during the 1980s and 1990s. Nevertheless, as this book tries to make clear, Wong's experimentation takes place within self-imposed formal constraints. Perhaps surprisingly, his films bear the hallmarks of organic unity. The films are formally experimental, but they are also characterized by compositional coherence and integrity. The tension between these impulses—toward disunity on the one hand and organicity on the other—contributes greatly to the films' fascination and dynamism. Contradictory impulses also obtain at the level of visual style. While sensuous imagery entices viewers toward passive absorption, a host of perceptual difficulties forces them to stay cognitively alert. The Wong Kar-wai film both exhilarates and exasperates. If the films are frustrating, this is due to Wong's roughening of popular norms. And here the very fact that Wong roughens— rather than radically subverts—established schemas behooves me to qualify the postmodernist claims of a radically new aesthetic. Instead, I conceive an aesthetic of disturbance; that is, an aesthetic that roughens existing norms in ways that both nourish and nonplus the eye, posing obstacles to the viewer's perception and understanding.

Why would Wong foster such an aesthetic? I can posit some gross hypotheses. Most crudely, Wong is a self-conscious auteur, and he seeks distinctiveness. From the start he defined a signature that marked him off from his contemporaries. Later, when the local industry responded with rip-offs, he reworked his stylistic program to outstrip his imitators. "Too many people are 'doing' Wong Kar-wai these days," he stated in 1997, "so I have to do something else" (Rayns 2008a: 33). He is also self-consciously a "world cinema" director, cognizant of the importance of the festival circuit. Wong understands that festival approval frequently goes to films probing the boundaries of film form, genre conventions, and norms of national cinema. In the late 1980s, local films like *Peking Opera Blues* (1986), *Rouge*, and *The Killer* proved that offbeat genre films could win international respect, preparing a path for Wong's own entry onto the festival market. Further, Wong is a passionate cinephile, well-versed in film history. He has cited as influences the modernist generation of European art filmmakers, including Antonioni, Godard, Truffaut, and Fellini. Like Wong, these auteurs pressed the limits of form without abandoning narrative. Their films evince a ludic approach to film style (compare Wong's topsy-turvy shots in *Happy Together* and the address to camera in *Fallen Angels*), they pose difficulties of perception and understanding (consider *Last Year at Marienbad* [1961] and *Hiroshima, mon amour* [1959]), and they can be visually sensuous (e.g., *Red Desert* [1964], *Le mépris* [1963], *Domicile conjugal* [1970], *La dolce vita* [1960]). More proximately, Wong was weaned on Hong Kong genre cinema (e.g., Shaw Brothers' *huangmei* operas and *wuxia pian*), a tradition of cinematic spectacle that was nothing if not visually sensuous. We might consider, then, Wong's aesthetic as drawing upon and blending these local and foreign influences. Another factor is Wong's background working in the commercial industry. Allied with his art film sensibility, the knowledge of popular filmmaking he acquired informs an aesthetic at once abstruse and accessible. In addition, we could identify different personalities at work within a collaboration. If Wong relishes improvisation, chance, and accident, his editors (William Chang, Patrick Tam) reassert the formalities of structure at the postproduction phase. As I argue throughout this book, Wong's aesthetic of disturbance springs in large degree from Wong's work routines and mode of production.

The Book's Structure

In *Poetics of Cinema*, Bordwell distinguishes among analytical poetics (concerned with such matters as audiovisual style, constructional form, and themes), historical poetics (studying the film's historical circumstances and its contexts of reception), and a poetics of effect (focusing upon the viewer's activity). The chapters that follow reside predominantly in the first and last of these domains. Each chapter considers how Wong's compositional strategies try to steer the viewer's uptake in particular ways. As such, the book presupposes a problem-solution heuristic governing the filmmaker's activity. Brian Boyd summarizes this perspective thus:

> We can see authors as problem-solvers with individual capacities and preferences making strategic choices within particular situations, by shaping different kinds of appeals to the cognitive preferences and expectations of audiences—preferences and expectations shaped at both specieswide and local levels—and balancing the costs against the benefits of authorial effort in composition and audience effort in comprehension and response. (2009: 396)

Filmmakers, like literary authors, compose the work so as to encourage particular kinds of pickup. (This assumption contrasts the culturalist trope of unconscious directorial activity.) In addition, the filmmaker may set *himself* problems in the form of artistic challenges. As Jacques Rivette rhetorically puts it:

> Is challenge too slim a criterion [for art]? But what was Michelangelo's fresco technique or Bach's fugue technique if not the compulsion to invent an answer to some vexing question (and I'll say nothing of the infinite challenges of technique and construction—often subtle to the point of seeming trivial—which all artists secretly impose on themselves, and which will never be known to the public). (1985: 277–78)

Wong's aesthetic of disturbance, reworked by the director throughout his career, might be perceived in terms of both kinds of problem-solution model. Most broadly, this book attempts to illuminate the interface among film, filmmaker, and viewer. That is not to say that the book slights historical matters.

On the contrary, it attempts throughout to identify historical norms and to situate Wong's cinema against pertinent historical traditions.

The questions I pursue range across Bordwell's three domains of poetics. What principles of composition characterize Wong's films? Why are they composed as they are? What continuities of style, story, and theme unify the oeuvre? How are the films designed to elicit particular responses? How do they draw upon and recast particular traditions? To this cluster of questions I would add: How have Wong's films been theorized by critics and scholars? These questions unify the chapters that follow. The book's overall structure mirrors the poetics method itself, beginning with close attention to specific features of the films and widening the scope to examine pertinent contexts (e.g., genre, historical poetics, appropriation, and influence). Each chapter takes as its primary focus a single aspect of Wong's filmmaking—musical style, visual style, narration, and genre. Treating each aspect separately enables the critic to provide detailed analyses of the films' functions and effects. Of course, all these filmic aspects work together, and I do not neglect how, say, Wong coordinates music with visual style. However, for analytical purposes, isolating distinct components gives a greater purchase on each one, and ultimately, on the whole. To isolate features of the work also enables a confrontation of critical assumptions about those features (for instance, that Wong flouts genre). Finally, the book's format lets me ask, "How does an aesthetic of disturbance manifest itself in each of these aspects of the work?"

The next chapter examines Wong's musical practices and principles of musical organization. It begins by surveying the critical frameworks customarily applied to Wong's musical style. Like the other main chapters, I treat Wong's corpus generally before presenting a case study. The analysis of *Chungking Express* in Chapter 2 introduces one of the book's thematic leitmotifs (indeed, a leitmotif braided throughout Wong's films)—that of authenticity, a key preoccupation for Wong and his protagonists. Chapter 3 treats visual style. Here I elaborate what I take to be Wong's stylistic "dominant," namely, his principle of disturbance. The salient feature of Wong's visual style, this chapter suggests, is its tactics of compositional and perceptual disturbance. In Chapter 4 I turn to the formal principles of Wong's storytelling, arguing that his films display robust formal unity. Chapter 5 centers on Wong's controversial engagement with popular genre. This chapter's main analysis of *In the Mood for Love* seeks to bring together this book's parameters of study—music, visual style, narrative discourse, and genre. The final chapter isolates and reviews the book's major claims. It reiterates the importance of a poetics approach to Wong's films (and to Chinese films generally). Put simply, the poetics approach helps us appreciate the art of Chinese cinema.

2 Romantic Overtures
Music in *Chungking Express*

Wong Kar-wai must be considered one of cinema's truly *cinematic* auteurs. A filmmaker immersed in sound and image, he taps the spectator's bimodal propensities for dramatic and expressive effect. He ascribes music special importance and no consideration of Wong as a cinematic stylist should neglect this aspect of his films. As an effort to elucidate Wong's musical engagement, this chapter examines the functions and effects of music in *Chungking Express* (1994). It aims to disclose how Wong marshals highly eclectic musical cues into a narratively coherent unity. Other, more general questions inform this chapter as well. What principles of musical scoring and spotting govern Wong's sound design, and to what extent do his methods typify standard Hong Kong practice? More broadly still, how have Wong's music tracks been theorized by critics?

This last question provides my point of departure. My general claim is that the critical reception of Wong's music tracks has been governed by reigning paradigms within academic film studies. To some extent, Wong's musical evolution has been assimilated, by critics, to the emerging trends in film theory and criticism. Consequently, these critical perspectives at times overstate (and oversimplify) certain aspects of Wong's music tracks, particularly at the level of cultural and sociological meaning. By contrast, the ways that music operates formally, narratively, and thematically have been qualitatively neglected. So, too, has the extent to which music permeates all stages of a Wong Kar-wai production. In this chapter, I aim to show that the importance of music in Wong's cinema extends far beyond what is heard on the sound track.

Critical Reception and Conceptual Frameworks

In the mid-1990s, Western critics subsumed Wong's music scores to broad conceptual and formal frameworks. Auteurists sought evidence of individual artistry in the compilation score, which seemed to exemplify directorial choice.

Song selection in *Chungking Express* and *Fallen Angels* was often interpreted as auteurist expression. Appropriated tunes, it was assumed, comprised a receptacle of personal themes, and specially commissioned scores embodied the director's intentions. Crucially, his collage practice fortified critics eager to construct Wong as a ranking auteur. That he cherry-picked songs and assumed "sole charge" of his films' sound tracks (Martinez 1997: 29) testified to a total authorial vision and design. In the same period Western critics gestured toward Wong's cinephilia, albeit largely ignoring non-Occidental influences upon his style. Several observers noted *Ashes of Time*'s borrowings from Ennio Morricone's "spaghetti western" scores (e.g., ibid.: 30). More generally, auteur-minded critics detected in Wong a kinship with cinephile directors that was predicated at least partly on musical style. If Wong's anachronistic pop songs evoked Scorsese (Morrison 1995), his abrasive spotting recalled Jean-Luc Godard (Leahy 1995: 45). Comparisons of this sort identified Wong's sound tracks not only with an aural salience at odds with traditional cinema's "inaudibility" but also with cultural connotations of hipness—an "indelible cinematic cool" (Charity 1995: 14) that formed a key component of Wong's entry into the West (and that was greatly enhanced by Tarantino's patronage). Not least, these comparisons were the fulcrum for the critic's auteur construction: musically, as in other respects, Wong was deemed heir apparent to an international legacy of virtuosic film stylists.

Another major framework applied to Wong's music scores was postmodernism. Already alert to Wong's affinities with Tarantino and the modernist nouvelle vague, critics realized that music in Wong's films could be assimilated to postmodern concepts. Thus, musical elements produce irony in *Happy Together* (Martinez 1997: 9), self-consciousness in *Chungking Express* (Morrison 1996), allusion in *Ashes of Time* (Martinez 1997: 30), and pastiche in *Fallen Angels* (Morrison 1995; Tsui 1995: 114). All these discoveries amounted to claims for a new (postmodern) mode of perception fostered by Wong's aesthetic—a line of argument developed, along predominantly visual lines, by Abbas (1997b)—and led critics to harness Wong's formal innovations to a cluster of ready-made if woolly concepts. Needless to say, the assertions of novelty and individualism also advanced the auteur-making efforts of Wong's advocates. More recent writings continue to place his scores firmly in a postmodernist context; one critic, for instance, discerns musical self-parody in *As Tears Go By* and *Fallen Angels* (Brunette 2005: 61); another perceives postmodern irony in *Chungking Express* and *Fallen Angels* (Binns 2008). One could also posit postmodernist strategies pervading Wong's aesthetic in the form of hybridity (the diversity—both cultural and idiomatic—within his compilation scores; see Dissanayake 2003: 65), surface structures (made palpable by sustained musical foregrounding), and acoustic fragmentation (the abruptly truncated use of music cues and the more encompassing principle of musical *collage*). For Teo (2005), as for many critics, Wong's heterogeneous musical style is but one dimension of a wholly postmodernist aesthetic.

For a time, critics grasped Wong's audiovisual style by reference to music video stylistics (Maslin 1994; Morrison 1995, 1996; Leahy 1995; Rohdie 1999). Wong, it was claimed, embraced a so-called MTV aesthetic characterized by the sorts of postmodernist tendencies noted above. Certainly Wong's use of music could be evocative of music video, conferring upon songs a rare degree of prominence and occasionally employing music cues to shape, determine, and direct the visual action. Moreover, the postmodernist emphasis on fragmentary experience found an apparent correlative in music-driven scenes: "As in Gene Kelly musicals," writes David Martinez, "the music in Wong Kar-wai's films always makes a break in the scene, interrupting the story-line" (1997: 34). Sometimes termed "MTV moments" (Romney and Wooton 1995), the music-led sequence, it was claimed, disrupts the film's narrative flow to allow a discrete musical composition to unfold. In addition, critics likened Wong's aesthetic to MTV's preoccupation with surfaces—though for Wong's detractors, the trappings of MTV stylistics simply furnished ammunition for the familiar charge of superficiality. (Paul Fonoroff's 1994 review of *Chungking Express* states, "It's brilliant MTV, but is it a movie? . . . Once you take off the wrapping, there isn't too much of substance inside" [1999: 406–7].) Postmodernism provided critics a framework by which to reconcile aesthetic contexts as diverse as MTV and Godard, which in Wong's case could sit cheek by jowl without contradiction. As Howard Hampton proclaimed, Wong's films (and *Chungking Express* in particular) constitute "a dazzlingly adroit synthesis of art cinema and MTV" (1996: 91)—in other words, a typically postmodernist hybridization of discourses.

Since the 1990s, the parallels with MTV have been iterated by some critics (e.g., Chaudhuri 2005: 123; de Carvalho 2008: 204–5). To an extent this correlation holds water; Wong has even ventured into music video production on occasion. However, I need to qualify some aspects of the postmodernist critic's claims. For instance, they have tended to overstate the MTV moment's disruptive effect upon narrative progression. Localized, music-led sequences seldom retard story action as Martinez and others contend. Their assumption overlooks how thoroughly Wong integrates music into the narrative and diegesis; for instance, by motivating a song diegetically (ascribing the song an identifiable source such as a jukebox) or establishing strong correspondence between story and song (as when song lyrics are yoked to character goals). Moreover, Wong's MTV moments typically transmit story information—indeed, they often convey much that is narratively essential.

Acknowledging Wong's debt to music video requires the recognition that his films also elicit a quite distinct sort of viewing activity. Neither the narrative nor the viewer's cognition is stymied by Wong's music-based sequences—the placement of such scenes within a large-scale narrative structure entails the spectator's engagement in an ongoing process of story construction. Clearly, this viewing process flies in the face of the "passive" spectatorship purportedly induced by music video. Prioritizing the viewer's story uptake also pushes the filmmaker toward greater clarity and continuity of time and space than is usually found in music videos. Analyzing a song-driven scene in *As Tears Go By*, Bordwell concludes that "Unlike most music videos, this sequence holds each image long enough to permit expressive elements to accumulate and step up the lyrical intensity" (2011: 177–78). By contrast, music videos often present audiovisual correspondences erratically, veering from lucid shot relations to opaque and ambiguous ones (Vernallis 2001: 34). Governed by narrative concerns, Wong's music-based sequences thus differ sharply from MTV: eschewing passive spectatorship, they temper MTV's incoherent form to rivet the viewer's attention to story matters.

Recent years have seen attempts to refine and redress the MTV comparison. Analyzing Hong Kong cinema, Brian Hu conceives the MTV aesthetic not simply as a set of stylistic conventions but as an economically shaped form of cross-media address, targeting a "cognoscenti audience" (2006: 422) and traversing television, karaoke (KTV), and other entertainment industries. Popular songs in Hong Kong movies, Hu argues, tap the extrafilmic knowledge of the local audience (and the cultural competency of the nonlocal viewer). The polysemous songs and singers *inform* the "knowing" viewer's grasp of narrative meaning, character traits, and so on (413). Hu demonstrates this thesis with reference to *Chungking Express*: here Wong exploits the local audience's familiarity with pop star Faye Wong, evoking memorable imagery from her music videos and plumbing her personal history to motivate song selection and story action (416–21). Hu proposes to substitute the term "MTV aesthetic" with "KTV aesthetic"—the better to replace connotations of viewer passivity with (inter)activity and to highlight the synergistic local contexts that govern the use of music in Asian films. Hu's approach mirrors a general disciplinary shift toward reception studies and transnationalism in film scholarship (see also Yeh 1999).

Authorship, cinephilia, postmodernism, MTV aesthetics—such were the contexts by which Wong's use of music was explicated in the mid-to late 1990s. Come the turn of the century, critics had to adapt their schemas to the case of *In the Mood for Love*, with which Wong shrugged off music video comparisons. Now the "MTV auteur" had emerged as an exponent of nostalgia cinema. Postmodernist critics could thus preserve Wong as an exemplar of postmodernity by downplaying music-video fragmentation in favor of another prized postmodernist concept—nostalgia. Wong's music score for *In the Mood for Love*, moreover, remained a model of hybridity. Wong contrived a melting pot of musical genres, idioms, and eras, of high-and low-culture musical forms. He was at once in thrall to American culture and nostalgic for old Shanghai. The "oldies" of *In the Mood for Love* function nostalgically (Yue 2008: 149; Polan 2001), constructing an imagined past and a yearning for a bygone age. As anachronistic objects, they are also apt to create the aesthetic distance common to postmodern artworks.

The concept of nostalgia has utility, but critics often neglected the oldie's fulfillment of primary functions, such as operating as a source of sheer romanticism or as a hint of the protagonists' asynchronous existence or as an index of a more general temporal salience in play. Often stressed was the local, sociological impetus for Wong's nostalgia. In the uncertain face of pre- and posthandover Hong Kong, archaic musical styles supplied a form of affective retreat (here a kinship with the culturalist line of criticism, explicated in the previous chapter, is evident). But from a transcultural vantage point (and from the perspective of a historical poetics), we might also recall the widespread use of anachronistic songs in Hollywood movies, supercharged in the 1980s by the influence of MTV (e.g., *Top Gun* [1986], *Ghost* [1990]). If we view Wong as an *international* auteur, assimilating both popular and high-art modes and both Western and Eastern influence, then this Hollywood trend constitutes a pertinent context for his nostalgic use of old songs. Postcolonial Hong Kong reverie, then, is not the whole story. Wong's musical anachronisms dovetail with those found in films like *Sleepless in Seattle* (1993) and *When Harry Met Sally* (1989) (see Krutnik 1998; Garwood 2000) and with the notion of "commodified nostalgia," David R. Shumway's term for "the revival by the culture industry of certain fashions and styles of a past era" (1999: 39). I am not claiming that Wong's *treatment* of oldies mirrors that of mainstream Hollywood directors, rather that his taste for old songs is symptomatic of an international cinematic interest in musical nostalgia.

Temporal salience also made Wong's films ideal fodder for Deleuzian scholars. Subsumed to ready-made categories (invariably, the *movement-image* and the *time-image*), Wong's musical cues could be grasped as expressing a new, specifically modern experience of temporality. Time here was not wholly past-oriented, but the postmodern concept of nostalgia was seldom very far away. Moreover, Deleuzian scholars revived arguments reminiscent of the MTV critics: Wong's narratives virtually stopped as the predominance of music asserted itself (de Carvalho 2008: 203). Seemingly operating outside of ordinary temporal experience, Wong's music and image combinations heralded a new form of cinema commensurate with specifically Deleuzian concepts of filmic experience (Wilson 2009; de Carvalho 2008).

Wong's music tracks are culturally as well as historically wide-ranging. As the 1990s wore on, the rise of transnationalist approaches sensitized theorists to Wong's pluralistic musical style. Emilie Yeh (1999) sets out to identify the transnational aspects of music in *Chungking Express* and *Fallen Angels*. She usefully distinguishes between international and cross-regional levels of musical engagement (128–29). Wong's use of music, Yeh points out, taps both international musical contexts (appropriating tunes from, say, America and Europe) and cross-regional musical contexts (mining the musics of Taiwan and other pan-Asian territories). Yeh therefore characterizes Wong's use of world music as both transnational and transcultural (129). Such musical variety invited theorists to note Wong's "global tastes" (Udden 2006: 67). For Julian Stringer, Wong's eclectic music constitutes a "global jukebox" (2002: 397), a neatly evocative phrase suggesting not only musical diversity but also the authorial element of choice and selection. Unlike postmodernist critics, to whom a cultural mix of music induces fragmentary experience, critics adopting transnational perspectives have emphasized cross-cultural accessibility. Thus a Westernized "pop sensibility" could account for Wong's successful penetration of American markets (Ventura 2005). As Stringer suggests, disparate music "provides consumers with diverse points of entry and helps a film travel far and wide" (2002: 398).

Though crucial, the international level of Wong's hybrid scores should not obscure local and cross-regional levels. Often Wong does not simply appropriate Western tunes—he reworks them, Sinicizes them, endows them with local features. Western vocals might be supplanted by a Chinese singer, as in Danny Chung's cover version of "Happy Together." Or Cantonese-language versions might be commissioned, as occurred with Massive Attack's "Karmacoma" in *Fallen Angels* (Toop 2005: 160). Various types of Asian music (e.g., Cantonese opera, Mandarin oldies) adorn Wong's sound tracks. In short, the local is as significant to Wong's scores as the nonlocal. Nowhere is this cultural synthesis better epitomized than in the genre of Cantopop, which recurs throughout Wong's oeuvre. Cantopop embodies cultural hybridity, fusing Chinese, Western, and Latin influences into a musical idiom unique to Hong Kong. Indeed Cantopop resembles Hong Kong itself in its mélange of influences, reminding us that Wong's eclectic scores also function at the primary level of narrative and setting. Postmodernist or not, a culturally mixed score accurately denotes the heterogeneity of Hong Kong space.

To examine the Western critical reception of Wong's film music is to encounter the prevailing theoretical frameworks of the day. Some critics isolated particular aspects of Wong's musical style in ways that served to reinforce the theories they invoked. Closer to home, local critics paralleled their Western counterparts, linking Wong to MTV (Li 1995), the nouvelle vague (Law Wai-ming, cited in ibid.: 29),[1] and postcolonial nostalgia (Sek Kei 1997: 124). Some critics posited Chinese precursors to Wong's style undiscovered by most Western critics (see Shu Kei 1991). However, only a handful of critics and scholars, from East or West, attempted to analyze Wong's musical techniques from a formal and narratological perspective. I will examine the formal strategies of a specific film example—*Chungking Express*—later in this chapter. But first I will lay bare some broad principles and tendencies characterizing Wong's use of music. What are the characteristic functions that music performs in Wong's oeuvre? What general principles govern his musical strategies?

Subjectivity, Sentimentality, Sensuousness

Film music's traditional narrative functions find expression in Wong's cinema, though there are notable deviations from convention. Wong's music fulfills the norms of scene setting, cuing the narrative milieu and constructing a historical period. It establishes mood, reinforces continuity, implies themes, and forges leitmotivic associations. It may be rhythmically dovetailed with ambient noise, yielding a holistically integrated soundscape—as when the opening segment of *Fallen Angels* alternates the rhythmic pulse of a passing train with a percussive musical beat. Or it may be subjected to large-scale patterning, presaging impending plot events. In *Fallen Angels*, a Leonesque music cue accompanies Killer's brush with death near the film's midpoint. Wong revives the cue toward the climax, when Killer is asked to commit a dangerous final murder. Wong thus engages in musical foreshadowing, hinting at the violence to come; indeed, when Killer is slain during the shooting, the somber music cue returns as a dirge. There is nothing innovative in employing film music this way, but such examples at least demonstrate a concern for narrational pattern, coherence, and unity.

Another standard function of film music—that of conveying a character's subjective state—also obtains in Wong's aesthetic, but it acquires unusual emphasis thanks to the subjectively opaque characters that Wong favors (think of Killer in *Fallen Angels*, the blonde woman in *Chungking Express*, and the circumspect neighbors of *In the Mood for Love*). Similarly, music's propensity to "speak for" a character becomes paramount when that character suffers from mutism, as does Ho Chi Moo in *Fallen Angels* (though Wong takes

---

1. Sometimes Wong's affinity with the nouvelle vague was made explicit by appropriation, as when *2046* borrows Georges Delerue's "Julien et Barbara" from François Truffaut's *Confidentially Yours* (1983). This musical quotation is itself symptomatic of Wong's cinephilia, discussed in Chapter 1. As Giorgio Biancorosso suggests, "cinephilia and musicophilia are for Wong closely intertwined" (2010: 238).

liberties with this character trait, which I discuss in Chapter 4). Here, music operates according to what I will call "expressive displacement" or diffusion—when character expressivity is not forthcoming, the burden of expression falls upon other diegetic or stylistic devices. Peter Brunette notes a cognate instance during *In the Mood for Love*, wherein the camera lingers upon curlicues of cigarette smoke: the moment "works precisely because of the evocative music that accompanies narratively 'empty' visuals and unleashes their expressivity" (2005: 97). I will address how *Chungking Express* puts music to subjective effect later.

Oftentimes, as I have noted, Wong motivates music diegetically. Characters "create their own sound environment" (Martinez 1997: 31), becoming immersed in jukebox songs, radio tunes, CD albums, and the like. More than this, for Wong's taciturn characters, music substitutes for verbal communication. In *Fallen Angels* the assassin obliquely conveys a message to his female contractor via a particular jukebox tune; the pair is condemned to indirect forms of interaction because of their mutual emotional and social reticence. Thus the song's presence on the sound track is motivated narratively by the quirks of character psychology. (As a "message," the tune is characteristically ambiguous—its refrain advises the contractor to "Forget Him," but the lyrics caution against doing so lest one "loses" oneself. Moreover, the assassin intends his message to convey his desire to quit his job, but is he also instructing his partner to "forget him" as a romantic prospect?) Frequently, character action motivates not only the presence of specific songs but also their salience on the sound track. Hence Agent's compulsive attraction to the song "Speak My Language" in *Fallen Angels* begets its conspicuous repetition. Likewise the thunderous strains of Italian opera in *2046* find justification in Mr. Wang's strategic preference for loud music (he pumps up the aria's volume to drown out the din of family quarrels).

Several of Wong's films seem to animate the "jukebox principle," whereby a range of popular songs dominate the sound track apparently without design. In Wong's cinema, I have said, the jukebox analogy holds good in certain respects—chiefly in terms of motivating musical diversity on the sound track. And yet the jukebox principle is ironically undercut in *Chungking Express*, for it serves to stress not random and miscellaneous tunes but, rather, the *same* few tunes repeated ad infinitum. The film's iterations of "California Dreamin'" imply Faye's almost pathological phobia of change (and, paradoxically, her unrelenting desire for change). Wong's use of music in such examples, motivated by character psychology and action, attests to the protagonists' all-consuming aversion to change. It is not enough that their romantic aspiration is constrained by habit; even their cultural consumption must be ritualistic and routinized.

Like other Hong Kong directors, Wong employs music to expressive ends, but he repudiates the sentimentality beloved of the region's directors. Highly emotive scenes tend to be shorn of musical accompaniment. Only ambient noise attends Leslie's tearful handling of her father's personal effects in *My Blueberry Nights*. In the same film, Sue Lynne's extended lament for her dead husband carries potential for sentimentality, but here again Wong rejects music as an intensifier of emotion. Both scenes present the character in close facial views, visibly expressing sadness. Wong thus resists emotional oversaturation by restricting the scenes' range of affective cues. Yet he finds alternative ways to subtly reinforce emotion. During Leslie's display of grief, he decelerates the imagery to a gentle staccato rhythm; and, as Sue Lynne's lament reaches its dramatic apogee, he incorporates a low thunder tremble into the ambient sound mix. Both devices function expressively, but without the emotional heavy-handedness that a music cue might bring. Through such unemphatic cues to emotion, Wong displays an affective restraint rare in Hong Kong cinema.

Not all of Wong's emotive scenes spurn musical accompaniment. But when music is employed, the effort to avoid sentimentalism remains a guiding principle. At times Wong averts sentimentalism by means of contrapuntal scoring, forging a disparity between the affective tenor of the music and that of the dramatic situation it accompanies. An example occurs in *Happy Together*. Poised to speak into a voice recorder, Lai Yiu-fai starts to sob uncontrollably, his loneliness now a wellspring of physical anguish. Here is a situation apt for sentimental treatment: private emotional distress unfolding against the energetic pulse of a Buenos Aires nightclub. Instead of paralleling this action with sad music, though, Wong counterpoints it with a jauntily up-tempo Latin tune emanating from the dance floor. The discord between song and situation precludes sentimentality and moreover makes Yiu-fai's isolation all the more palpable (Figure 2.1). Consider also the climax of the film, set to a Cantopop version of the Turtles' "Happy Together." The song is contagiously euphoric, but the narrative situation is relatively ambivalent—for one critic the ending conveys "alienation" (Tambling 2003: 62), as if Yiu-fai's sense of isolation is not wholly vanquished. Still, the rousing tune works its irresistible effect upon the closing imagery and situation. This is close to what theorists call polarization, the music's affective qualities influencing the viewer's interpretation of emotionally ambiguous visual information (see Smith 1999: 161). In such ways, an equivocal denouement is infused with affirmative feeling. At the same time, the tension between song and story keeps sentimentality at bay.

In short, sentimentality is too "pure" an emotion for Wong, who typically trades in complex, composite, and generally low-level feeling states. He is alert to music's potential for melodramatic excess and discovers ways to diffuse inherently emotive story action. In *Fallen Angels*, the scenes linking Ho Chi

Moo's father to Chyi Chin's "Thinking of You" are moving but not sentimental—Wong undercuts sentimentality with ingratiating humor (the father's exasperation at his son's harassment). He also motivates the ballad by character action, tracing it to a CD selection by Ho Chi Moo. Thus the *scene's* apparent sentimentality is transferred to the mute young man, as he displays open affection for his father and later mourns his passing. The scene's emotivity, in other words, is focalized around (and motivated by) the grieving son. Rejecting sentimentality is one way that Wong distinguishes himself from Hong Kong filmmakers, but he also eschews the austerity dear to certain European art directors. In Wong's cinema, music suffuses the soundscape, but it is apt to perform sensuously, not sentimentally. Again and again, music and image combine to sensuous effect—think of Sue Lynne floating through the Memphis bar to the strains of "Try a Little Tenderness" (*My Blueberry Nights*), the sensual tango that segues into erotic lovemaking in Yiu-fai's kitchen (*Happy Together*), or Agent's tactile bond with the jukebox from which "Speak My Language" issues (*Fallen Angels*). Wong employs music to sensuous and expressive effect, but he negates both the emotional manipulations of sentimental cinema and the affective detachment of the art film.

Music also mobilizes what I have called a strategy of aesthetic disturbance. One traditional narrative function of film music is, as one theorist states, "to cover temporal ellipses" (Smith 1998: 177). A music cue may serve as a sound bridge between scenes, ensuring smooth continuity of actions set some time apart. In Wong's ludic storytelling, however, music not only "covers" temporal ellipses but disguises them, and those ellipses may elide significant passages of story time. Consider an instance from *In the Mood for Love*. Su and Chow carry out their pantomime in a restaurant, augmented by the lush sound of a Nat King Cole tune. A visual cut occurs but indicates no noteworthy shift in story time; after the cut we are still with the protagonists in the restaurant. Cole's ballad continues across the shot change without any break in its continuity, thus de-emphasizing the cut's significance and implying continuous action. Yet the music disguises a significant ellipsis—following the cut, Su is shown wearing a different cheongsam, the only overt indication that story time has skipped forward. Cole's tune, indifferent to the advancement of story time, has rendered temporal progression discreet. It has been subsumed to the film's restricted discourse, neglecting to cue us to the narration's forward leap. (If the alert viewer does notice the time shift, the narration's reticence in signaling this ellipsis creates temporal salience—the passage of time becomes more prominent than if this scene transition were indicated by, say, a dissolve or an intertitle.) In effect, Cole's song constitutes a narrationally restricted device that disturbs our confident grasp of narrative time. As such, it participates in Wong's aesthetic of disturbance, where we find an interplay of repressive or "difficult" elements (the tacit use of ellipsis reinforced by the continuous performance of the song) and aids to comprehension (the change in Su's appearance). Here again, Wong adapts a traditional function of film music—the "smoothing down" of temporal ellipses—to his own aesthetic style, challenging the preeminence of dramatic clarity and stimulating cognitive effort.

When we "hear" a Wong Kar-wai film, we are aware of the conspicuous absence of any overarching, predominant sound. Postmodernist theorists might pronounce Wong's sound tracks incoherent on the basis of this musical heterogeneity. By fixating on diversity, however, we pay no heed to the music track's continuities. As the above tendencies indicate, Wong's music tracks are unified by consistent principles, to which at least two further tendencies can be added. First is what might be called the thematic unity of the music track. Despite their disparate idioms and places of origin, most of Wong's music tracks accord with a thematic concern with romantic love (of a certain sort). This thematic raison d' être is typically embedded diegetically, with romantic music affixed to the psychology and action of romance-absorbed characters. Most broadly, Wong accords music an intensity and formal salience that defies the "inaudibility" of traditional film scoring. If there is one overarching principle governing Wong's music design, it might be this—*audibility*, music that is rendered "probient" rather than ambient. Throughout Wong's oeuvre, music comes palpably forward by way of loudness, repetition, incongruity, cultural otherness, and other strategies. For all the imputed incoherence of Wong's collage scores—their postmodern fragmentation and hybridity—the principles, traits, and tendencies shaping them remain remarkably consistent from film to film. Here, as in other aspects of Wong's cinema, randomness and disparity give way to traditional principles of unity, order, and coherence.

Musical Practice

I have shown that Wong not only adopts film music's traditional functions but intensifies them. The standard use of music to convey subjective states, bridge temporal gaps, or motivate music diegetically assumes heightened importance and prominence in Wong's films. To take the full measure of his musical engagement, however, it is necessary to alight on his methods of production. Put simply, music permeates every aspect of Wong's film practice. It serves initially as a generative element in the film's inception—the filmmaker commences preproduction equipped with preexisting music containing the kernel of potential narratives. Notes editor William Chang, "Wong Kar-wai usually compiles the music before the shoot and let[s] the music carry the story" (Lee 2004: 46). Music influences casting too, both as a commercial imperative (a troupe of pop idols attracts financiers and audiences) and as a prototype for character traits and action (the actor-musician's actual life supplies raw material for characterization). Also prior to shooting, Wong instructs actors to glean character traits from recommended tunes. At the preproduction phase, then, music is at once a point of departure and a communicative tool among collaborators.

During shooting, music fulfills a number of tasks. Wong typically plays music on the set "to establish the mood" of the dramatic action (Wong 2007). At other times, he uses on-set music to induce the actor to a desired emotional state. "It's very difficult for me to cry," says Faye Wong. "During filming [of *2046*, Wong] used music . . . that helped me a lot" (*2046* DVD Sony). Live music also enjoins players to choreograph their gestures and behavior to the tune's rhythmic and tonal qualities. The on-set score similarly establishes a musical tempo with or against which the cinematographer can interact. As Wong Kar-wai states, "When I try to explain to a camera operator the speed I want for a certain move, a piece of music will often communicate it better than a thousand words" (quoted in Tirard 2002: 198; see also Lim 2006). Editing takes place during the shooting phase as well as in postproduction, and here again Wong recruits music (often "temp tracks") to determine the scene's visual tempo (Stokes 2002: 132).

Wong's reliance on music at all phases of production is not without precedent, but it departs from standard practice in Hong Kong cinema. Until recently the local industry's refusal of direct sound gave voice dubbing priority at the postproduction phase, with music added relatively late in the process (see Bettinson 2013). By contrast, Wong's entire production process is imbued with a musical sensibility. Considerations of rhythm shape his storytelling style. In interviews, Wong and his collaborators stress the need to discover the rhythm of the preproduction script ("rhythm is the essence of a script," Doyle states; Greenhalgh 2005: 209), of acting performance and camera movement ("the actors' rhythms pace our shots"; Doyle 2003: 8), and of production design and editing (according to Chang, "All the techniques I use are based on . . . emotions and rhythm"; McGrath 2001: 157). Each dimension of the film is brought into rhythmic harmony. This attempt toward, in Sergei Eisenstein's words, "binding [sound and image] organically *through movement*" (1986: 136; italics in original) reminds us that Wong prizes aesthetic principles of order, pattern, and unity. Another lesson must be noted here: Wong's musical practice is not reducible to the process of selecting or commissioning music and arranging it into cues. Rather, a musical sense shapes each level of Wong's artistic creation, from the germination of a narrative to the film's completed look and feel. It would be reductive, therefore, to conceptualize Wong's musical practice purely on the basis of what is heard on the music track.

The rest of this chapter examines Wong's musical strategies in *Chungking Express*, with particular emphasis on the score's narrative, formal, and thematic unity. With a few notable exceptions (Hu 2006; Yeh 1999), critics have tended to subsume this film's musical strategies to the sociological, postmodernist, and other "grand" theories of film and culture discussed earlier. Bordwell, however, argues that *Chungking Express* possesses a "formal finesse" that intrinsically deserves study (2000: 283). In what follows I analyze how Wong formally integrates music into discrete sequences and how music is distributed across the film as a whole. Not only does a poetics analysis reveal Wong's effort to unify musical style and story; it also spotlights the characters' psychological traits and shifting relationships. As I will show, *Chungking Express* (scored mostly with appropriated music but also featuring two specially composed cues) exhibits a sophisticated engagement with the music track, assigning myriad "intensified" functions to its diversified score.

Changing Tunes: *Chungking Express*

Chungking Express splices together two narrative phases. In the first block of action, Officer 223 (Takeshi Kaneshiro) almost collides with a blonde woman as he chases a suspect through central Kowloon. Later 223, recently estranged from his girlfriend, gorges on expired pineapple. Meanwhile the blonde woman (Brigitte Lin) recruits a cadre of Indian smugglers to ferry a shipment of cocaine out of Hong Kong. When the smugglers abscond with the drugs, the blonde woman begins a desperate search before word of the heist reaches her supplier. 223, looking for companionship, approaches the blonde woman at a bar, whereupon they drink whisky, rent a room, and spend a chaste night together. The next morning, the cop goes jogging and is heartened when the woman pages him a birthday greeting. Later the woman, unsuccessful in her search for the Indian smugglers, shoots the drug supplier dead. This first plot phase culminates when 223 physically stumbles against Faye (Faye Wong), an incident recalling the opening scene and prompting a shift in the film's "interest-focus."[2]

Four musical themes appear in this first plot phase. Wong organizes these themes into leitmotivic arrangements: up-tempo, percussive Bhangra accompanies action involving the Indian contrabandists; a languorous jazz theme attends the night shared by 223 and the blonde woman; electronic violin music is allied chiefly to the blonde woman's drug trafficking; and a sprightly reggae song denotes the drug peddler's milieu. Clearly, in this plot phase, characters are individuated not only by discrete musical themes but by strikingly distinct musical idioms. A postmodernist critic might here claim evidence of fragmentation and incoherence (the score is a miscellaneous hybrid), but Wong's

---

2. Seymour Chatman coins the term "interest-focus" to denote a figure or figures in a narrative whose point of view the spectator shares (at least temporarily) and with whom they are led to identify to some degree. See Chatman (1990: 148).

leitmotivic patterning of the score's diverse themes attests to an overarching, *systematized* sound design. Characterizing the score as incoherent obscures the unifying functions to which Wong's musical cues are molded. Take the film's opening sequence. Its action moves through three phases—the blonde woman is introduced, 223 is brought into the action, and both characters converge in a fleeting encounter. Accompanying this sequence is a synthesized violin theme (Michael Galasso's "Baroque") that unfolds as a coherent and unified text, its coda precisely synchronized with the end of the scene's action. Wong, therefore, calibrates visual action to the musical cue's rhythm and duration. The formal unity of "Baroque" also reinforces the structural coherence evident in the scene's image track (seen, for instance, in the latter's consistent use of step printing). Far from evoking postmodern disintegration, Galasso's musical theme mounts a formally unified story episode.

This plot phase's reggae song goes beyond the functions of unity and mood to fulfill additional tasks. Wong motivates Dennis Brown's "Things in Life" diegetically—it emanates from a jukebox in the drug peddler's bar—but the song's memorable trumpet intro, along with its dynamics and clarity in the sound mix, afford it nondiegetic prominence. "Things in Life" next appears when the blonde woman arrives at the bar; in a restricted framing she obliquely asks a bartender "where he is." This visual and narrative action may be enigmatic (Who does the blonde woman refer to? Where is this action taking place?), but the presence of "Things in Life" disambiguates matters. Relying principally on the tune's trumpet hook to denote character and place, this scene establishes "Things in Life" in motivic relation to both the drug peddler and the bar he presides over.[3] Now the song bridges an elliptical cut to the blonde woman wandering Kowloon's streets. Lowering its dynamics to accommodate both ambient traffic noise and the woman's voice-over, the trumpet melody loosely synchronizes with screaming car horns and other nonmusical sounds. As the voice-over ends, the narration cuts to another line of action. "Things in Life" straddles both action lines and "sneaks" out as 223's voice-over initiates a new stage in the drama. Consuming barely a minute of screen duration, this leitmotif displays a plurality characteristic of Wong's musical cues: it denotes character and place, provides underscoring of dialogue, evokes the musicality of diegetic noise, and lends continuity to parallel lines of action.

"Things in Life" is also here afforded commentative purpose. Like many Wong protagonists, the blonde woman not only recoils from change but inauthentically strives to conquer it. Even the minutiae of her behavior manifest this compulsion, as her voice-over in this sequence reveals: "Somehow I've started being very cautious. Whenever I wear a raincoat I put on sunglasses. You never know when it'll rain and when it'll be sunny." In resolving to

---

3. Consequently "Things in Life" disappears from the film after the drug-peddler's death.

preempt, outstrip, and master change, the blonde woman compulsively repudiates the fundamental nature of the world. Hence she represents (like the main agents of *In the Mood for Love*) another of Wong's inauthentic protagonists. If the blonde trafficker safeguards against change, however, "Things in Life" mildly rebukes her: "It's not every day we're gonna be the same way," sings Dennis Brown. "There must be a change somehow." Counterpointing the blonde woman's narration, Brown's song hints at the essential futility of her worldview. It is also worth noting that this musical counterpoint is not so much audiovisual as primarily aural. Music here functions as a strategy of disturbance; the sound track divides the viewer's aural attention, juxtaposing divergent points of view simultaneously. In subtle ways, Wong's sound design refuses the viewer a univocal meaning.

If popular film music typically "speaks for" the character, here it contradicts what the character says. When the blonde woman first meets 223 at a bar, a sultry sax motif underscores her voice-over: "Knowing a person doesn't mean they'll love you. They change. They may like pineapple today and something else tomorrow." Wong intercuts this scene with action set inside the drug peddler's bar, a maneuver that curtails the saxophone cue and motivates the opening bars of "Things in Life," including Brown's exhortation that "there must be a change somehow." On the image track, the drug peddler passionately kisses a woman (Dennis Brown's appeal for "change" here implying sexual promiscuity). This steamy clinch underlines the chasteness of the blonde woman's encounter with 223, itself unfolding against the sexually evocative lilt of the jazz saxophone. While crosscutting foregrounds contrasting activity, the sound track mounts a dialogue between voice-over (which equates change with emotional heartache) and music (which implies a romantic desire suppressed by the blonde woman in "bad faith"). It is through this disparity between voice-over and music that Wong's judgment of the blonde woman can be inferred.

The second phase of *Chungking Express* centers on Faye and Officer 633 (Tony Leung Chiu-wai), a cop who patronizes the fast-food counter where Faye works. Abandoned by his stewardess lover, 633 becomes the oblivious object of Faye's desire. Eventually 633 discovers that Faye has been sneaking into his apartment, refurbishing and domesticating its décor. Officer 633 asks Faye on a date, but the waitress decamps to the United States and finds work as a stewardess. A year later, Faye returns to the fast-food counter to discover 633 installed as its owner. At the cop's request, she makes out a fake boarding pass in his name.

A host of formal and narrative parallels links the film's two plot phases, but only one music cue recurs in both stories. The jazz theme, marked by a steady drumbeat and sensual saxophone melody, first appears when 223 and the blonde woman meet in a bar, and it is reprised during their wholesome night together. Subsequently it resurfaces in the second story, as 633 waits for Faye to arrive on their aborted date. Each of these situations centers on a promise of romance now stymied. Once more, Wong employs the jazz idiom ironically. Its cultural connotations of sexuality pointedly contradict the characters' nonsexual relationships. Moreover, by establishing this leitmotif as the film's musical lynchpin, Wong identifies its accompanying scenes as especially meaningful—appropriately so, since the frustration of romantic fulfillment is a major theme in *Chungking Express*, as in Wong's other films. Again, Wong's ironic use of this crucial leitmotif might arouse proponents of postmodernism, but top-down postmodernist readings are inadequate here. Wong's ironic scoring, and the authorial commentary it animates, does not of necessity engender aesthetic distance or other postmodernist effects. Furthermore, postmodern notions such as incoherence fail to describe Wong's treatment of the jazz motif. As the film's musical hinge, this leitmotif contributes structural and thematic cohesion.

With characteristic symmetry, *Chungking Express* furnishes four musical themes in each plot phase, but the second story's themes are much closer in idiom than those in Part 1. Aside from the unifying jazz motif, the score of Part 2 is comprised wholly of popular songs: the West Coast folk tune "California Dreamin'" by the Mamas and the Papas, Dinah Washington's wistful ballad "What a Difference a Day Makes," and Faye Wong's Cantopop reworking of the Cranberries' "Dreams." As their titles imply, all these tunes evoke private reverie, making them apt correlatives for Wong's distracted, insular protagonists. More specifically, their lyrics converge on themes of change and transition; as such, they mirror the conceptual basis of the first story's musical themes. Each of these songs warrants closer attention.

Like all preexisting songs, "California Dreamin'"—a buoyant slice of 1960s folk-rock—possesses what Jeff Smith calls "formal autonomy" (1998: 175), an intrinsic structural integrity not easily assimilated to narrative film sequences. Hence, preexisting songs, unlike specially composed themes, present a problem to filmmakers seeking unity between sound and image. In addition, narrative assimilation may be problematized by a song's *cultural* autonomy. Appropriated by the 1960s American counterculture as an anti–Vietnam War anthem, "California Dreamin'" harbors cultural associations far removed from Wong's modern-day tale of Chinese romance. In what ways does Wong embrace or subdue this tune's formal and cultural qualities?

At a formal level, Wong's scoring practice typically subjects sequences to either musical or narrative principles of organization. The appropriated song is as likely to be carved into cue-like segments (subordinated to the narrative scene) as it is to be left formally "intact" (dictating the scene's rhythm and duration). A more complex application of these strategies occurs when

Chungking Express switches stories. "California Dreamin'" bridges the two plot phases, its opening guitar hook synched to the closing freeze-frame and fade-out of Part 1. Initially, Wong foregrounds the tune: its dynamics suffuse the soundscape, despite the diegetic source supplied by a stereo at the fast-food counter. And as Cop 663 approaches the counter, he acknowledges the song's salience: "Like noisy music?" he asks waitress Faye rhetorically. If the song seems to dominate matters, soon its primacy is qualified and its integrity dismantled. Midway through its flute-led middle eight, the song is made to perform a kind of sonic jump cut, alerting us to a temporal shift in the action. (Subtle changes in Faye's physical appearance confirm the story's shift forward.)[4] This imposed ellipsis enables Wong to signal an advance in story time, but the song's flute interlude is spliced against its opening verse, now destined to start over. While the narrative action jumps forward through time, therefore, the song shuttles backward.

This perhaps seems an odd scoring tactic. Given that the scene skips forward in time, the song could have reinforced this narrative ellipsis by likewise skipping ahead. But the tune skips backward, not forward. How can this unusual tactic be accounted for? One might surmise that Wong's intention is simply to dilate the music cue's length, expanding its duration to match that of the narrative action. But this explanation falters when Faye pauses the stereo, restarting the tune a few seconds later. I suggest, rather, that Wong disturbs the song's formal autonomy not primarily for structural purposes but to tacitly reveal character traits. Iterating an earlier section from "California Dreamin'" allows Wong to imply Faye's tendency to listen to this tune ad infinitum. *Chungking Express* will soon underline this trait by repeating the song insistently, but already it cues us to Faye's proclivity for routine and her unabated fixation with this song.

Ultimately, neither the song nor the image track is granted structural primacy. Noting that the contours of the sequence roughly coincide with the song's start and end points (indicating that the song is retrofitted to the scene's formal structure), it becomes apparent that "California Dreamin'" is heard in its entirety, albeit in disjunctive fashion (indicating that the song is structurally paramount). Indeed, partly because its integrity is so palpably disfigured, the song is as prominent here as if it were showcased in a music video sequence—but devoid of the formal limitations imposed by such sequences. In essence, Wong manages to disrupt the formal integrity of the song without relegating it

---

4. This case effectively reverses an elliptical strategy from *In the Mood for Love* described earlier in this chapter. Whereas the latter tactic is reticent about conveying a shift forward in story time, this instance in *Chungking Express* announces temporal progression quite baldly. In each case, the respective continuity and discontinuity of the accompanying music is crucial to the narration's degree of communicativeness.

to a subordinate position; throughout the sequence, it retains an acoustic and expressive salience.

What of those extrafilmic and extramusical associations wedded to "California Dreamin'"? How does *Chungking Express* divorce this song from its prior meanings? *Forrest Gump* (1994), released in the same year as *Chungking Express*, appropriates "California Dreamin'" precisely to exploit this army of connotations. As well as designating the drama's historical epoch, the song underscores images both of American troops in Vietnam and a commune of hippies in the United States. It thereby evokes not only the soldiers' desire for homecoming that the counterculture recognized in the song's refrain but also the antiwar attitudes (and affiliation with folk-rock) embodied by the hippie movement.[5]

Such meanings rely, of course, on the cultural competency of the viewer. The preexisting tune fills in narrative information by way of its familiar cultural associations. *Chungking Express*, by contrast, is indifferent to its appropriated tune's prior meanings. Not demanding cultural knowledge, it suppresses the song's associational baggage and historical specificity. It achieves this not only by recontextualizing and defamiliarizing "California Dreamin'" (refusing a narrative context consonant with the song's cultural meanings) but also by throwing weight on the literal meanings embodied in the song's lyrics. Faye fantasizes about departing for California, and her obsession with the song both reflects and nourishes that fantasy. Thus "California Dreamin'" does fill in narrative detail, but it does so by means of its intrinsic musical features not (as *Forrest Gump* does) through its extratextual associations.

At least two other tactics subjugate the tune's associational baggage. Emilie Yeh (1999: 125) has argued that *Chungking Express* at times induces the spectator toward "reduced listening," Michel Chion's term for a mode of audition focused exclusively on a sound's acoustic traits rather than on its meanings or source (1994: 29). When Faye cleans 633's apartment, Yeh contends, "California Dreamin'" largely effaces ambient noise and "creates a somewhat exclusive aural field" (1999: 126). Auditory attention thereby favors musical properties. If, as Yeh argues, the tune's sonic primacy constitutes an "invitation to reduced listening for the film spectator" (ibid.), it is reasonable to conclude that the song's extramusical meanings recede as its purely sonic qualities grow conspicuous. Yeh might also have noted that musical repetition, too, encourages reduced listening. Alternatively "hip" (Charity 1995: 75) or "annoying" (Hu 2006: 416), Wong's restless iterations of "California Dreamin'" dilute the viewer's attention to the song's referential and cultural meanings. At the same time, this repetition triggers the viewer's inferential activity. Reduced listening

---

5. "California Dreamin'" is similarly allied to the social and historical setting of Vietnam in an earlier US drama, *Air America* (1990).

might prompt us to appreciate the tune's sensuous qualities, but this is not all we do; we also engage critically, postulating narrative and thematic explanations for the tune's prominence. The sheer repetition imposed on the song does not allow us simply to bathe in the leitmotif's dense, consonant harmonies and breezily lilting melody. Rather, it compels us to elucidate musical repetition in ways consonant with the film's narrative and themes.

What narrative themes does "California Dreamin'" animate? Most broadly, it crystallizes the topos of transition and change, a theme resonant for culturalist critics but also informative of character psychology and story action. In *Chungking Express*, the protagonists' neurotic attachment to reassuringly familiar objects (Faye's favorite pop tune, the blonde woman's raincoat and sunglasses, 633's customary fast-food meal) signifies an inauthentic retreat from change, hence from life itself. More, Wong's characters are critically alienated from a modern Hong Kong milieu popularly dubbed "Asia's transit lounge"—an apt ascription for a film that makes flight its key metaphor. References to airline travel abound in the film's dialogue and mise-en-scène (model planes, flight uniforms, boarding passes), and "California Dreamin'" elaborates the flight motif as a metaphor for change.

Consider the following pair of shots, both underscored by Faye's leitmotif. First, an airplane soars overhead while an airline uniform flutters on a clothesline; second, Faye lounges on the balcony of 633's apartment, launching paper planes into the air (Figures 2.2 and 2.3). Juxtaposed, these shots imply Faye's stunted desire for change, indicating the separation between action (actual transportation) and mere reverie (ersatz flight). But "California Dreamin'" endows these shots with further specificity. If the first image schematizes the visualizable aspects of Faye's fantasy (aircraft, flight uniform), "California Dreamin'" specifies that which is not readily expressed pictorially: Faye's dreamed-of destination. The tune's leitmotivic tendency, moreover, links these images to Faye's subjectivity. Overall, this sequence foreshadows Faye's active pursuit of change. Before long, she adopts a flight outfit, boards an airplane, and pursues the song's promise of "safe and warm" contentment in California.

The flight metaphor finds further expression in "What a Difference a Day Makes." Like "Things in Life" and "California Dreamin'," Dinah Washington's string-heavy ballad muses on change: "What a difference a day makes / Twenty-four little hours." In contrast to his use of "California Dreamin'," though, Wong works against the tune's explicit meaning. No longer does the lyric celebrate the birth of a love affair; now it eulogizes an expired romance, yoked to nostalgic images of 633 cavorting with his stewardess lover (played by Valerie Chow). When 633's rueful voice-over exclaims, "I thought we'd fly all the way, like a plane with a full tank. . . . I didn't expect it to change course," the song's title and refrain adopt the affective tenor of a lament. Thanks to dialogue and mise-en-scène (toy airplanes, the sound of flight safety instructions), "What a Difference a Day Makes" becomes inextricable from both the film's flight motif and the couple's failed romance.

And yet Wong will find reason to disrupt the song's motivic patterning. Later in *Chungking Express*, "What a Difference a Day Makes" recurs at the fast-food counter. Its placement here is purposely disorienting, since by now the viewer is primed to expect only "California Dreamin'" to trumpet from Faye's stereo. Yet again, Wong adopts a tactic of disturbance: if leitmotifs are characterized by *consistent* associations, *Chungking Express* here short-circuits its own motivic system. Consequently, the music track once more achieves self-consciousness. "That song doesn't suit you," 633 tells Faye, intensifying the viewer's auditory attention still further. Most significantly, Faye's substitution of "California Dreamin'" with "What a Difference a Day Makes" suggests not only that Faye finally welcomes change but that important parallels link Faye and the stewardess. Both women enter the airline industry, cling to favorite songs, and develop romantic feelings for Cop 633. Faye acts inauthentically, however, by hijacking the stewardess' trademark tune and poring over the woman's vestiges in 633's apartment (the model airplane, flight uniform, stands of hair)—by flirting, in short, with the assumption of another identity. In this respect, Faye anticipates the protagonists of *In the Mood for Love* and their penchant for role play. Finally unable to quell her urge for change, Faye discards the ill-fitting Dinah Washington tune, relinquishes the emotional fulcrum of "California Dreamin'," and fulfills her "authentic" goal to migrate to the United States.

The sense of converging identities is germane to a film teeming with parallel actions, motifs, shot compositions, and music cues (see Bordwell 2011: 181). As noted above, Faye returns from overseas at the film's climax to find 633 the proprietor of the fast-food outlet, "California Dreamin'" booming from his stereo. The cop's newfound affinity for "California Dreamin'" might imply an inauthentic retreat from self, but on the contrary it is best grasped as representing a turn toward authenticity. Like Faye, 633 has come around to the prospect of change, forfeiting mechanical routine in favor of an enhanced engagement with the world and himself. *Chungking Express* strikes an optimistic final note with Faye's boarding pass. "Where to?" she asks, sketching an itinerary. "Wherever you want to take me," 633 replies. At last in sync, the two characters can venture toward an unknown future together.[6]

---

6. That Faye remains a flight attendant at the climax does not indicate that she remains inauthentically closeted in a false identity. Her dream of traveling to California *precedes* her obsession with 633's ex-lover, and we know this thanks to her musical leitmotif—she listens to "California Dreamin'" at the start of the second story and only later comes to learn of Valerie Chow's stewardess.

How, finally, does "Dreams" function in terms of form, theme, and cultural meaning? Stringer construes this tune—the film's only Cantonese-language song—as a "shrewd marketing" gesture (2002: 398), and the fiscal advantage of exploiting local music is not to be downplayed. Outside of Hong Kong itself exists a populous diasporic following for androgynous pop idols crooning apolitical and "hummable" laments to love (Hewett 1997: 28). That "Dreams" is recorded by pop star Faye Wong (the actor who plays Faye) bolsters the music's local appeal. Economic principles are significant, but still Wong Kar-wai must confront the song's formal and cultural autonomy. "Dreams" is first heard at length when Faye covertly renovates 633's apartment. Since "Dreams" accompanies shots of its vocalist, this scene's link to music video is augmented—assuming, that is, that the viewer is competent to recognize the star's voice. Faye's methodical behavior also evokes music video imagery: as Torben Grodal notes, "Many music videos make extensive use of images depicting unfree, obsessive behavior . . . with the aim of generating a strong lyrical toning" (2009: 284). Yet the sequence is sharply different from MTV. Not least, Wong embeds "Dreams" within the diegesis, integrating nonmusical ambient sounds into the tune's texture. Thus, when Faye sweeps the cloth from a table, the clatter of objects lends "Dreams" a kind of ambient percussion. In such ways the primacy of narrative action is affirmed; the viewer's attention is guided toward matters of narrative import. When "Dreams" sneaks out at the start of the next scene, its distinction from music video is explicit. Whereas music videos are formally unified and self-contained, Wong's so-called MTV moments minister to a broad narrative system, underpinned by a concern for narrative continuity and progression. The music-based sequence in Wong's cinema, therefore, is ontologically divorced from music video.

Culturally and thematically, "Dreams" offers a complex case. Hu (2006: 418–19) has shown that Faye Wong's Cantopop reworking of "Dreams" not only transforms the original track culturally but alters its thematic meaning too. The Cranberries' English-language verse fits neatly into the thematic logic of *Chungking Express*: "Life is changing every day / In every possible way." Yet Faye Wong's interpretation, Hu demonstrates, eliminates the tune's explicit reference to change (418). Once again, cultural competency comes into play. For example, the Western viewer unversed in Cantonese may recollect the tune's English lyric and apply it, by default, to the narrative sequence. If it purges the theme of change, however, the Cantonese lyric also dovetails with Wong's major themes. Certain clauses reverberate with Wong's trademark sensitivity to time: "Let's embrace for a minute / Then kiss for ten minutes"; other phrases evoke the allure of strangers in *Chungking Express*: "How can a stranger walk into my heart / And cause this ecstasy?" Despite the song's varied cross-cultural meanings, Wong ensures that both versions of "Dreams" evoke the film's overarching themes: romantic possibility, time, and change (itself an inherently temporal phenomenon).

Music in *Chungking Express* is channeled into a network of leitmotifs. This network furnishes an apparently fragmented narrative with sonic coherence, foregrounds character parallels, and converges upon a thematic preoccupation with change. Preexisting songs, replete with formal constraints, demonstrate surprising malleability. Cultural meanings are tamed or triggered, and they are contingent upon cultural knowledge. Above all, Wong makes music indispensable to narrative meaning. Martinez has written that Wong's films "constantly flirt with the musical genre without ever slipping into it completely" (1997: 31), a claim evoking the salience with which Wong's cinema affords film music. Like certain musicals, the songs in *Chungking Express* seem to be directly wired to the characters' subjective states. For all its apparent arbitrariness, incoherence, and superficiality, the music score of *Chungking Express*—like those of all Wong's films—displays a rigorous obedience to logic, unity, and aesthetic purpose.

3 | Partial Views
Visual Style and the Aesthetic of Disturbance

Many of Asian cinema's most renowned auteurs have mounted stylistic programs optimizing a narrow range of techniques. Ozu Yasujiro mines the expressive possibilities of frontal staging, fixed shot perspective, and low camera height. Hou Hsiao-hsien, Tsai Ming-liang, and Jia Zhangke test the inexhaustibility of extended takes and distanced framings. Zhang Che and John Woo explore the kinesthetic effects of camera-speed juxtapositions and rapid zoom shots. In Bordwell's terms, these filmmakers are "stubborn stylists," faithful to their stylistic signatures (2007). Unlike these counterparts, Wong Kar-wai holds fast to no stable stylistic repertoire. And yet Wong's films—even those as stylistically dissimilar as *Chungking Express* and *In the Mood for Love*—seem unified by a consistent visual sensibility.

In this chapter I argue that Wong is a director wedded not so much to a privileged set of visual techniques as to an elevated narrational *principle*, to which an array of stylistic techniques is subordinated. This governing principle—Wong's stylistic *dominant*, in neoformalist parlance—involves complicating (or *roughening*) the viewer's perception and comprehension without sacrificing overall dramatic clarity. Pledged to making the image "difficult" yet intelligible, Wong revises, recombines, and repurposes standard schemas of visual style. This authorial strategy contributes to an overall aesthetic of perceptual and cognitive disturbance.

By promoting a formal principle above favored devices, Wong outstrips aesthetic pigeonholing—hence he is no more a "long-take director" than he is a devotee of MTV-style editing. And yet, while Wong is in a sense properly characterized as a "polystylistic" filmmaker (Bordwell 2011: 176), he stays monogamous to a stylistic (and narrative) norm of roughened form and perceptual difficulty. In other words, Wong embraces stylistic pluralism, but his films are unified by an enduring aesthetic principle. For Wong, the film experience involves perceptual and cognitive challenge. Since the early 1990s, he has sought to set dramatically legible devices against tactics that disturb the viewer's perception and comprehension. While his local contemporaries sustained a popular cinema based on maximally readable visual design (Bordwell 2011), Wong inclined toward a different approach, elaborating an interplay of visual clarity and obscurity. He quickly tired of the perspicuous close-ups employed in *As Tears Go By*. He grew still less fond of neatly symmetrical staging, which in his maiden film hierarchizes the characters and foregrounds visual and dramatic clarity (Figure 3.1). Although such schematic layouts would continue to flourish in films by Johnnie To, Soi Cheang, and other Hong Kong mainstream directors, Wong's subsequent films press toward other possibilities. This chapter sets out to illuminate Wong's dynamic of opacity and clarity, examining its effects upon narrative meaning and spectator response.

I begin by surveying the theoretical claims advanced with respect to Wong's visual style. Examining the previous claims of scholars and critics enables one to identify the salient features of Wong's visual aesthetic, redress widely accepted yet flawed assumptions, and relate the key scholarly exegeses to research trends within the academy. This starting point also brings the chapter's main preoccupations to light. How successfully has symptomatic explication illuminated Wong's visual stratagems? To what extent can the films be subsumed to "parametric," or style-centered, form? What is the role and significance of sensuousness in Wong's aesthetic? And what are the general principles, functions, and effects governing his visual style? These concerns inform the analyses of *Happy Together* and *My Blueberry Nights* that follow later in this chapter. As I will demonstrate, Wong's visual style is no less committed to narrative, formal, and thematic unity than is his film's musical design.

Theorizing Wong's Visual Style

Wong's visual style has attracted the attention of many scholars, but the work of Abbas looms large over the literature. Abbas assimilates Wong to a "new Hong Kong cinema" that surfaces in the 1980s and whose distinctiveness lies in indirect representations of Hong Kong's unique historical situation. These films speak to and about a Hong Kong population at the threshold of historical change. In the face of the 1997 handover, nothing less than the disappearance of Hong Kong's cultural identity and traditions is at stake. For Abbas, disappearance is articulated through this cinema's play with genre and narrative structure, but most especially through its visual images. He writes, "It is in the images of the new cinema that the history of contemporary Hong Kong with all its anxieties and contradictions can be read" (Abbas 1997b: 17). Visual style becomes a vehicle not only for social comment but for social critique—the visual strategies Abbas identifies obliquely undermine the ruling colonial power. By problematizing the viewer's perception of the visible, the new Hong

Kong filmmakers implicitly critique that which is visible, that is, colonial space (36). Abbas is preoccupied with Wong's visual style chiefly insofar as it reflects, or "responds to," the collective experience of Hong Kong's inhabitants at a key moment of political, economic, and cultural change. For instance, Wong's accelerated shots of traffic "show us how at the level of everyday life the global is experienced not only as a greater degree of connection, but also as disconnection" (Abbas 2001: 624). Wong's films in particular fascinate Abbas because they furnish images problematizing "the act of looking itself" (1997b: 26). Ephemeral, irresolute, and ambiguous, Wong's images evoke the threat of disappearance, echoing the Hong Konger's desire to arrest the historical moment and postpone cultural change.

Abbas's thesis proved highly influential upon film critics seeking to theorize Wong's visual aesthetic. The propagation of Abbas's ideas coincided not only with an intensified, cross-disciplinary attention to prehandover Hong Kong but also with the concomitant shift within film studies toward culturalist hermeneutics described in Chapter 1. Increasingly, Wong's visual strategies were explicated as sociological critique. Reflectionism proved a favorite explanatory method, proposing direct correlation between Wong's visual storytelling and the 1997 situation. For instance, *Ashes of Time*'s somber palette and fragmentary editing implied a sense of "hopelessness" and "uncertainty" about Hong Kong's postcolonial fate (Chan 2001: 500; Dissanayake 2003: 146). Most compelling for film scholars was Abbas's notion of disappearance, which Wong's trademark visual devices were held to embody. Slow motion and dilatory fades (Stokes 2002: 142), rapid cutting (Tambling 2003: 4), and smudge motion (Tsui 1995: 98–99; Tong 2008: 67) all evoke for these critics the territory's precarious cultural heritage and identity. Following Abbas, Wong's commentators argued that the unique situation of colonial Hong Kongers—anxiously anticipating the future, nostalgically recalling the past, helpless to arrest the ephemeral present—was perfectly captured by Wong's visual manipulations of cinematic time.

Exemplary here is Joelle Collier's examination of editing practices in Hong Kong cinema. Tracing the region's cinema to Oriental traditions of art, she identifies certain discontinuity devices as local stylistic norms. Violation of the 180-degree rule and rejection of match cutting, unusual in Hollywood movies, are "simply part of the common grammar of Hong Kong cinema" (Collier 1999: 73). Collier isolates two further tendencies within Hong Kong film practice: overlapping editing and "serial repetition," whereby "an action is presented in its entirety two or more times in succession, either by means of looping a single take, or editing a number of different takes into a series" (ibid.). If such tactics are rarely witnessed in Hollywood films, Collier finds them prevalent in Hong Kong cinema, persuasively citing a range of films including *A Better*

Tomorrow (1986) and *Project A* (1983). Subsequently, she extends her analysis onto allegorical terrain by way of Abbas's cultural disappearance. The local cinema's discontinuity devices, Collier argues, can be grasped as expressive correlatives for Hong Kong's collective unconscious. She writes, "Faced with the date of Jun. 30, 1997—as Wong Kar-wai reminds us in *Chungking Express*, what a difference a day makes—what power could a Hong Konger desire more than to control time itself?" (77). This collective desire—to conserve a culture threatened with disappearance—is articulated cinematically by overlapping editing and serial repetition:

> these devices . . . call time back. . . . the ubiquity of these devices in Hong Kong films constitutes if not a conscious strategy of reappearance, as an act of defense against the coming disappearance, at least an unconscious urge. With overlapping editing and serial repetition, one holds on to time or holds it back; the future is postponed while the present or the past is savored. (ibid.)

Like Abbas, Collier finds Wong an exemplar of this strategy. That the mute hero of *Fallen Angels* repeatedly screens video footage of his dead father not only conveys the character's personal loss; it also reflects a widespread and deep-seated desire among "Hong Kong Belongers" to savor what is already or soon to be lost (ibid.).

Collier's essay offers valuable insights into Hong Kong cinema's editing norms, but her thesis falters in one or two respects.[1] Explaining textual features by recourse to the filmmaker's "unconscious urge" is a heuristic bearing theoretical and empirical shortcomings. This rhetorical maneuver removes any barrier to ascribing all manner of meanings to filmmakers on the grounds that the imputed meaning operates in their unconscious. Even contradictory testimony from filmmakers themselves can be discounted, for the imputed meaning resides beyond their conscious awareness. In other words, the critic presumes to know filmmakers' minds better than filmmakers themselves. For his part, Wong has offered a plausible rationale for his films' visual repetitions:

> Most of my films deal with people who are stuck in certain routines and habits that don't make them happy. They want to change, but they need something to push them. I think it's mostly love that causes them to break their routines and move on. That's why we always want to repeat shots, to show the routines and the changes as they happen. (Tobias 2001)

If this represents Wong's *conscious* impetus for shot repetition, it only belies an unconscious impulse to resist China's reclamation of Hong Kong—such is

---

1. For one thing, homogenizing Hong Kongers is problematic, since this view presupposes a unity of political attitudes and opinions. In Collier's essay, this is especially unexpected given that she begins by castigating monolithic theorizing (here disclaiming notions of a singular "Chinese" film aesthetic).

Collier's thesis. This line of argument ought to perturb critics generally troubled by the intentional fallacy. For, in Collier's methodology, the film's aesthetic features are explicated by reference to not merely authorial intentions but to intentions authors do not even know they have.[2]

In at least one more respect, Collier's essay typifies critical writing on Wong's visual style. Scholars have primarily centered on the ways Wong's visual tactics manipulate time. (The authorial motif of clocks/watches also cues this pre-occupation with time.) Time is conceived in terms of both the viewer's temporal experience (Chow 2006: 180–181; K.-f. Yau 2001: 552–53) and the deformations imposed upon the profilmic event (Cook 2005; Yue 2008: 145; Ma 2010). A notable intervention here has been staged by Deleuzian film scholars, who found in Wong's cinema a fundamentally new cinematic style, which collapses the virtual and the actual into a mélange of past, present, and future (K.-f. Yau 2001: 553; E. Yau 2001: 9–10). Wong rejects classical cinema's stylistics, they argue, in favor of exemplary time-images (Rushton 2012: 149) and movement-images (Teo 2005: 62) that furnish drastically new ways of seeing. Both image types purportedly compel the viewer to active engagement and critical reflection (Dissanayake 2003: 63), chiefly by foregrounding time and rendering it in unfamiliar ways (Tong 2008: 65). Ever conscious of Hong Kong's geohistorical situation, several scholars were able to mesh Deleuzian concepts with cultural-ist allegory (see, for example, Tong 2008).

Indeed, the Deleuzian approach has proven not so distant from the cultur-alist perspective. In rhetorical strategy and hermeneutic findings, the respective readings of Wong's style are remarkably alike. Like Collier, Tong isolates an aspect of Wong's visual style—smudge motion, as deployed in *Chungking Express*—and examines it only insofar as it defamiliarizes time; from here the interpretive leap to socio-allegorical meaning is a straightforward, and by now familiar, maneuver (2008: 70–71). Similarly, in a discussion of Deleuze's perception-image, Seung-hoon Jeong specifies a visual device (the mirror motif in *Chungking Express*) and subjects it to top-down, socio-reflectionist

---

2. At a more general level, Collier's approach bears the limitations of top-down hermeneutics. Onto the film is mapped an a priori cultural theory—namely, that Hong Kong film style embodies the trope of cultural disappearance—with the result that every notable visual device hypostatizes Hong Kong's tenuous identity. Consequently, the culturalist critic forsakes the individual functions and effects of particular visual devices. In Wong's aesthetic program, repeated shots (Collier 1999) and stop-motion effects (Tsui 1995: 98–99) surely perform discrete functions, but the culturalist distills them to a single allegorical function. By ascrib-ing a univocal meaning, moreover, the culturalist sharply downplays the films' differences. For Curtis K. Tsui, optical printing harbors the same thematic connotations in *Chungking Express* as in *As Tears Go By* and *Ashes of Time*, regardless of the varied narrative contexts it accompanies (*wuxia* battle, romantic clinch, chase-and-fight sequence) (113). Destined to map the same interpretive frame ad infinitum, the allegorical approach becomes hermeneutically moribund. Sacrificed is nothing less than the unique specificity of—and fundamental distinc-tions among—a diverse and complex set of films.

interpretation. Furthermore, Jeong's hypothesis is commensurate with that of culturalists like Collier and Tong: the mirror motif, he claims, reveals the film-maker's obsession with national identity vis-à-vis Hong Kong's retrocession to China (2012: 221). Though not all Deleuzian analyses revert to allegory, these two approaches have treated Wong's style in strikingly similar ways.

A major alternative to understanding Wong's visual aesthetic emerged in the form of film poetics. As noted in Chapter 1, Bordwell's *Planet Hong Kong* epitomizes this approach. Subsequently, a few other scholars pursued a poetics of Wong's film style. In his essay "The Stubborn Persistence of the Local in Wong Kar-wai," James Udden explores similar terrain to that of the culturalists and Deleuzians, concentrating principally on the temporal dimension of Wong's style (2006). Like these critics, Udden itemizes stylistic devices whose traits alter the profilmic reality: in-camera slow motion, postproduction step printing, time-lapse cinematography, and freeze frames. Yet Udden goes beyond the mere linkage of these devices with sociocultural processes, or with abstract concepts such as disappearance, to situate them within concrete traditions of cinematic storytelling. Wong's aesthetic does not coalesce wholly and inextricably from cultural instability. Rather, it develops out of cinematic norms prevalent within that historically specific milieu. Put differently, Wong's stylistics spring not from the zeitgeist but from the "concrete conditions of the Hong Kong film industry" (69). To substantiate this claim, Udden surveys Hong Kong filmmaking during Wong's entry into the industry. He recalls that the 1980s saw local directors such as Tsui Hark, John Woo, and Ringo Lam experimenting with time-deforming visual techniques. Wong, Udden argues, inventively recasts these practices "for his own aesthetic ends" (77). For Udden, then, "the core of [Wong's] aesthetic"—and the key to his global appeal—"comes from his transformation of local practices" (77). Contextually and critically sensitive, Udden's essay has the virtue not only of stressing the local foundations of a filmmaker often subsumed to an amorphous "world cinema" category but also of qualifying claims of "newness" as regards Wong's visual aesthetic—an aesthetic, Udden concludes, that draws upon fairly widespread practices in contemporary Hong Kong cinema.

A poetics of Wong's cinema also accommodated what culturalist readings were wont to neglect—attention to the ways that film practice shapes film style. The logistics of location shooting, Chris Doyle has stressed in interviews, constrain stylistic options and inform aesthetic choices. Edge framing and mirror reflections in *2046* provided practical solutions to shooting in CinemaScope in a small playing area (Davis 2005: 28). Camera movement and cutting rhythms might be led by music played during shooting and postproduction editing. "In all our collaborations," says Doyle, "the music informs the camera" (Bosley 2001: 28). Wong's tendency to shoot many takes, moreover, invites elliptical editing to emerge as a major strategy, thanks partly to continuity gaps arising from assembled takes. The poetician is alert to the filmmaker's practical constraints and choices, which are conceptualized on a problem-solution model. How far the solutions are anchored in story, form, and theme also occupies exponents of the poetics approach.

The poetics approach offered a fresh departure from two further theoretical perspectives applied to Wong: postmodernism and transnationalism. Critics invoking postmodernity explicated Wong's visual aesthetic much as they did his musical style—as an expressive vehicle for nostalgia, specifically as regards Hong Kong's colonial past. Postmodernist accounts thus converged with broadly culturalist preoccupations. More generally, critics routinely mapped postmodernism's salient concepts, such as pastiche and fragmentation, onto Wong's often self-conscious and elliptical visual narration (Leung 2000: 244).[3] As an interpretive framework, postmodernism supplied tools fit for top-down application. Its proponents, preoccupied with extracting cultural commentary, have tended to marginalize other stylistic motivations, meanings, and effects. In this respect, the poetics approach stands apart from postmodernist and other Grand Theories of cinema.

If social allegory underpinned culturalist and postmodernist studies of Wong, so too did it permeate transnationalist accounts. Here again there is strong convergence among apparently disparate approaches. Most of the theoretical paradigms I have addressed—culturalist, postmodernist, transnationalist—are centrally concerned with the politics of identity. This politics looks beyond the film's story world and its universal or cross-cultural appeals to specify a cultural situation unique to Hong Kong.[4] In the transnationalist model, as in the culturalist approach, identity is conceptualized broadly in relation to the nation and the individual as social subject. The identity of a

---

3. In one respect, postmodernism provided a familiar if loose rubric by which to categorize the filmmaker; hence Teo can classify Wong as "a post-modern visual stylist" (2005: 88). In another respect, it provided critics a rhetorical basis from which to "read" particular visual techniques. Nostalgia, for instance, becomes an a priori trope adopted to explain both the mise-en-scène of *In the Mood for Love* (Needham 2006: 66) and the visual motif of the train in *2046* and *Happy Together* (Teo 2005: 141). None of this is to suggest that nostalgia lacks relevance to Wong's cinema. On the contrary, several of his characters appear nostalgic for former romances now consigned to the past, and the 1960s milieu to which Wong returns is certainly significant, whatever the influence of the 1997 handover.

4. Gina Marchetti reads *Chungking Express* as a film that yokes the transnationalist concern of "American commodities, consumerism, and the shaping of Hong Kong identity . . . to the issue of the 1997 changeover and emigration" (2000: 308). Marchetti is less concerned to examine the film's primary level than to excavate "another story about economics and the politics of identity" (289). This embedded commentary, she suggests, is partly to be found at the level of visual style, particularly within the film's mise-en-scène (model airplanes, canned food, and various other commodified objects). Marchetti constructs a compelling reading of *Chungking Express*, but the film's primary level—its depiction of, in Bordwell's words, "young people in search of love" (2000: 274)—inevitably becomes an object of limited interest.

film's characters—their idiosyncratic psychologies, goals, and obsessions—is of significance only to the extent that it reveals a perspective on this wider milieu. By the same token, visual devices, such as Wong's ubiquitous use of mirrors, are noteworthy insofar as they "highlight play with identity" (Cameron 2007). (This constitutes a reading close to that posited—from a Deleuzian standpoint—by Jeong, described above.) Above and beyond their narrative functions, such visual devices are absorbed into the critic's chief preoccupation with (trans)national identity.

In sum, Wong scholarship has, to date, been dominated by Grand Theories promoting top-down culturalist readings of the director's visual style. Distinct in theoretical scope and emphasis, these approaches nevertheless alight upon mutual thematic territory (e.g., identity, time), utilizing shared schemas (e.g., nostalgia) and symptomatically concentrating analysis on secondary levels of the text. The poetics approach is undoubtedly a minority practice within this research context. Yet by insisting on the virtues of bottom-up analysis, and with no paradigmatic commitment to allegorical exposition or tropes such as identity or nostalgia, it carries the potential to avert Wong scholarship from repetitive readings and reflectionist platitudes.

Parametric Form

In analyzing Wong's aesthetic, critics and scholars have pondered to what extent style supersedes story. Often this has led them to make sharp distinctions between form and content. Local critic Paul Fonoroff, one of Wong's most outspoken detractors, reprimands *Days of Being Wild* for "an imbalance of form over content," claiming that Wong's films, though "beautifully packaged," are "long on style but short on substance" (1999: 123, 634). *Variety* critic Todd McCarthy titles his negative appraisal of *In the Mood for Love* "Cannes Unspools More Style Than Content" (2000). Most criticisms hinge on a simplistic dualism of story and style. For US critic Justin Chang, Wong's cinema is "predicated less on narrative and dialogue than on mood and style" (2007). For certain film scholars, moreover, Wong's films subordinate plot and characterization to stylistic concerns (Cheng 2000: 20) and foreground images that cannot be fully grasped through narrative analysis (Tong 2008: 65).

Brunette observes Wong's tendency toward images "that are, strictly speaking, narratively and cognitively unnecessary" (2005: 9). For Brunette, these visual excursions from narrative demands are evidence of a purely "graphic expressivity" (54). In his exegesis, however, it is too often unclear precisely what Wong's images are expressive *of*, if not of narrative concerns.[5] Moreover,

---

5. Writing of *Chungking Express*, Brunette states, "More blatantly expressive techniques are used elsewhere to indicate interior psychological states, as when a blurry, repeated reflection

Brunette gravitates toward the fallacious style/story dichotomy noted above. *Fallen Angels*, for instance, places emphasis on "visual expressivity . . . rather than on narrative or theme per se" (61). This dualistic inclination similarly emerges in Jeremy Tambling's study of *Happy Together*. Writing of this film's "half-replacement of narrative by image, as in all of Wong Kar-wai['s] films," he argues that certain (unspecified) shots "do not further a narrative" (Tambling 2003: 15). Tambling evidently conceives these images as independent to some extent of narrative concerns: "The image comes first [while] the narrative, usually established by a voice-over, is like an afterthought" (ibid.).

What Tambling and Brunette seem to deny is that Wong's images function within the context of a story and thus are *narrative* images, even if their contribution to plot progression seems negligible. As such, their expressivity is inseparable from matters of narrative. Even those images that look wholly abstract frequently reveal motivation and meaning at the level of narrative. A similar counterargument can be set against Allan Cameron's claim that *Chungking Express* emphasizes "style over [character] psychology" (2007). As demonstrated in the previous chapter, which analyzed this film's stylistic repetition and organization of popular music, style in Wong's cinema invariably *is* character psychology. Overwhelmingly, Wong's visual and musical techniques are motivated by and expressive of the protagonists' psychological traits and temperaments. The straightforward demarcation of style and character (narrative) does not hold water. Finally, Jean Ma commits a similar fallacy by asserting that Wong's incoherent visual tactics "seem to call for a perceptual rather than cognitive grasp" (2010: 127)—that is, a response founded less on narrative comprehension than on some kind of expressive or affective engagement. Here again the implied binarism is fundamentally superficial. Perceiving and cognizing are practically inextricable processes; the narrative and cognitive, on the one hand, cannot be easily divorced from the abstract and perceptual, on the other hand. Such cut-and-dried distinctions obscure the ways that Wong's images function narratively.

Underlying these critics' style/narrative distinction is an implicit skepticism that Wong's films transcend prettification. A *Sight & Sound* review of *My Blueberry Nights* amply exemplifies this skepticism: "the frequent step-printed slow-motion effects are overdone, suggesting post-production attempts to add resonance to material that otherwise lacked it" (Brooke 2008: 74). Wong's perceived elevation of style above story apparently betokens a reversal of priorities, rendering the films attractive but insubstantial (Brooks 2007; Romney

---

of Faye in a metal wall on screen right eventually takes over nearly the whole of the image. One hesitates to assign a precise narrative or symbolic meaning here" (2005: 53). But Faye's psychological state *is* a narrative concern. Brunette's discussion rests on an artificial distinction between narrative and visual expressivity.

2005: 17). Even Wong's supporters have ventured doubts about his outré style. "*Fallen Angels*," writes Abbas, " . . . verges on being a mere exercise in style . . . a stylish film that runs the risk of being too stylized" (1997a: 71). Brunette, moreover, considers Wong's first five films to be stylistically self-indulgent; not until *Happy Together* and *In the Mood for Love* does the auteur successfully harmonize form and content (2005: 71–72). That Wong is synonymous primarily with style is reflected in the epithets critics have attached to him, such as "ultraformalist" (Douchet 1998: 17) and "aesthete" (Sailer 2005)—terms that, though reasonable, pejoratively imply a neglect of narrative, not to mention a neglect of cultural critique or allegory. Less judgmentally, some scholars describe Wong's style as "parametric," a mode of narration in which technique comes noticeably forward as a result of being wholly or largely unmotivated by the narrative (see Bordwell 1985: 274–310). Dana Polan hints at this concept by claiming that *In the Mood for Love*'s décor "takes off from story and even takes it over" (2001). The film's costume design, according to Lynda Chapple, displays an excessive "over-investment in the representation of the *qipao* which transcends any diegetic need" (2011: 215). Mark Betz, meanwhile, explicitly defines *In the Mood for Love* as parametric, analyzing its systematic patterning of aural and visual devices (2010: 41–44).

Yet the concept of parametric form seems only partly adequate to summarize Wong's stylistic program. Though it aptly indicates the stylistic foregrounding typical of Wong—in terms of both "active" and understated expressions of style—it is liable to mislead, for parametric form encompasses varying degrees of stylistic salience and narrative motivation. Wong's visual technique is generally self-conscious and noticeable; but it is also generally motivated by story concerns, compositionally rooted in narrative, character, and theme. I do not wish to deny that some images might elude narrative justification. However, Wong typically ensures that visual technique is harnessed to narrative signification and story-bound effects. Contra Brunette, moreover, I submit that Wong's unity of story and style is in evidence from his earliest films (even if, as I will discuss shortly, his visual strategies and production practices have varied over time).

Wong's defenders have roundly dismissed the charge of superficiality (e.g., Tsui 1995: 94). Yet some of their strategies of defense seem misplaced. Disclaiming the comparison with MTV, Teo reasons that "Wong's [films] have not vitiated to the level of MTV because of the contexts they invoke: their historical nexus with past eras, their identification with the times, their interconnectedness of the local with the global, and, above all, their depth of meaning and feeling" (2005: 158). In other words, Teo looks to the films' *extra*textual contexts—to the cultural sphere and its attendant conceptual tropes of nostalgia, zeitgeist, and diaspora—to demonstrate the films' depth and significance.

I propose, however, that Wong's aesthetic can be defended by looking closely at the films themselves, examining the internal motivations, functions, and effects of their visual techniques. We need no recourse to "significant" cultural resonances to legitimize Wong (though such contexts, properly animated, may enrich our appreciation). The films themselves are evidence of the filmmaker's artistry. In Wong's cinema (to borrow from Jean Cocteau), "the depth breathes on the surface" (Cocteau and Fraigneau 1972: 130).

Motivated Sensuousness and the Aesthetic of Disturbance

Central to the prominence of Wong's aesthetic is an overall sensuousness of visual design. Every aspect of mise-en-scène and cinematography seems keyed to engender what one scholar calls an "aesthetic of sensuous experience" (Robinson 2006: 194). William Chang's art direction famously weaves sumptuous textures into everything from curtains to cheongsams, but a languid camera pan is no less apt to produce a frisson of sensuality. The films' high-end look led critics to ascribe to Wong a "fashion magazine sensibility" (Scott 2008), stressing affinities with advertising and MTV—often as confirmation of Wong's "emptiness" (Thomson 2010: 1053). To some degree, such comparisons are plausible: Wong, a graduate in graphic design, has often declared an interest in photography and periodically produces promotional materials for fashion and beauty products, as well as music videos. Yet Wong's aesthetic is not reducible to these multimedia forms. I have already established in Chapter 2 that, despite the prevalent use of rapid and erratic cutting, fundamental contrasts obtain between music video and *Chungking Express* (as with any of Wong's films). In any case, no criteria of art could justly posit a necessary correlation between stylistic sensuousness and artistic destitution.

Partly what ails some critics, I suspect, is the notion that sensuousness in artworks seduces the spectator in ways that desensitize or disable critical functions. Connotations of viewer passivity infuse the language employed to describe Wong's aesthetic. His films are said to display a "hypnotic quality" (Hunter 2005), "a drug-taker's immersion in the narcotic of cinema" (Thomson 2010: 1053), a dreamlike progression rendering the spectator "totally spellbound" (Teo 2005: 149). Wong's spectator is often characterized, at least tacitly, as being enticed into a somnambulistic dream state by a suite of intoxicating, oneiric images. As Amy Taubin asserts in a favorable account of *2046*, "It's a film to get lost in" (2005: 28). Indeed this immersive potential may hold one key to Wong's appeal: viewers can become absorbed in the film at a purely aesthetic level. But while aestheticism is an undeniable feature of these films, many critics overstate its primacy within Wong's aesthetic program; consequently, they exaggerate the passivity of the viewer. These films may be dreamlike but they are not dreams. To ascribe to the viewer a dream state is to confuse representation and reception. Moreover, sensuousness is but one component of Wong's aesthetic of disturbance. Against the films' lush visual design are imposed blocked compositions, facial masking, opaque cuts, and a host of other complicating strategies, all of which deter the viewer from sheer aesthetic absorption. Notwithstanding Wong's invitation to aesthetic engrossment, these perceptual and cognitive challenges must be confronted if the viewer is to fully grasp a narrative that is in itself complex and enigmatic. In sum, Wong's aesthetic demands a cognitively alert viewer. The challenge to aesthetic absorption springs directly from within that aesthetic itself—what I am calling an aesthetic of disturbance.

Scholars have so far concentrated on William Chang's production design and Chris Doyle's camerawork as pivotal components of the films' seductiveness (see, for example, Lee 2004; Greenhalgh 2005). Yet we should not forget Wong's assimilation of photogenic players to this program of sensuousness. Wong populates his films with a roster of handsome players: Maggie Cheung, Tony Leung, Faye Wong, Takeshi Kaneshiro, Gong Li, Zhang Ziyi, Norah Jones, and others. These figures mesh neatly with an aesthetic in which all stylistic parameters—mise-en-scène, cinematography, editing, music—are marshaled to conjure a ravishing film world. The critic claiming that "the performances [in *Chungking Express*] are strong but they do take second place to the aesthetic of the film" (Leahy 1995: 44) not only misrepresents *Chungking Express* as a parametric work but fails to appreciate that performance in Wong's cinema becomes integrally absorbed into a sensuous aesthetic.

At times, Wong's camera cannot resist lingering on the star's flawless physiognomy. Such intimate views are the basic currency of screen stardom. The flattering facial close-up is as ingrained a convention of star construction in Hong Kong cinema as it is in Hollywood film. "The primary objective" of such compositions, notes Joe McElhaney, "is to beautify the face" (2004: 67). Pam Cook suggests that the close-up aids "the process of idealization of stars," proffering the star as an ideal figure of desire and identification (1979/1980: 83). Wong's films similarly frame the star in admiring close-up. Critics probably have such images in mind when comparing the films to fashion photography, but Wong's star tableaus are seldom gratuitous or merely ornamental. Just as Wong motivates pop music by character psychology in *Chungking Express*, so he justifies the sensuous star close-up by matters in the story world.

We might call this a strategy of motivated sensuousness. In *Ashes of Time*, for instance, Wong furnishes a close-up of Maggie Cheung that is in every sense a star composition—legible, lingering, and luminous (Figure 3.2). Yet this image is perspectivally aligned with the woman's lover, whose romantic memory confers upon her an almost unnatural beauty. Wong's star portrait, then, cannot be understood except in relation to its narrative context; moreover, it is this signification within a wider narrative structure that sets it apart from typical fashion photography. Then there are those Wong protagonists prone to self-admiration. The self-assured and sensual poses affected by Leslie Cheung in *Days of Being Wild* find justification in Yuddy's all-consuming narcissism. In such cases, the seductive star image is motivated less by shallow ornamentation than by the psychological states and traits of the characters.

The sensuous star portrait can be understood in the context of a larger dynamic governing Wong's visual narration, one that sets eye-pleasing detail against obstacles to perceptual uptake. Legible star close-ups exist in counterpoint to less instantly readable images designed to block or obscure the human face. In *Days of Being Wild*, close singles and frontal staging offer no guarantee of legible facial views; oblique body posture, intrusive shadows, or impinging foreground figures often disturb visibility. Nor is the over-the-shoulder shot (OTS) exempt from obfuscating treatment. The anamorphically filmed *2046* strangulates the OTS schema, occluding much of the frontal character's face by obstructive back-to-camera figures. As if defied by the widescreen format to flout spaciousness, Wong perversely jams the onscreen pair together, wedging them against the frame edge to conjure unnaturally oppressive framings; in the process, the characters' faces are abbreviated as beguiling fragments. Even the freeze-frame—traditionally an aid to dramatic clarity—is in Wong's repertoire an available source of obfuscation. *Chungking Express* violates cinematic tradition by arresting an indistinct image: fleeing a murder, the blonde-wigged woman, suspended in motion, becomes an off-center, murky figure. (Perceptual and narrative frustration coalesces here: the oblique image flagrantly blocks revelation just as the enigmatic woman sheds her noirish disguise.) Wong's strategy of facial masking reminds us that traditionally informative devices such as facial close-ups, OTS staging, and freeze frames possess no essential property of legibility.

Much as Wong establishes narrative justification for his films' lustrous look, he motivates these obstructive tactics compositionally. Stalking away from his birth mother's mansion, Yuddy refuses to grant this woman (and the camera) a glimpse of his face. In a display of tit-for-tat petulance, he reveals in voice-over: "As I was leaving, I could feel a pair of eyes watching me from behind, but I was determined not to turn around. I just wanted to look at her face. Since she wouldn't give me that chance, I wouldn't give it to her either." The back-to-camera framing obscures the look of wounded emotion we infer on Yuddy's face, even as he strives obdurately to conceal it. In *The Hand*, a foreground object blocks facial access to Xiao (Chang Chen), who eavesdrops on a colleague's phone call to Hua (Gong Li) (Figure 3.3). Strategically masking Xiao's face not only frustrates the viewer's line of sight; it also ambiguates Xiao's reaction to what he hears, extending his subjective opacity and preserving the narrative's suspense as to Xiao's feelings for Hua (does he love her, loathe her, pity her?). Finally, *In the Mood for Love* motivates facial masking by narrative setting, the cramped apartment interiors squeezing characters into nooks and crevices, a clutter of objects impinging upon private space (Figure 3.4). The film's occlusion of faces and figures testifies to a space devoid of privacy and hints at a world in which the characters' authentic selves are mutually inaccessible.

These compositions may present perceptual difficulty, but this does not mean that they are not also sensuous. On the contrary, such images are simultaneously sensuous and "difficult," placing incompatible demands upon the viewer's comprehension. Recurrently, the image's enticement toward aesthetic absorption is undercut—within the selfsame image—by stimuli to perceptual and cognitive effort. Wong's characteristic visual scheme, in other words, harbors a dynamic narrational tension, meshing sensuous appeals (intended to enthrall, and seduce) with perceptual obfuscations (designed to disorient and frustrate).

The demotion of facial access gives rise to a kind of displacement or diffusion of character emotion. Most commercial cinema makes the human face the prime site of character revelation, but Wong throws expressive weight onto bodily attributes (hands, feet), features of setting (landscape, décor), and parameters of style (cinematography, sound). As a result, he diffuses the conventional center of character emotion and affectively saturates the diegetic terrain. Here is another strategy whereby the visual image is at once narratively motivated, sensuous, and cognitively demanding. In *2046*, *In the Mood for Love*, and *The Hand*, Wong often cuts to parts of the body (midsections, fingers, the nape of a neck), investing scenes with a potent sensual charge. But these images are not motivated by sensuousness alone. They also bear narrative significance, inviting the viewer to reflect upon the story milieu. Expressive diffusion, in all three films, aids the construction of place and time—specifically a 1960s Hong Kong shot through with conservative mores. From the oblique image, the viewer infers the cultural "display rules" (Ekman 1982) governing the characters' behavior. These norms of behavior constrain facial expression to within a very circumscribed range; consequently, the strategy of expressive diffusion implies character emotion from a repertoire of body language.

Emotion bleeds into the narrative setting too. The physical environment becomes an expressive, rather than simply mimetic, element.[6] "The very walls

---

6. The narratively expressive function of Wong's landscape shots distinguishes them from Ozu's "pillow shots," which function parametrically, and the "empty shots" in Chen Kaige's *Yellow Earth* (1984) that, according to Chris Berry and Mary Ann Farquhar, "suspend the development of narrative" (1994: 90, 108).

of rooms [in *The Hand*] seem erotic," notes Stanley Kauffmann (2005: 24). Vibrant colors, emblazoned onto costumes or features of décor, compensate for the protagonists' emotional reticence. The pathetic fallacy comes forward as a favorite device, supplementing or supplanting shots of the face. Facial masking also places greater burden on cinematography to execute expressive tasks. A languorous panning shot skims surfaces like a soft caress. Disjunctive cuts embody moments of anxiety, disorientation, or shock. In all, facial masking diverts the characters' feelings of desire, melancholy, and loneliness into other expressive channels. Neither coldly objective nor emotionally direct, this authorial strategy elicits cognitive arousal suffused with feeling.

Wong's critics might regard these tactics as mannerisms, but his aesthetic of disturbance plays a crucial role in the viewer's narrative uptake. The staccato duels in *Ashes of Time*, for instance, retard the viewer's individuation of characters by minimizing clear facial close-ups and recruiting smudge motion to vitiate or occlude the action's specificity. When Wong blends this device with discontinuity editing, canted angles, whip pans, fast cutting, sudden figure movement, and febrile camerawork, the action's legibility emerges only in brief spasmodic bursts. As often in Wong, the viewer's perception is roughened but not wholly stymied; decelerated shots and communicative sound provide vital aids to intelligibility. Yet the welter of gestures and bodies ambiguates key phases of combat—amid the ferment, the superior swordsman is impossible to identify. Such strategies both intensify suspense (e.g., which of the duelists will prevail?) and powerfully convey the fighter's stunning, whipcrack agility. Only in the abrupt aftermath of battle is the action's key information made apparent.

In Brunette's view, these scenes amount to a parametric foregrounding of cinematic style:

> The result of all this is that the viewer can momentarily forget the specific twists of narrative and causality and become simply immersed in the flow of the blurred images in any given sequence. (2005: 38–39)

But the array of visual obliquities in such sequences cannot help but stimulate the viewer to perceptual and cognitive effort. It is not simply that we want to distinguish one swordsman from another but that our construction of the narrative depends upon our doing so. Some viewers may immerse themselves "in the flow of the blurred images," but Wong's tactics of disturbance sanction against it. The scenes' concurrent push-pull of seduction and provocation attests to an ambivalent and dynamic visual narration. In any event, *Ashes of Time* differs sharply from the pictorial norms governing Hong Kong action cinema. This tradition, Bordwell states, puts "the graceful body at the center of its mise-en-scène" and aims to maximize the actor's gestural clarity (2008b:

401). By contrast, *Ashes of Time* reduces the combatant's body to an amorphous blur.[7] This aesthetic choice is partly (but not wholly) corollary to Wong's ambivalence toward facial close-ups. The studied masking of faces pushes Wong into fresh areas of character expressivity, extending the visual norms of Hong Kong genre storytelling.[8]

In what other ways does Wong roughen the viewer's perception? One method is to combine cluttered foregrounds with staging in depth. *Happy Together* introduces a compositional trope in which window inscriptions festoon the foreground, embroidering the mise-en-scène but also obscuring figures tucked into farther regions of space. The image yields niches of visibility. Slit-staging, similarly, presents narrow apertures in which characters are barely glimpsed in deep space. Nowhere is this device more obliquely deployed than in one shot in *Fallen Angels* that depicts Agent plotting an assassination over the telephone. Wong blends staging in depth, figure movement, tilting handheld camera, and an extremely slender foreground aperture into an abbreviated take. Thanks to the shot's brevity and perceptual obstacles, the viewer is permitted only a tenuous purchase on Agent as she occupies deep space; Agent's elliptical dialogue, moreover, demands the viewer's full attention. Once more, a flagrant pictorial device is far from narratively superfluous: in this case, it reinforces the enigmatic Agent's mystique, while the hint of voyeurism underscores the covert nature of her activity.

Deep staging nudges Wong toward telephoto shooting, allowing fuzzy foregrounds to encroach upon the characters placed in depth. In *My Blueberry Nights*, Wong routinely situates the camera outside the zone of action, thus promoting the long lens option. Action staged within the café interior is often observed through windows; likewise, Wong shoots exterior scenes from inside the locale. As a result, the obtrusive window patterns are frequently admitted into frame, blurrily disrupting the spectator's view of figures in the recessional playing space. *In the Mood for Love*'s multiplanar staging similarly compels our visual attention to scan planes of depth. At the same time, the patterned cheongsams and décor not only ravish the eye but stimulate perceptual effort. *Fallen Angels* allies deep staging with extreme wide angles. The result is a drastic warping of dramatic space, causing foreground objects to bulge at the edges and taper off sharply into receding planes. Such shots exaggerate distances between foreground and background planes. As Teo suggests, this

---

7. In contrast, *Ashes of Time*'s dialogue scenes, which in a traditional film would prioritize facial performance, invariably obfuscate, obstruct, or displace the human face with other expressive elements.

8. Wong's reworking of Hong Kong cinema's "clarity" can be generalized to other textual features and effects, such as emotional appeals (which tend to convey and elicit complex, diffuse, compound emotion states, rather than the basic emotions traditionally exploited by local mainstream films).

optical distortion is motivated at a narrative level. Wong, says Teo, finds a visual correlative for the protagonists' remote intimacy that "captures the essence of two people close to each other, yet distant" (2005: 86).

Then there is Wong's fondness for elliptical editing, whether overt (flaunting gaps) or tacit (suppressing gaps). Most demanding is the ellipsis that skirts our attention. Hong Kong movies typically mark scenes off from one another by striking shifts in tone and action, but Wong subdues explicit scene demarcations. Instead, tacitly elliptical cuts disguise scene transitions, conceal significant leaps forward in the *fabula*, and lead the viewer into errors of comprehension. Once alert to the narration's elliptical gambits, the viewer refocuses attention to that which *is* reliably communicative of *fabula* progression, such as changes in the characters' dress and appearance.[9] Critics describe such editing tactics as "incoherent" (e.g., Tsui 1995: 113), but this does not necessarily mean that the films themselves are incoherent. Indeed, discontinuity cutting emerges as an internal norm in each film, supplying a consistent principle of visual design.

Slit-staging, blocked foregrounds, telephoto shooting, elliptical cutting—each of these tactics contributes to Wong's aesthetic of perceptual disturbance. For all these obstructive elements, however, the visual action is not wholly opaque or abstruse. An aesthetic of disturbance entails the delicate negotiation of retardatory and legibility devices. Again, this dynamic tension is manifested at the level of visual style. A single shot may exhibit a tendency to both obscure important action and to present it perspicuously. Consider again the strategy of facial masking. By *Ashes of Time*, Wong had perfected what I will call a disturb-and-refresh schema, temporarily masking a clear facial view before restoring visibility. A representative instance occurs in the protagonist's ramshackle hut. Here, staging and framing are wholly communicative: Ouyang Feng (Leslie Cheung) is frontally positioned in a telephoto medium shot. As he addresses an offscreen figure, a foreground curtain periodically billows into frame, obscuring Ouyang's face. (Apart from generating pictorial and perceptual disturbance, this obscuring element accents a wider narrational suppressiveness—tantalizingly, Wong never supplies the reverse shot of the unseen figure.) In characteristic fashion, Wong discovers a means by which to flout the clarity promised by traditionally communicative devices (frontality, close framing) while also preserving enough communicativeness to ensure perceptual comprehension. Visual perception is disturbed, but at no permanent cost to narrative intelligibility.

---

9. By contrast, Wong often announces key plot moments with an overt stylistic flourish. In *Chungking Express*, Brigitte Lin's first and final scenes are marked by freeze frames, as is the film's bifurcating plot switch. Freeze frames also mark decisive plot developments in *Happy Together*. And *Fallen Angels* launches its second plotline by means of an elaborate long take unlike any previous shot in the film.

Bordwell argues that Wong cultivates an "aesthetic of the glimpse," switching between a sidelong presentation and relatively transparent views:

> Wong, like von Sternberg, shifts between a nearly hypnotic stare and a teasing glimpse. The landscape shots, the lengthy close-ups of the characters . . . , and the long tracking shots following a crowd or up a staircase invite the spectator to study a slowly unfolding spectacle. By contrast, the film will reward us with a perversely blocked view. (2011: 178)

The teasing glimpses, Bordwell suggests, are stylistically apposite for Wong's stories of shy and flirtatious young lovers (182). Symptomatic of a filmmaker Bordwell describes as polystylistic, this visual dichotomy advances Wong's dynamic of opacity and clarity—though, as I have demonstrated, even a stare can be frustratingly uninformative (as when a face is obscured by hair and shadow, despite a long take close-up treatment).

Wong's visual aesthetic, I am arguing, is neither wholly opaque nor wholly informative. Equally, it refuses both the direct emotional payoffs of Hong Kong's popular cinema and the affective "distance" of the art film. Contrary to his detractors' claims, Wong's stylistic traits are not gratuitous or self-indulgent, nor do they testify to artistic incoherence or postmodern fragmentation. A strategy of motivated sensuousness endows Wong's alluring surfaces with narrative significance. Moreover, his visual stratagems do not betoken textual incoherence but the opposite: they unify the film, lending continuity to discrete locales and plotlines. The overall visual design is not incoherent, and it does not blunt the viewer's cognitive processes. Wong's films refuse to let us slip into dreamlike trances, even as they tempt us with the possibility. Rather, our construction of the narrative crucially depends upon our perceptual pickup—it depends, that is, on our ability to individuate faces, spot tacit ellipses, perceive changes in costume and appearance, read images quickly, infer narrative significance from abstract imagery (say, of landscapes or limbs), and so on. That our grasp of the story relies so intimately on perceiving and grasping these visual cues demonstrates the rigor with which Wong's visual design and narrative are integrated. The charge that his visual tactics are merely superficial, then, falls far wide of the mark.

The rest of this chapter examines specific instances of the techniques I have described. *Happy Together* and *My Blueberry Nights* are characteristic of Wong's visual style inasmuch as they exemplify the auteur's aesthetic of disturbance. Yet the personnel behind each film differ: *Happy Together* was shot by Chris Doyle, while Darius Khondji photographed *My Blueberry Nights*. However, the films' overwhelming affinities—not least, their stylistic dominant of disturbance and their demonstration of stylistic coherence and overall compositional unity—attest to the authorial hand of Wong Kar-wai and the organizing influence of William Chang (here responsible for production design and editing). Both films, moreover, are putative road movies—though, as I will show, each is concerned as much with stagnation as with progress.

Happy Together

Notwithstanding a brief credits sequence, the opening phase of *Happy Together* announces a marked shift from the brisk preliminary expositions of *Chungking Express* and *Fallen Angels*. Chris Doyle's handheld camera aims for steadiness; shot length is increased; monochrome supplies a sober palette; normal motion reigns, rejecting the kinetic propulsion of the two previous films—in all, *Happy Together*'s opening segment exhibits an altogether more sedate look than that of Wong's recent films, presaging the visual restraint of the films to follow (*In the Mood for Love*, 2046, and *The Hand*). Critics attributed this temperate style to Wong's growing "maturity" as a filmmaker, but the muted register is perfectly apt to convey the protagonists' stasis at the film's start. Exiled to Argentina and consigned to a roadside in their broken-down car, Ho Po-wing (Leslie Cheung) and Lai Yiu-fai (Tony Leung Chiu-wai) can barely sustain a relationship bereft of direction or purpose.

If the visual tenor has changed, the strategy of facial masking remains active, and Wong must find fresh ways to cue the protagonists' subjectivities. Once the central couple separates, the profound isolation of the taciturn Yiu-fai finds powerful expression at the visual level. In an Argentine tango bar, Po-wing passionately kisses a "trick"; Yiu-fai, alone in the street outside, can only observe the pair through a window. Stationing the camera inside the bar, Wong shoots Yiu-fai through the glass surface, a prominent window inscription partially blocking the protagonist from view (Figure 3.5). The inscription does more than obfuscate, however—it has the effect of embedding Yiu-fai farther into deep space, augmenting his exclusion from the bar interior (and the cozy aura of warmth and intimacy inside). Depth staging and the inscription motif compound the impression that Yiu-fai is literally and emotionally shut out in the cold. Po-wing, however, revels in the warm interior, apparently unmoved by his estrangement from Yiu-fai. No mere decorative flourish, the window inscription—together with the camera's interior vantage point—expressively conveys Yiu-fai's emotional situation, a kind of psychological exile reflected and exacerbated by his physical displacement from home. Furthermore, *Happy Together*'s inscription motif not only designates specific locales and animates the disturb-and-refresh schema. As in *My Blueberry Nights*, it also becomes a compositional element defining the film's overall design. Buttressing the film's total unity, it coheres places and plotlines in motivic fashion.

Situating the protagonist on background planes accentuates his emotional isolation, but so too do other visual techniques. One brief sequence shot begins with a close-up of the lamp in Yiu-fai's apartment; the camera pans away from the object to find Yiu-fai in the far distance, alone. The lamp is a thematically charged item of décor—it depicts the Iguaçu Falls, a personal nirvana for the estranged couple. As a motivic element, the lamp periodically resurfaces to mark the figurative distance between the protagonists' relationship and their attainment of this adopted idyll. In this particular shot, Wong uses the foreground element to comment on the background element, though the lamp and Yiu-fai do not share the frame—the panning camera is instrumental in juxtaposing the two elements. Without recourse to dialogue or facial close-ups, Wong palpably conveys Yiu-fai's existential solitude.

In Wong's films the point-of-view (POV) structure is demoted, thus marginalizing a major source of subjective access. It seems to me that the conventional POV structure—comprised of a glance and object shot—furnishes subjective information that Wong prefers to conjure in other ways (for example, by a strategy of expressive diffusion). At times, Wong wants to withhold or ambiguate subjective states, hence the legible glance shot is anathema. In *Happy Together*, Wong reworks the POV schema in a way that is evocative of Yiu-fai's alienation. Po-wing glides past Yiu-fai at the tango bar's entrance but does not acknowledge him. Has Po-wing failed to notice him? Or is this a pointed slight? Ostensibly, a medium close-up of Yiu-fai supplies Po-wing's POV. That Yiu-fai looks directly at the camera, and thus inferably at Po-wing, makes the image very compelling as a subjective POV shot. Yet the reverse shot of Po-wing reveals that Yiu-fai's gaze is not reciprocated, thus disconfirming our POV inference. What this juxtaposition of shots very effectively registers is that Po-wing is peripherally aware of Yiu-fai's presence but trenchantly, cruelly, rebuffs him (an inference confirmed later, when Po-wing glances at his ex-lover through a taxi's rear windshield). Revising the traditional POV schema roughens both a stylistic norm and the viewer's perceptual habits. But it also conveys Yiu-fai's isolation, in sidelong but potent fashion, by purely visual means.

Happy Together traces a narrative of character interchangeability so endemic to Wong's films. Near the climax, Po-wing moves back into the apartment, but Yiu-fai has gone. Like Faye in *Chungking Express* and Agent in *Fallen Angels*, he cleans the empty apartment of the man he pines for and adopts this absent figure's routines. Wong depicts Po-wing residing in the apartment alone, as Yiu-fai had. He also revives the lamp motif, now looked upon forlornly by Po-wing instead of Yiu-fai. For Po-wing—self-centered, uncaring, narcissistic—the utopia represented on the lamp is now an impossible pipe dream. Only Yiu-fai will reach the falls and bathe in their sublime spectacle. Yiu-fai's solitude has been vividly portrayed throughout the film, and at the climax he remains alone. Yet the closing images are euphoric—Yiu-fai stands aboard a speeding train (a signature visual motif) as it hurtles along at an invigorating clip. In sharp contrast to his inertia at the film's start, Yiu-fai is at last engaged in exhilarating motion, making progress.

My Blueberry Nights

Just as *Happy Together* roughens the traditional POV norm, so *My Blueberry Nights* exploits disjunctive editing to roughen the viewer's perceptual habits. Jump cuts, tacit ellipses, and violations of the 180-degree rule enliven the film's more energetic sequences. Drastic shifts in shot scale and angle carry disjunctive force, but even relatively minute shifts in perspective have the power to disorient. The film makes little use of deep focus, favoring a limited playing area; selected planes are sharpened, with others put out of focus. Characters seldom walk toward the camera or retreat into depth. Instead Wong rivets them to the spot and cuts around them, typically in a woozy fashion. Tight close-ups jostle with oblique long shots; reverse perspectives unsettle our spatial bearings; and a single action may be presented from several angles, as if to suggest that even slight variations in vantage point might yield significant revelations in the drama. Thanks to a breathless cutting rate, the viewer must strain to process incoming information before the next shot arrives. In all, Wong's restless visual narration invigorates dialogue scenes and plays pinball with the viewer's eye.

My Blueberry Nights' editing techniques successfully roughen perception, but they may also be attributable to Wong's distinctive shooting practice. An exponent of multicam filming, Wong shoots a single take from a host of vantage points and distances. He is also fond of repeated takes, subjecting a single scene to fresh renditions (Chang 2007). These shooting protocols promote the likelihood of cutting, multiplying choices at the postproduction stage, and yielding copious shots that can be spliced together in infinite combinations. William Chang speaks to this point:

> Wong likes taking a few master shots, which is good news for an editor. His shots are very fluid—they can be used alone, broken down into individual units or joined up—unlike the rigid and detailed shot breakdowns in some other films. (Lee 2004: 47)

It is worth stressing that Wong's production practices—multiple camera setups, high shooting ratio—invite but do not prescribe the often disjunctive patterns on display in *My Blueberry Nights*. Other directors insist on varied camera setups yet strictly adhere to traditional continuity principles. Still, Wong could not as effectively dynamize his scenes with unexpected shifts in scale and angle were it not for his multicam approach. The perceptual difficulties at the film's surface find their genesis in the working methods of this fastidious filmmaker.

From the start, *My Blueberry Nights* announces self-consciousness and perceptual disturbance as internal stylistic norms. Its opening phase deploys a visual tactic that occupied the earlier portion of this chapter: the partial blocking of faces. Broadly, this recurring motif executes a roughening of traditional schemas, chiefly, the facial close-up, the OTS shot, and the shot / reverse shot—all mainstays of international film style. At its limit, the practice of obscuring faces yields almost abstract compositions. In one OTS shot in *My Blueberry Nights*, Elizabeth is situated in the extreme foreground, tucked against the frame edge and out of focus; the back of her head largely obscures Arnie (David Strathairn), the lovelorn cop, positioned frontally. The shallow depth of field produced by the anamorphic lens casts Arnie in crisp focus, while a string of bleary lights dances across the frame's rear horizon. Concrete features of mise-en-scène dissolve into indeterminate, abstract patterns of color and light. Compositions like this tease us with partial views of the protagonists, but they also hint at a general fascination with substantially graphic or abstract configurations.

This tendency toward pictorial abstraction is embodied in several of the film's visual motifs. The window art adorning Jeremy's café yields brightly colored curlicues that swirl sinuously around the characters. Mottled lights within the décor amplify the romantic tenor of dialogue scenes. Bold, saturated colors fall into motivic alignment—in the café, Jeremy's blue shirt complements features of setting (such as a blue pillar and the blue window inscriptions stretched across the frame's foreground). When the café's surveillance camera malfunctions, the entire image is flooded in blue tones, preserving the locale's dominant color scheme (Figure 3.6). (The saturated blue tones hark back to Andrew Lau's vibrant cinematography in *As Tears Go By* and *Chungking Express*.) At times, *My Blueberry Nights* foregrounds images that are, of themselves, purely abstract, as when the camera bathes in the reflected shapes and colors sweeping over a Jaguar's bodywork. Extreme close-ups of blueberry pie, stressing rich colors and sticky textures, similarly revel in sensuously graphic play (Figure 3.7). Contrary to the charge of pure aestheticism, the presence of abstract imagery does not mean that such imagery is devoid of narrative function or meaning. In Wong's aesthetic program, style services story. Opaque or abstract images tax the viewer's eye, but the film makes dramatic clarity an aesthetic priority.

The window inscriptions in Jeremy's café, for all their apparent decorativeness, do more than embroider the image. More so than in *Happy Together*, Wong exploits this feature of mise-en-scène for narrational purposes, creating visual payoffs by masking and revealing faces and by guiding the eye toward

Figure 1.1. *Ashes of Time Redux* (2008). Artificial Eye.

Figure 1.2. Smudge motion in *Chungking Express* (1994). Artificial Eye.

Figure 2.1. Contrapuntal music negates sentimentality in *Happy Together* (1997). Kino DVD.

Figure 2.2. In *Chungking Express* (1994), an airline uniform flutters on a clothesline and an airplane streaks through the sky, as "California Dreamin'" fills the soundscape. Artificial Eye.

Figure 2.3. Faye throws a paper plane in *Chungking Express* (1994). Artificial Eye.

Figure 3.1. *As Tears Go By* (1989) displays the kind of perspicuous symmetrical staging that Wong would abandon in subsequent films. Mega Star Video Distribution (HK).

Figure 3.2. The star player as sensuous spectacle: Maggie Cheung in *Ashes of Time* (1994). Artificial Eye.

Figure 3.3. In *The Hand* (2004), obtrusive foreground objects conceal and ambiguate character emotion. Mei Ah Entertainment.

Figure 3.4. *In the Mood for Love* (2000) motivates facial masking naturalistically, by items of setting and décor. Tartan DVD.

Figure 3.5. Depth staging isolates Tony Leung's protagonist in *Happy Together* (1997). Kino DVD.

Figure 3.6. A malfunctioning surveillance camera in *My Blueberry Nights* (2007) motivates a blue-saturated image, preserving the film's patterned color scheme. Optimum DVD.

Figure 3.7. In *My Blueberry Nights* (2007), the title sequence's extreme close-ups of a pie announce a fascination with sensuousness and abstraction. Optimum DVD.

Figure 4.1. Yuddy admires his own reflection while dancing the cha-cha in *Days of Being Wild* (1990), a film laying bare the influence of Tennessee Williams. Tartan DVD.

Figure 4.2. Spectacle versus story in *Fallen Angels* (1995). Kino DVD.

Figure 4.3. In *Fallen Angels* (1995), ebullient characters offset Killer's taciturnity. Kino DVD.

Figure 5.1. Gong Li's Su Lizhen, in a typically off-center framing, raises the romantic stakes in *2046* (2004). Sony Pictures Classics.

Figure 5.2. *In the Mood for Love* (2000): Mrs. Suen lectures Su on social decorum, the latter's emotional reaction typically withheld by back-to-camera staging. Tartan DVD.

Figure 5.3. *In the Mood for Love* (2000) misdirects the viewer with restricted narration, triggering false inferences. Tartan DVD.

Figure 6.1. Zhang Ziyi as Gong Er in *The Grandmaster* (2013). Mei Ah Entertainment.

Figure 6.2. *The Grandmaster* (2013) furnishes a "family portrait" visual motif, tracing Ip Man's shifting fortunes. Mei Ah Entertainment.

relevant niches of action. But Wong also patterns this motif across the film's distinct plotlines. The window art figures most prominently in Jeremy's café, but it surfaces in the film's other major plot strands too: in the second episode, set in Memphis, illuminating the windows of Travis's bar; and in the subsequent action line, set in Nevada, attending the hospital setting. Constituting a cohesion device, the window motif cannot be dismissed as a mere stylistic flourish; rather, it emerges as a function of large-scale narration, serving to knit the episodic plot phases together.

Wong invests the film's aleatory plot with a lush pictorial consistency. Each major locale is assigned a dominant color scheme. Deep blues and greens saturate the New York setting; hot reds and oranges mark the Memphis milieu; golds and tans pervade Nevada and Vegas. Wong's bold color palette owes a debt to both Hong Kong's popular cinema (recall the splashy Eastmancolor spectacle of the Shaw Brothers output, as well as the 1980s work of John Woo and Ringo Lam) and European art cinema (think of the startling color schemes in certain films by Godard, Antonioni, and Bergman). Like the exponents of those traditions, Wong handles film color expressively. In *My Blueberry Nights*, the colored lights that coruscate in background planes—as when Elizabeth and Jeremy are reunited on a New York City street—endow the action with a tender, romantic quality. When Arnie is publicly spurned by his estranged wife, a bright red wall simmers behind him. Most generally, the film's sensuous color design is motivated by the diegesis as ambient features of setting and location. Motivated from within the story world, Wong's saturated color design is hardly superfluous to story and plot.

Even the most abstract compositions are granted narrative justification. A perceptual fascination arises from the colored lights refracted on the Jaguar, but the purpose of these shots is not wholly or gratuitously graphic. The car itself holds narrative importance—it facilitates Elizabeth's road trip, represents a central character goal (Elizabeth works several jobs to earn money for a car), and constitutes a plot device bringing two protagonists (Elizabeth and Leslie) together. When the abstract images appear, moreover, the vehicle represents the coveted stakes in a gambling wager. Wong's sensuous treatment of the car is entirely apt to convey the allure that the object holds for Elizabeth. Wong's pictorial abstraction is one instance of what I have called expressive displacement; a byproduct of facial masking (or facial opacity, as with the poker-faced gamblers here), it conveys subjective states and prompts the viewer to undertake active inference making.

Like Wong's other films, *My Blueberry Nights* follows a logic of motivated sensuousness. By claiming this, I do not wish to demote the role of sensuousness in *My Blueberry Nights* nor to deny that formal saliency is an integral part of its interest. The film's sensuousness does indeed gratify the eye. But, instead of elevating visual style above thematic and narrative concerns, as Wong's detractors allege, Wong endows the stylistic flourish with narrative meanings and effects. In denying that Wong is a pure aesthete, moreover, I am not arguing that a wholly stylistic use of the medium would necessarily degrade Wong—or indeed any filmmaker so inclined. Purely stylistic exercises can be innately valuable, not least for their capacity to revivify perceptual skills gone stale. But the mantle of pure aestheticism does not fit Wong. Far from privileging ornamentation, *My Blueberry Nights* exemplifies the harmonious integration of story and style.

There are surely other visual tactics in *My Blueberry Nights* that deserve attention—the prevalence of the profiled shot / reverse shot, the tendency to carve the wide picture format into discriminable zones—but I hope to have indicated some important features of the film's complex aesthetic. Just as Wong's cinema cannot be summarized by reference to favorite techniques (e.g., smudge motion, MTV-style editing, alienating long takes), it cannot be reduced to a simple aestheticism inducing viewer passivity. Typical of Wong's films, *My Blueberry Nights* roughens the viewer's perception, but it does so without detriment to either cognitive arousal or perceptual gratification.

This chapter has been concerned to demonstrate the primacy of visual disturbance to Wong's aesthetic program, and to show how his characteristic tactics animate a dynamic of clarity and obfuscation. A cluster of visual maneuvers—e.g., facial masking, expressive displacement, the disturb-and-refresh schema—conspire to buttress a stylistic dominant of disturbance. At the same time, an overall strategy of motivated sensuousness belies the impression of superficiality, and tantalizes the viewer with the possibility of aesthetic absorption. The consistency of these tactics across Wong's oeuvre qualifies the teleological assumption that meditative films such as *In the Mood for Love* bear witness to the "maturing" of Wong's technique over time, as if energetic expressions of film style, as deployed in *Chungking Express*, are somehow less sophisticated or technically accomplished. In sum, Wong has cultivated a visual style both robust and flexible. Some of his techniques have endured across his oeuvre and others have fallen into disuse, but the principle of disturbance prevails. As a result, his cinema bears a stylistic signature that is at once steadfast and subtle.

4 | Parallel Lives
Poetics of the Postproduction Plot

I have examined the significance of style in Wong's cinema, but what of story? What convinces critics of the negligibility, even the absence, of plot in Wong's films? Consider this representative but hardly exhaustive sample: *Chungking Express* is "minimally plotted" (Taubin 2008), displaying a "breezy disregard for plot structure" (Cameron 2007); *My Blueberry Nights* constructs a narrative "so vaporous it barely exists" (Brooke 2008: 74); *Happy Together* is "almost plotless" (Elley 1997: 50); *Days of Being Wild* "uneventful" (Brunette 2005: 21); and *As Tears Go By* narratively "sparse" (2). In this context, identifying *storytelling* as a central enterprise in Wong's cinema seems wrongheaded. Yet perhaps some critics miscalculate Wong's engagement with norms of story and narration, however popular or rarefied these norms might be.

Part of the problem stems from conceptual imprecision. Just as some critics rely upon a spurious antithesis between story and style, so they presuppose an opposition between story and character. Thus, for instance, "all of Wong's films . . . [are] more interested in the nature of human relationships than in narrative momentum" (Davis 2005: 26), while *Days of Being Wild* is a case whereby "character prevails over story" (Teo 2005: 35). Such claims may seem intuitively correct, but they lack the exactness of more conceptually fine-grained distinctions. For the purposes of this chapter, I adopt the narratological concepts of *fabula* (the story in its linear abstract form), *syuzhet* (the plotting of the story events in a particular way), and narration (the ongoing maintenance of story information). As differential tools of analysis, these distinctions enable a more specific examination of the apparently diffuse, attenuated, or nonexistent narratives in Wong's oeuvre.

This chapter regards story patterning as fundamental in shaping audience interest, stimulating cognitive effort, and counterpointing sensuous absorption. The complexity of Wong's films owes as much to story materials (e.g., opaque and contradictory characters), plot structure (e.g., deforming the story in ways that make narrative chronology ambiguous), and narration (e.g., implying omniscience while eliding crucial narrative facts) as to perceptual disturbances at the visual level. Further, certain complex features of storytelling find their genesis in Wong's unique production methods. The chapter also considers narrative organization as an integral component in the films' overall coherence and unity. Later in this chapter I examine how narrative functions in a film that critics have primarily treated as a showcase for Wong's audiovisual style—*Fallen Angels*. Here I argue that Wong not only contrives a *syuzhet* as self-conscious as the film's sensuous sound and image tracks but also that he deflects allegations of parametric excess by anchoring narrational strategies in textual elements such as character and theme. The "architectural pleasure" provided by the film's structure is explicitly motivated by matters pertaining to the diegetic world.[1]

Aesthetics in Practice

Wong's production method embraces chance and experiment to a degree that is unusual even for Hong Kong film production. "People are more and more interested in the way we make a film than [in] the film itself," Wong stated during promotion of *In the Mood for Love* (Forde 2000: 23). Indeed, at first glance a disproportionate critical emphasis upon Wong's distinctive mode of film production might stand out. But the films' narrative architecture is palpably shaped by Wong's mode of film practice. These practices are well known, but they bear repeating here. During the 1990s Wong favored schematic story outlines over full-fledged scripts. Tentative scenarios, character delineations, and genre tropes took the place of advance script construction, providing a sketchy template from which to fashion a plot. In preproduction, Wong apprizes the principal players of their respective roles and storylines. Each shooting day is dedicated to developing and filming two or three scenes, the action and dialogue of which Wong devises just days or hours before. Postproduction editing is a misnomer in Hong Kong cinema, and William Chang's scene construction accompanies the shooting phase. A painstaking editing process continues after shooting is completed. Here Wong and Chang arrange footage in numerous combinations until a plot coalesces. Entire action lines are discarded, relegating major stars to mere cameos. Crucial narrative exposition might be shoved to the denouement or eliminated altogether. Plot order is repeatedly reworked, sometimes quite radically, as Chang testifies: "we often spend more time discussing whether the last scene should be the opening scene or whether the middle scene should really be the last, rather than deciding how a particular scene should be edited

---

1.   The phrase "architectural pleasure," denoting the viewing pleasures wrought by a *fabula*'s deformation, derives from Murray Smith (2001: 156).

or re-edited" (McGrath 2001: 160). The narrative's shape and structure is repeatedly fine-tuned until notoriously late in the film's production schedule.

Call this a strategy of postproduction plotting—only by methodical trial and error does the narrative's fundamental shape come into focus. This remains Wong's preferred work method today, though shifting industrial norms have made financiers anxious for preproduction scripts. As international coproduction has moved to the center of Hong Kong filmmaking and overseas financiers have multiplied, risk has been reduced by a completed script shared among all parties. An experienced scenarist, Wong compromises by supplying investors expanded story outlines, though with a caveat allowing him to revise the story during shooting and postproduction (Rayns 2000: 35). *My Blueberry Nights*—a first foray into English-language cinema, shot on American locations with Hollywood stars—necessitated a preproduction screenplay to attract Western personnel and capital. (Wong devised the script with American novelist Lawrence Block.) Nevertheless, Wong is still privileged with a degree of narrative license, at all stages of production, that is rare in contemporary cinema.

Some critics equate Wong's aleatory practice with narrative incoherence. Postproduction plotting results not only in wispy, threadbare narratives but also, for these critics, in an "almost ramshackle" story design (Rohdie 1997: 121). Yet this basic assumption—that a working method open to chance yields inevitably desultory and disorganized narratives—does not withstand scrutiny. Again we alight on an argument rehearsed elsewhere in this book, namely, that Wong's films follow a logic of organic unity demonstrable at all levels of form and style. Unifying Wong's footage may be the purview of the film's editor, but the formalities of narrative are an important consideration from the start. Hence Chris Doyle's production log for *Happy Together* betrays a commitment to the classical underpinnings of the film's structure: the synopsis "looks a little feeble in this form: few 'motivations,' little apparent action, no subplot" (Doyle and Rayns 1998: 156). Governed by traditional storytelling principles, Wong's plotting is by no means as unruly as his working method might imply. Indeed, the films' protracted editing stage—whereby plot order is fastidiously worked on—betrays a fine-grained and overarching attention to narrative structure. When Teo (2005) characterizes Wong as a "literary" filmmaker, he refers to nothing less than Wong's deep fascination with plot architecture.

In sum, the films themselves contradict the aleatory nature of their creation. Whereas Wong prizes exploratory shooting practices, the nominal postproduction phase—supervised by Chang—evidently prioritizes Aristotelian principles of coherence and unity, subjecting creative experiment to formal constraints. For all their capricious, mazy gestations, Wong's films display remarkable internal unity at every level of design. Episodic plotting, ellipticality, audacious shifts in tone, coincidental encounters, chance events, repeated actions, voice-over narration—Wong Kar-wai's storytelling signature is etched upon these devices. How firmly these features are grounded in Wong's work practices can be better grasped by considering an anomalous case—*As Tears Go By*, which originated from a precomposed screenplay. Wong's maiden film evidently relied upon a degree of preplanning eschewed in much of his subsequent work.

Partway through the film, gangster Wah (Andy Lau) randomly encounters a former girlfriend, now heavily pregnant. The scene begins with a distant view of Wah dashing through a downpour. As he arrives close to frame, the camera glides laterally to reveal the woman standing nearby. The arcing camera comes to rest, framing the pair in frontal two-shot. This setup presents the characters' stilted conversation as they take refuge from the rain, the woman assuring Wah that he is not her child's father. Assuaged, Wah bids farewell and ventures back into the rainstorm. Now the camera reverses its original path, tracking away from the woman and reclaiming its initial vantage point as Wah darts into the distance. Bracketed by rhyming tracking shots, this sequence evinces a formal unity consistent with the film's generally episodic construction.

In some respects this scene is prototypical Wong Kar-wai. The fondness for story action motivated by chance, the use of inclement rainfall as pathetic fallacy, the interruption of genre plotting by apparently incidental action, the expression of interior states through subtle implication (Wong hints that the woman might be lying about her child's paternity)—all these features have become cornerstones of Wong's cinema. Yet the scene's visual symmetry betrays a degree of detailed calculation, perhaps even storyboarding, uncharacteristic of Wong's subsequent films. In other words, the episode's formal neatness indicates careful advance plotting, rather than postproduction scene construction. Here, the indications are of economical shooting and cutting-in-the-camera, not least because the scene's visual bookends were evidently conceived prior to editing. Wong's next film, *Days of Being Wild*, signals a decisive shift toward the director's now-customary film practice: an experimental preference for shooting many improvised variants of a scene. Now a rich lode of footage multiplies options for scene construction, and this fund of possibilities—afforded by Wong's spontaneous method of shooting, which does not presuppose how the finished scene will be structured—effectively relegates the sort of neatly symmetrical sequence found in *As Tears Go By*.

As it makes one aesthetic option less likely, however, Wong's production method promotes other formal choices. Ellipticality now emerges as a primary strategy, thanks partly to continuity gaps arising from assembled takes. If scenic symmetry in *As Tears Go By* yields crisp scene divisions and formal finesse, ellipticality fosters ambiguous effects more in tune with Wong's sensibilities. As I will discuss in the next chapter, the romantic role plays of *In the Mood for*

Love register disorientation largely by elliptical cutting, which blends discrete scenes together almost imperceptibly; the resulting temporal ambiguity renders the protagonists' ostensibly platonic relationship indeterminate. Noting this early shift in Wong's production methods—from advance scripting and cutting-in-camera to on-set spontaneity—recalls not only that Wong often favors complication over clarity but that his films' formal complexity stems in part from his distinctive, mercurial mode of production. At a more abstract theoretical level, moreover, any attempt to account for stylistic change in Wong's filmmaking is positioned within the domain of *historical* poetics, exploring patterns of continuity and change against a historically specific background and proposing causal explanations for such patterns.

Other storytelling strategies find an impetus in Wong's work habits. A high shooting ratio yields repeated takes that may be distributed motivically across the film. As Bordwell has noted, such motifs supply structural ballast to a narrative whose causal links fall slack (2011: 118); in Wong's films, moreover, they suggest the insular routines traced by the protagonists. Similarly, episodic plotting owes something to William Chang's piecemeal approach to cutting. "I do not cut the film in a sequential order following the storyline," Chang attests. "I cut the scenes I am editing *as if they were self-contained*" (McGrath 2001: 160, emphasis added). Such block-by-block editing sharpens the films' episodic texture and probably reveals the influence of Hong Kong cinema's norms of reel construction (Bordwell 2011: 175). Further, the need to impose coherence and order upon semidiscrete episodes promotes the option of voice-over narration. Detractors of this device brand it the lazy filmmaker's exit strategy, but Wong typically pushes voice-over beyond mere cohesiveness to perform additional narrative functions, such as imparting thematic commentary or character subjectivity, or exacerbating the film's narrational complexity and strategy of disturbance (as in the polyphonic *Ashes of Time*). I am not arguing that Wong's method of production exerts a deterministic influence upon his films' features of narrative and narration. But I am suggesting that this method to some extent accounts for these features, pushing certain structural options (ellipticality, motivic patterning, and so on) into prime contention.

Fabula, Syuzhet, Narration

A fiction's *fabula* consists of a set of events usually enacted by or upon one or more narrative agents. As Meir Sternberg points out, from one *fabula* can be constructed myriad different *syuzhets*, "each with its own temporal structure and narrative strategy and consequently with its own peculiar effect on the reader" (1978: 9). The ways to tell a given story are potentially inexhaustible. Teo has traced Wong's *syuzhet* structures to a literary background set that is appropriately pluralistic (2005). But Teo reveals that Wong plumbs literary models for *fabulaic* material as well. For instance, *In the Mood for Love* culls passages from Liu Yichang's novella *Intersections* [*Duidao*] (1972), while *2046* owes a narrative and thematic debt to the same author's *The Drunkard* (1962) (126–27). *Ashes of Time* resurrects and reworks the *wuxia* universe of Jin Yong swordplay sagas (69). And *Days of Being Wild* mounts characterization on the model of Manuel Puig's 1969 novel *Heartbreak Tango* (38). Other critics have laid in further literary backgrounds. For Tony Rayns, *Happy Together* borrows from Puig the subject matter of a destructive homosexual romance, played out on Argentinian territory (2000: 36). And while Teo finds Puig's protagonist a progenitor of Yuddy, Ma links the character to Chow in *2046* (2010: 145).

Teo's survey in particular deftly reveals the historical and cultural breadth of Wong's literary appropriation and allusion. Yet almost wholly overlooked in these accounts is the influence of Tennessee Williams upon Wong's *fabula* material, particularly at the levels of characterization and milieu. We can trace, for instance, the genesis of the seminal bird fable in *Days of Being Wild* and *2046* to both Williams's 1950 novel *The Roman Spring of Mrs. Stone* and his 1955 three-act play *Orpheus Descending* (as well as Sidney Lumet's film adaptation, *The Fugitive Kind* [1959]). The novel's male protagonist—Paolo, an Italian libertine—bears striking affinities with Yuddy, delineated by Williams as a flawed, "petulant" gigolo whose spiritual desolation manifests itself in a tendency to "drift" (1987: 93; 20). Like Yuddy, Paolo is in thrall to his own image (Figure 4.1): in one passage he "turned a startled look from the mirror on which [Mrs. Stone] had interrupted his Narcissean gaze" (66). And he shares with several Wong protagonists—most notably those in *Ashes of Time*—an inauthentic desire to vanquish painful memories, stating, "A bad memory is a great convenience" (107).[2]

The novel's most explicit connection to *Days of Being Wild* and *2046* is the parable of the wayward bird doomed to perpetual flight. "Speaking of birds," Paolo is asked, "is it true that the rondini don't have legs and that is the reason they stay in the air all the time?" (Williams 1987: 56). Williams recycles this motif in *Orpheus Descending*, connoting a "fugitive kind" of individual bereft of a place to "belong"—here again foreshadowing Yuddy's rootlessness. Williams articulates the bird metaphor by means of his male protagonist, Val:

> You know they's a kind of bird that don't have no legs so it can't light on nothing but has to stay all its life on its wings in the sky? . . . those little birds, they don't have no legs at all and they live their whole lives on the

---

2. Other examples in the Wong canon include Killer and Charlie (*Fallen Angels*) and Lulu (*2046*). Typically Wong's forgetful protagonists seek to banish unhappy memories as a way of self-anesthetizing; in most cases, this trait signals an inauthentic withdrawal from the world and its emotional travails.

wing, and they sleep on the wind. . . . They sleep on the wind and . . . never light on this earth but one time when they die. (1961: 49–50)

Both *Days of Being Wild* and *2046* invoke this legend, but Wong goes beyond mere appropriation. Apart from adumbrating character traits, the bird fable extends an authorial motif of *flight* as a metaphor for authentic existence. From this angle, the myth of the sky-bound bird shares a comparable function with the airplane motif of *Chungking Express*. As Joseph Campbell asserts, "the flight of the airplane . . . is in the imagination as the release from earth. This is the same thing that birds symbolize. . . . The bird is symbolic of the release of the spirit from bondage to the earth. . . . The airplane plays that role now" (Campbell and Moyers 1988: 18). Faye's actual flight to California, transforming reverie into reality, represents an act borne of authentic desire. In Yuddy's case, however, spending his life "on the wind" only apparently signifies personal freedom. In a trenchant postscript to Williams's fable, the bird without legs turns out to be stillborn: "the bird was dead all along" is Yuddy's *anagnorisis*. Far from derivative, Wong's use of Williams's folktale facilitates oblique character delineation and authorial themes.

Other Wong Kar-wai films present *fabula* material reminiscent of Tennessee Williams. *My Blueberry Nights*, Wong affirms, carries "a tribute" to the dramatist (Rayns 2008a: 34). The hothouse atmosphere of the film's Memphis episode, fueled by domestic conflicts between Rachel Weisz's sexualized Southern belle and her impotent spouse, is highly evocative of Williams's melodramas.[3] Then there is Brigitte Lin's drug trafficker in *Chungking Express*. According to Wong, the initial prototype for Lin's protagonist was Vivien Leigh's Blanche DuBois in *A Streetcar Named Desire* (Elia Kazan, 1951). In the final analysis, Williams' influence upon Wong should not be surprising: this most American of dramatists holds an irresistible appeal for a cinephile filmmaker fascinated by US cinema and culture. Throughout his oeuvre, Wong embraces both Hollywood cinema and American iconography and, across his films, drapes like bunting the raw materials of this American influence.[4]

So far I have noted Wong's preference for narcissistic and aimless protagonists. What other features of characterization determine the *fabula* events? Most broadly, Wong's characters refuse both the clear-cut goal orientation

---

3. An intriguing companion piece to *My Blueberry Nights* is Ethan Hawke's *The Hottest State* (2006). Steeped in Americana, both films evoke Tennessee Williams and the road movie genre (utilizing trains and cars as staple motifs) and foreground Cat Powers and Norah Jones on the music track.

4. Several critics have noted the influence of another American author, Raymond Chandler, on Wong. I might add that Chandler's fiction permeates Wong's *fabulas*, as well as his *syuzhets*. In *2046*, for instance, Chow must negotiate his feelings toward Mr. Wang's two daughters, the youngest of whom is sexually precocious—a narrative situation paralleled in Chandler's *The Big Sleep* (1939).

of the Hollywood hero and the apathetic passivity of the art-film protagonist. Unlike the art-film agent, Wong's protagonist *does* conceive objectives, but this goal formation consists of contradictory and even negative plans of action. Thus we find hesitant characters equivocating about future alternatives. Indeed, the protagonist is often prostrate before forking paths, disinclined to precipitate change. Take the protagonists of *In the Mood for Love*, who do not so much define purposeful goals as state negative ones. "We won't be like [our spouses]," they assert, resolute in their monogamy. Here, purposeful goal orientation gives way to a course of action that will decisively not be pursued. Concurrently, the viewer is cued to infer an antithetical—and more "authentic"—desire for romantic union largely subdued by the protagonists. The film's narrative futures thereby hinge on the protagonists' effort *not* to act, and Wong generates remarkable suspense from the clash between the viewer's generic expectations (i.e., romantic protagonists will be united) and the protagonists' negative and contradictory desires.

Whereas the classical hero pursues mutually harmonious goals, Wong's characters conceive incompatible ones. The mutually exclusive desires that both Chow and Su possess give rise to the emotional intensity ingredient to the melodrama genre. In *Chungking Express*, Faye's obliquely expressed goal to migrate to the United States confounds her desire for romantic domestication with 663. Andy Lau's reluctant gangster in *As Tears Go By* is beset by divided loyalties. Characteristically, Wong populates the *fabula* with internally conflicted agents warring with their own desires. Equivocating over goals retards the protagonists' purposeful action—hence the *temps morts* and *longueurs* identified with Wong's narratives.

Alternatively, ostensibly major goals fizzle out, diverting plotlines along unexpected paths. In *Fallen Angels*, Charlie's hysterical search for Blondie never bears fruit, the focus shifting from the elusive blonde to the romantic incompatibility of Charlie and the mute Ho. And, in *Days of Being Wild*, Yuddy's goal to reconcile with his birth mother effectively dissipates, which, as Bordwell points out, allows the film to shift narrative focus onto the chance network of characters affected by Yuddy's actions (2008b: 220). That Yuddy's goal evaporates, moreover, demonstrates the character's self-denial—spurned by his mother, Yuddy sacrifices purposeful goal pursuit for personal pride. Invariably in Wong's films, the protagonists' activity or inactivity stems from their capacity, at any given instant, to acknowledge their own genuine desires. Teo (2005: 88–89) characterizes these protagonists as "pathological," but they might be alternatively perceived as grappling with inauthentic modes of existence—a point I elaborate in the following chapter. Inevitably, Wong's conflicted characters motivate distinctive lines of action. Located at a point between classical and art cinema norms of characterization, Wong's protagonists are goal-oriented agents, yet their psychological complexity engenders paralysis. The corollary is a kind of stasis that enervates the *fabula*'s "eventfulness" and predictability.

Above all, Wong's characters hesitate on the precipice of authentic existence, and he upbraids his protagonists for lapsing into inauthentic ways. Recurrently, these figures retreat into self-denial—they may repress genuine desire and emotion, ostracize themselves from society, reject their own agency as free individuals, shirk personal responsibility, and falsely adduce "fate" as a substitute for purposeful action. In *2046*, for instance, Chow invites Black Spider to accompany him to Singapore. The heroine stakes her decision on a card game, apparently assigning her future to fate. That Black Spider will draw the ace, however, is a foregone conclusion; as the defeated Chow states in voice-over, "She found an indirect way of rejecting me." Such oblique and evasive feints are typical of Wong's protagonists, who recoil from change by denying their own capacity to act. Their withdrawal from social encounters, moreover, often leads to circuitous methods of interaction, as when Killer jilts Agent by means of a jukebox song in *Fallen Angels*. Against the irredeemably inauthentic protagonist, Wong sets characters with the potential for authentic change. I have already argued that Faye and 633 come to live more authentically as the *syuzhet* of *Chungking Express* unfolds, effectuating purposeful action and personal communication. The theme of authenticity, then, is a key component of Wong's *fabula* material.

Just as Wong's protagonists embody differing degrees of authenticity, so they embody contrasting attitudes to romance. Whether fanatical or frivolous about romantic love, however, all Wong's characters broil with intense feeling. Occasionally Wong limns these figures by their sensory traits; they possess a surfeit or deficit of physical sensation. They may be deprived of sight (the blind swordsman in *Ashes of Time*), voice (Ho in *Fallen Angels*), or touch (Po-wing in parts of *Happy Together*, arguably Black Spider in *2046*). Conversely, their senses may be abnormally sharp (Chang's auditory pickup in *Happy Together*, Zhang's tactility in *The Hand*). In every case, these characters feel things acutely—even the ostensibly impregnable protagonist "leaks" heartfelt emotion occasionally (think of Yuddy in *Days of Being Wild* or Killer in *Fallen Angels*). Understood this way, Wong's affectively suffused diegesis—gilded by sensuous production design and source music—materializes the inner states of profoundly emotional agents. Thus, in Wong's cinema, psychological causation not only initiates action lines but wields affective purpose too.

Of course the *fabula* consists not merely of characters. But this brings me to the character-story binarism alluded to earlier on. As I have been implying, the narrative, and the characters enmeshed within it, are functionally inextricable. One does no better to polarize character and story than to insist on a sharp-edged distinction between story and style. In Wong's mode of story-telling, character *is* story. This is far, therefore, from describing fictions in which "nothing happens" (Brunette 2005: 97). On the contrary, the arcs of psychological change traced by Faye (*Chungking Express*), Lai Yiu-fai (*Happy Together*), or Elizabeth (*My Blueberry Nights*) constitute, in Wong's terms, momentous *fabula* events. Wong's viewer must acclimate to an apparently non-classical dramaturgy whereby gradual character change, rather than dramatic conflict, constitutes the basic narrative action. Within this framework, the bold dramatic climax favored by Hollywood films can find a powerful alternative in an action as subtle as whispering into a crevice in a wall.

What principles of organization govern the *fabula*? Wong's *syuzhet* structures typically adhere to episodic principles. (Bordwell has suggested that Wong's episodic form springs from a local custom of reel-by-reel plotting, whereby blocks of action are correlated to the length of a film reel [2008b: 104].) A new action unit may be an occasion for skipping forward or backward through the *fabula*'s chronology. The *syuzhet* may run distinct action lines together, generating simultaneous parallelism (in which each plotline is understood to occur concurrently in *fabula* or *syuzhet* terms or both) or successive parallel-ism (whereby one plotline precedes another at the level of *fabula*, *syuzhet*, or both).[5] While the juxtaposed plotlines expose rhyming situations and char-acter affinities, converging plotlines reveal the interwoven fates of familiars and strangers. In Wong's multiple-protagonist plots, the encounters between characters typically unfold sequentially, until all the main characters have been weighed up as potential couples or allies. Finally, as Richard Rushton observes, Wong's films end as they begin, in medias res (2012: 145).

At a broader level, Wong has been both an exponent and a prime mover in the contemporary vogue for complex storytelling. Foremost among his films in this regard is *Chungking Express*, whose audacious *syuzhet* disobeys some standard principles of classical construction. As indebted as *Chungking Express* surely is to local norms of construction, the film also bears the imprint of European art-film plotting. At the level of plot, *Chungking Express* arranges its two stories consecutively, avoiding the option of interweaving plotlines. With the displacement of the first story comes an unexpected shift in interest focus, a late-arriving event reminiscent of Antonioni's *L'avventura* (1960). Wong's *syuzhet* structure is even more radical than *L'avventura*, insofar as the emergent protagonists of Part 2 have hardly been adumbrated before the second story supplants the first. Yet as Curtis K. Tsui and others have noted, the principal agents of the film's second story briefly appear before the *syuzhet* launches Part 2 (1995: 113). A brief cutaway shows us Tony Leung's on-duty cop, and a

---

5.   For detailed discussion of these formal options in contemporary cinema, see Smith (2001) and Bordwell (2008b: 99).

single long shot presents Faye passing the blonde woman outside a store. For Ma, this tactic suggests that the two stories "in fact take place simultaneously" (2010: 130). *Chungking Express* remains ambiguous on this point—its stories may be simultaneous at the *fabula* level and successive at the *syuzhet* level, as Ma argues; or, as it seems on first viewing, the action may be successive at the levels of both *fabula* and *syuzhet*. The important point is that Wong tantalizes us with counterfactual alternatives, engineering the kind of tacit narrative ambiguities that compel the puzzle-film viewer to repeat viewings.

The early glimpses of Faye and 633 may foreshadow the plot switch to come, but this is foreshadowing of a highly oblique order. Again, the European art cinema provides a precedent: in Antonioni's *The Passenger* (1975), Jack Nicholson passingly glimpses Maria Schneider long before she emerges as a key figure in the drama. As in *The Passenger*, *Chungking Express* inaugurates protagonists into the film in oblique and acausal fashion—when first introduced, Faye and 633 are neither causally motivated (by foregoing *syuzhet* action) nor causally motivating (of future action). Only in retrospect does the tactic come forward as a cohesive device. Further, the classical principles of legible character individuation and the primacy effect—upon which we conceive initial judgments about the agents—operate only retrospectively, on repeat viewings. In art-film tradition, Wong handles narrative exposition in offhand ways, postponing the primacy effect and forfeiting the suspense that can derive from concrete foreshadowing. At the same time, his tactic of foreshadowing—obscure as it is—reveals an overarching concern with formal cohesion, binding the episodes together into an organic whole.

In *2046*, Wong subjects the primacy effect to puzzle-film misdirection. Characterization in *2046* hinges on transworld identity—the novelist Chow invents Tak as his futuristic counterpart, a *fabula* situation that the *syuzhet* and narration initially suppress. Consequently, the viewer individuates Chow and Tak as discrete agents. The exposition's misdirection rests on *syuzhet* structure (which chronologically rearranges the *fabula* so that *2046* initially seems an autonomous world, not one imagined by Chow) and the narration (which presents Chow and Tak as physically distinct figures). The latter gambit exploits a norm of film viewing and everyday perception that psychologists call the "person schema"—a heuristic whereby we recognize, individuate, and ascribe discrete traits to different human bodies (M. Smith 1995: 20–24). Irresistible textual cues thus trigger everyday habits of perception and cognition, prompting the viewer to discriminate Chow and Tak as wholly distinct figures. Wong's narrative stratagem, moreover, not only evokes art film complexity but assimilates *2046* to the modern puzzle-film trend. *Fight Club* (1999) and *Secret Window* (2004) stake narrative surprise on the viewer individuating a single protagonist as two discrete persons. Further, in each of these films, one of the individuated figures (Tak, Tyler Durgen, Shooter) is wholly illusory within the story world. The *syuzhet* and narration conceals these figures' tenuous ontology, at least until the primacy effect has lured us down false inferential paths. Indeed, in *2046* the entire futuristic universe is only belatedly revealed as a synthetic, wholly imaginary space. Like puzzle films generally, *2046* adopts a strategy of delayed exposition. Wong belatedly reveals the viewing strategies appropriate to comprehending the drama in ways that oblige us to mentally revise our understanding of early *syuzhet* action.

If Wong's *fabula* unspools in episodes, his films' piecemeal structure betokens the cultural fragmentation of a transnational city—such is the top-down assumption of some postmodernist and culturalist critics (Teo 2005: 75). As Bordwell has shown, however, episodic plotting yields more immediate effects on a film's structure, texture, and viewer activity (2011: 114–26).[6] A plot built out of episodes, for instance, may engender "tonal ruptures" (117). This tendency permeates Hong Kong movies, but tonal fluctuations hold particular appeal for a filmmaker mounting an aesthetic of disturbance. Not surprisingly, then, Wong's films tend to shift tonal gears abruptly. Tonal ruptures are liable to disconcert the uninitiated spectator and trigger curiosity hypotheses, but one need not presuppose the affective "distance" identified with the art film. On the contrary, tonal counterpoint might be grasped as another oblique device whereby Wong elicits strong spectator emotion. The emotional tone of one episode can set in vivid relief the contrasting tone of the next. As Ed Tan suggests, juxtaposed affective tones may "lead to an optimum evocation of emotion during each of those scenes" (1996: 62). Wong rejects both the explicit emotionality of Hollywood cinema and the objective detachment of art cinema.

Episodic plots substitute chance incidents for tight causal linkages (Bordwell 2011: 116). Here again Wong hovers at the hinge of Hollywood melodrama and the European art film, where chance and coincidence are staple devices. But there are more proximate contexts too, not least the indigenous "civilized play" of the 1930s and the butterfly fiction of the early twentieth century. In several films, Wong elevates the chance encounter to a major structural device, but he also employs it to comment upon the characters. In place of the deus ex machina found in Hollywood melodrama, Wong's films present chance events in more mundane ways that highlight the decisions facing his protagonists. Recall the chance encounter between Wah and his ex-lover Mabel in *As Tears Go By*. Mabel's advanced pregnancy represents the affirmative pathway that Wah forsakes in favor of triad loyalty.[7] Again and again, the film implies, Wah

---

6. Wong's fondness for episodic plotting may also explain his affinity for the short-film format (e.g., *The Hand*, his contribution to the portmanteau film *Eros* [2004]) and advertising shorts (e.g., *The Follow*, an eight-minute segment in the BMW commercial, *The Hire* [2001]).

7. Interestingly—and presumably not by chance—*Infernal Affairs* (2002) furnishes a similar coincidental encounter, whereby Tony Leung's undercover cop happens upon his ex-lover

makes wrong choices. At the climax, with Wah mortally wounded, the narration confirms the affirmative path not chosen. Here Wong employs a recurring narrational device, what one might call the rueful flashback—a burst of retrospective action that both signifies a character's subjective memory and elicits pity for the figure in question.[8] A fleeting replay of Wah's romantic clinch with Ngor reminds the viewer of a forking pathway now irrevocably closed to him. Wah's chance meeting with Mabel revives the film's romance plotline, recently sidelined by the crime story. More generally, chance and coincidence augment the episodic plot's robustness, linking the *syuzhet*'s main segments. Finally, the chance event can retard narrative predictability. In *Fallen Angels* the assassin flees the scene of his latest carnage by bus. Coincidentally onboard is Hoi, the paid killer's former classmate. Wong imbues the sequence with comedic overtones, not only creating a tonal disparity with the violent preceding episode but thwarting the predictability of the ongoing narrative. The incongruous chance encounter warns us not to expect a generic rendition of the conventional gangster plot.

Lacking tight causal linkages from scene to scene, then, episodic plots foster unpredictability (Bordwell 2011: 117). For Ma, however, the *syuzhets* of *In the Mood for Love* and *2046* "acquire a cast of inevitability," gravitating toward "hyper-predictability" (2010: 139). Ma's claim requires qualification. What she recognizes here is, in effect, the underlying orderliness of Wong's plotting. Still, if the organized plot enables the viewer to predict narrative outcomes, it does so only gradually, in stairstep fashion. The viewer of *Fallen Angels* might hypothesize that Ho Chi Moo and Charlie will furnish narrative closure, but this hypothesis coalesces only once we become aware of the *syuzhet*'s systematic shuffling of couples. In some cases, by contrast, Wong seems actively to repel predictability. Indeed, he often embraces the kind of retardatory suspense favored by puzzle films. The *syuzhet*'s chronological deformation of *fabula* events, the opening of temporary gaps, the elicitation of mutually incompatible hypotheses, the salience of chance events, and the proclivity for delayed exposition—by all such means the *syuzhet* and narration deflect predictable story

---

and her daughter by another relationship. (The film's codirector, Andrew Lau, served as the cinematographer of *As Tears Go By*.) As in Wong's sequence, the spurned woman's poker face implies that the male protagonist is her child's father—thereby weighting the losses of the personal pathway not pursued by the protagonist. Wong's sequence also recalls a scene in François Truffaut's *Baisers volés* [*Stolen Kisses*] (1968). In a chance event typical of the modernist art film, the carefree Antoine Doinel (Jean-Pierre Léaud) runs into his former girlfriend, now a mother. Truffaut employs the scene to convey both Antoine's immaturity and the relatively stable—albeit conventional—lifestyle he studiously avoids.

8. Other examples of the rueful flashback include Blind Swordsman's memory of Peach Blossom in *Ashes of Time* and the extended reprisal of a sensual tango between Lai Yiu-fai and Ho Po-wing in *Happy Together*. In such cases, the flashback laments forsaken courses of action that, had they been pursued, might have prevented the protagonist's dire situation.

outcomes. In the case of *In the Mood for Love*, predictability is further stymied by a deliberately suppressive and misleading narration (as I aim to show in the next chapter). Just as tonal ruptures trigger cognitive curiosity (what logic links incongruous plot episodes?), so unpredictable plot progression invites suspense hypotheses (where is the story heading?). Wong's episodic *syuzhet* emerges as a fundamental component in his films' cognitive difficulty.

Cognitive complexity emerges above all from the films' narration. The complexly organized plot becomes still more formidable thanks to unmarked ellipses, flashbacks within flashbacks, ambiguous points of view, arcane intertitles, and polyphonic voice-over. Despite the narration's apparent omniscience—moving us freely among a cross-section of protagonists in *Ashes of Time* and *2046*—the viewer is often granted only limited access to *fabula* information. The narration's range and depth tends to be self-consciously restricted. Subjective access to characters' inner states remains scarce, prompting what I have called expressive displacement—the transference of character emotion to features of mise-en-scène and audiovisual style. When voice-over commentary and intertitles suggest character subjectivity, the viewer must reckon with willfully abstract epigrams that render the subjective information enigmatic. Despite the preponderance of repeated motifs, moreover, the narration does not aim for the maximal redundancy sought by the Hollywood film. Ellipses hollow out *fabula* information even further, typically with narrational élan; Wong's narration flaunts overt and initially unmarked gaps with a high level of self-consciousness. And major *fabula* information may be permanently elided, begetting the open-endedness of art-film narration—as when the climax of *In the Mood for Love* suspends the ambiguity marking the protagonists' (chaste? sexual?) relationship.

At times, the narration generates complex effects from parallel plotting. *2046* alternates between two time levels, with several of Wong's players embodying doppelgängers on each level. Bodily resemblances encourage us to compare characters across the two plotlines. The narration does not merely ask us to comprehend action on the 2046 level in its own right—itself a daunting task, given the narration's elliptical and suppressive maneuvers. But the narration also obliges us to perceive the 2046 plotline as illuminating character psychology and relationships on the 1960s level. For instance, Wong reveals Chow's romantic attraction to Jingwen (Faye Wong) with characteristic obliqueness. It is only by noticing the parallel encounters between Tak and the android, their 2046 counterparts, that the viewer first discovers Chow's affections. As well as staying abreast of the moment-to-moment action, then, the viewer must constantly cross-reference characters and actions across the parallel plotlines. Failure to perceive the connections between doppelgängers or to map agents' emotions and attitudes onto their counterparts risks losing track of character relationships in the 1960s sequences.

For all their obstacles to comprehension, however, Wong's narrational tactics mostly hover at the junction of classical and art-film storytelling. The polyphonic and enigmatic voice-over narration in *Ashes of Time* conjures the ambiguity familiar to art cinema, but it also functions classically as a cohesion device, binding multiple plot strands together. Flashbacks generally remain perspicuous as focalizing devices, funneling character subjectivity. Here again Wong aims not to violate but to disturb classical storytelling norms. As the film's overall organizing system, the narration marshals roughened schemas of visual style, music, *syuzhet* patterns, and genre tropes into organic form, both aiding and complicating the process of narrative construction and comprehension.

Routine Crimes: *Fallen Angels*

The complex storytelling strategies on display in *Fallen Angels* have received little attention even from the film's admirers. Not surprisingly, its vivid panoply of visual devices—including fish-eye lenses, slit staging, distorted motion, split-screen imagery, shifts in color and film stock, and canted angles—has imposed itself as the primary object of critical attention. Brunette's critique of *Fallen Angels* epitomizes the film's wider critical reception: he regards *Fallen Angels* as a predominantly reflexive enterprise, a mesh of allusions to Wong's own work. Style, not story, provides the film's raison d'être. Brunette subsumes the film's narrative, themes, and generic strategies to Wong's broader program of self-parody, another index of a postmodernist sensibility (2005: 57–70). More generally, he balks at the notion that Wong's films engage plot or narrative. For Brunette, too little "happens" in a Wong Kar-wai film. Wong's plotting is too desultory and diffuse to constitute a narrative in the conventional sense (61; 72). How, then, does the *fabula, syuzhet,* and narration function in a film regarded as a purely "stylistic" exercise?

It is useful at this point to recall the narrative of *Fallen Angels*. In modern-day Hong Kong, Killer (Leon Lai), a paid assassin, performs contract killings arranged by Agent (Michele Reis), his female accomplice. Killer insists that their relationship remain purely professional, but Agent harbors a secret affection for him. In his absence, she tidies his apartment, alert for clues to his personality. At Chungking Mansions, the flophouse where Agent lodges, the mute Ho Chi Moo (Takeshi Kaneshiro) is arrested by police; looking for extra income, Ho has illegally commandeered business premises during closing hours. He becomes attracted to Charlie (Charlie Young), a feisty drifter seeking revenge on Blondie, the fiancée of the man she loves. Killer rekindles a fling with a former lover, Baby (Karen Mok). When a crime goes wrong, he decides to terminate his partnership with Agent. Ho, meanwhile, also resolves to renounce crime, acquiring a job at a bar where, by coincidence, he encounters Killer. Agent asks Killer to carry out one last execution before retiring, but the assassin perishes in the attempt. After Ho's father passes away, the bereft youth slips into old routines, trespassing on private properties. In a diner he encounters the solitary Agent, and the pair finds solace speeding through the cross-harbor tunnel on Ho's motorcycle.

Formally, *Fallen Angels* consists of two major plotlines, between which the narration alternates. Whereas *Chungking Express* splices its dual stories one after the other, *Fallen Angels* interweaves its two *fabula* strands. The first story, involving Agent and Killer, alternates and occasionally intersects with the second story, centered on Ho. Most of the first story also forks into two lines of action, as Wong toggles between the protagonists' separate trajectories. Wong motivates this bifurcation by character psychology. Early in the plot, Killer explains his separation from Agent: "Partners should never get emotionally involved with each other," he reveals in voice-over. Thus the protagonists' exclusive pathways emanate from their own attitudes and are apparently not attributable to the narration as such. *Fallen Angels* teems with attention-getting devices, but Wong disguises his role in this structural conceit by motivating it diegetically. Once more, Wong exemplifies the inextricability of character and story. Part of the film's organic unity stems from the close imbrication of characterization and narrative form.

Wong's preliminary exposition establishes the protagonists' itinerary, as Agent and Killer traverse the same space separately. At times, their estrangement gives rise to misleading narrational effects but in ways that sharpen character psychology. In the fourth reel, the narration crosscuts between Killer and Agent in a barbershop. Though Wong's crosscutting implies simultaneity—as does the salon space through which both characters maneuver—the characters' paths do not once intersect. Gradually it becomes evident that a significant ellipsis separates the parallel lines, disqualifying our assumption of synchronicity. If this narrational gambit initially bewilders, it harbors important character meaning. Most simply, it foregrounds the protagonists' mutual isolation, the pair having pledged to seldom meet in person. But it also accents the fact that one protagonist follows a spatial path set by another. Just as the yearning figures of *In the Mood for Love* restage the adulterous activity of their spouses, so Killer and Agent each trace itineraries laid out in advance. Both Agent (who privately adopts the assassin's routines) and Killer (whose work patterns are supplied by Agent) avoid mapping purposeful trajectories of their own. They obliquely renounce purposeful activity and personal responsibility ("I like others to arrange things for me," proclaims the assassin). Like the protagonists of *In the Mood for Love* (as I will show in Chapter 5), Agent and Killer seek emancipation from the burden of human choice and action.

The film's second story will not be initiated until Reel 3, but Wong plants elements from that story in earlier blocks of action. Already the film seeks to unify its plot strands into a coherent whole. Reviving a formal tactic from *Chungking Express*, Wong gives a key character from the second story a brief appearance in the preliminary exposition. We first glimpse Ho's father as he fleetingly crosses paths with Agent at Chungking Mansions, but so unemphatic is this character exposition that the primacy effect can hardly be mobilized. Consequently, the first-time viewer fails to reidentify Ho's father when the second plotline properly gets underway. Here again, a tactic to unify plotlines becomes evident only retrospectively, on subsequent viewings. If this tactic lends a certain robustness to narrative architecture, it also delineates a degrees-of-separation story world, whereby protagonists share spatial proximity but remain (at least for a period) strangers to one another. All the same, within this social network lies the possibility of new intimacies being formed. ("We rub shoulders with people every day," Ho announces at one point. "Strangers who may even become friends of confidants.") Against this milieu Wong ironically situates Agent and Killer, their lives intimately "connected" yet spatially divorced. As so often, Wong sets his protagonists at odds with their environment and implies a psychological inauthenticity at the root of their social estrangement.

The protagonists' degree of inauthenticity is sharpened by the *syuzhet*'s split structure, which impels us to compare character attitudes and behavior. The first story brings forth affinities between Agent and Killer—both characters, for instance, are denied proper names, the *fabula* identifying them solely by profession. This impersonal labeling suggests Brechtian *Verfremdung* as a narrational maneuver, commensurate with the film's wider reflexive strategies. But at the *fabula* level it both accentuates the agents' psychological opacity and reflects their effort to eliminate the "personal" from their partnership. Gradually the *syuzhet*, by alternating the paths of Agent and Killer, reveals contrasts too. Emotionally withdrawn, Killer epitomizes the inauthentic hero. By abdicating decision making to Agent, he renounces the freedom of action and choice that defines authentic existence. His abstention from personal communion with Agent, moreover, signals an inauthentic retreat from social intercourse. By contrast, Agent betrays a yearning for intimacy. Her fixation on the possessions in Killer's apartment, her autoerotic revelry in his bed, her habit of frequenting his favorite bar (because "it makes me feel closer to him")—through all such actions, Agent flouts the pair's pact not to become "emotionally involved with each other." Though they adopt each other's itinerary, then, Agent and Killer harbor sharply different (if similarly inauthentic) attitudes. Wong obliges us to decide which of these fallen angels is the least authentic—the assassin who rejects personal responsibility or the agent who consents to personal distance but who privately craves emotional intimacy.

The film's parallelisms become more elaborate in the third reel, which launches the second plotline. Prima facie, Ho appears comparable to Killer and Agent, a wrongdoer hiding out from the law. The three characters are also aligned formally, each assigned a voice-over track. (This narrational maneuver is crucial inasmuch as it grants subjective access to a mute and two subjectively opaque protagonists.) The primacy effect thus establishes Ho as somewhat akin to Agent and Killer. These are but superficial affinities, however. Whereas Killer's voice-over espouses detachment, Ho's narration affirms intimacy: "strangers [may] become friends or confidants," he says. Wong establishes all three characters as outsiders, but here again their situations are not analogous. Ho's social alienation stems not from an inauthentic aversion to intimacy, as in the case of Killer, but from his own condition of muteness—"for this reason," he explains, "I have very few friends." His desire for intimate relationships endows him with purposefulness; Killer, by contrast, studiously avoids both intimacy and goal formation. By a principle of simultaneous parallelism, *Fallen Angels* registers contrasting attitudes toward social existence.

Once Ho's story initiates its own line of action, we become alert for moments when the branching plotlines might intersect. The second story starts with one such intersection—at Chungking Mansions, Agent conceals Ho during a police raid. But for several reels thereafter, Wong keeps the protagonists on separate tracks. Gradually the *syuzhet* whittles away our expectations of plot convergence. We might predict, for instance, that Agent and Ho will cross paths regularly, given their early complicity and their mutual place of residence. We might hypothesize that the trio of protagonists will become enmeshed in a romance triangle or conspire in a criminal scheme. But Wong substitutes such generic hypotheses with a premise altogether more mundane—Ho and Agent are linked only tangentially, as neighbors. If Wong lets genre expectations fizzle out, he also heightens the impression of loose plotting by foregrounding coincidence as the primary connecting force.

Indeed, the contingent nature of the intersecting plotlines has led critics to remember *Fallen Angels* as being more loosely plotted than it is. Ma claims that the dual plotlines intersect only twice during the film (2010: 130), while Bordwell suggests that Ho and Killer "never meet" in the course of the narrative (Bordwell 2008b: 200). In fact the *syuzhet*'s twin plotlines intersect on at least three occasions:[9] first, at the launch of the second story line, when Agent shelters Ho from the cops; second, when Ho encounters Killer at the

---

9. The plotlines converge four times, if one counts the oblique introduction of Ho's father in the lobby of Chungking Mansions.

restaurant where he works; and, last, at the film's conclusion, when Agent and Ho reunite by chance. The second point of connection—Ho's chance meeting with Killer—is motivated by analogous shifts in character psychology. Echoing the character arc of Wah in *As Tears Go By*, both Killer and Ho separately pledge to end their lawless ways and pursue purposeful plans of action. For Killer in particular, this resolution constitutes a major volte-face. No longer content to leave decisions to others, Killer—like Ho—now gravitates toward purposeful and authentic action, his goal formation a marker of choice and responsibility.

Parallel character development, then, cues the *syuzhet* to dovetail its dual plotlines. Consequently, the affinities between Killer and Ho become quite salient. Following their unplanned encounter, both characters resume their separate spatiotemporal paths, thus obliging the *syuzhet* to continue its parallel structure. By once again setting Killer and Ho on parallel tracks, Wong is best able to highlight how two protagonists proceed from an analogous situation along sharply different paths. Yet, at the same time, parallelism renders contrasts between the protagonists relatively less explicit; hence, the viewer must be alert to rhyming actions and situations across both plotlines. After Killer and Ho part ways, for instance, the assassin reluctantly consents to one last job, during which he is slain. Shortly after, the *syuzhet* switches to Ho at the fast-food counter, where he endeavors to impress Charlie. Substituting ketchup for blood and lapsing into theatrical paroxysms, Ho melodramatically stages his own death. The attentive viewer perceives the *syuzhet*'s ironic parallelism. Ho's playacting comes forth as a parodic restaging of Killer's actual demise minutes earlier in the *syuzhet*.

These juxtaposed events produce a tonal rupture, yet they also preserve the contrasting tones of the foregoing action—for instance, a ludic, surreal atmosphere predominantly accompanies Ho's plotline throughout *Fallen Angels*. More importantly, however, these distinct episodes reflect the different fates and psychologies distinguishing Killer from Ho. On the one hand, these contrasts pertain to authenticity and responsibility. After Killer briefly encounters Ho, he accepts Agent's request to commit an assassination. Killer's submission to Agent proves both inauthentic and fatal: he not only regresses to a position of passivity vis-à-vis his own activity but follows a path of action that ends his life. Wong places responsibility for this tragic outcome squarely at the assassin's door, for Killer has once again rejected authentic desire—he has, in other words, negated his own desire to repudiate crime and reclaim personal autonomy. Understood this way, Killer's death is a comeuppance for his backslide into inauthentic behavior. On the other hand, the difference between Killer and Ho is one of morality. At no time does the assassin reflect upon the immorality of his crimes. ("I love my job," he announces near the start of the film.) His decision to go straight stems not from an awakening of moral conscience but from a fear of physical injury. By contrast, Ho's desire to change springs from moral self-reflection. "I realized how irresponsible I had been in the past," he remarks. "I shouldn't have taken over people's shops the way I did." Ho's moral reflection sets him apart from Killer and earns the film's approbation—as evidenced by the happy end afforded the mute hero.

Fallen Angels also arranges its parallel plot to highlight affinities between Ho and Agent. Echoic situations cue us to notice correspondences, as when both characters are stood up by their prospective partners. More meaningful are the psychological affinities highlighted during the course of the film. Both Agent and Ho are distinguished by their authentic capacity for intimacy, a kinship hinting at their romantic compatibility. Parallelism—and genre expectations—here arouses the viewer's desire for well-matched protagonists to be united. Wong relies on this desire to motivate narrative closure, as the climactic reunion of Agent and Ho concludes a series of character pairings that the *syuzhet* has systematically worked through. The culminating and long-deferred intersection of plotlines, moreover, creates strong narrative closure. Structurally, Wong finesses the second story with a symmetrical opening and end. "We rub shoulders with people every day," Ho observes at the start of the story when he briefly encounters Agent. "Strangers who may even become friends or confidants." The second plotline, having kept Agent and Ho apart throughout, reunites both protagonists at the climax—no longer "strangers," and with intimacy a genuine prospect.

If Wong's parallelism suggests structural looseness, this impression is compounded by the plotlines' parsing into episodes. Critic Stephen Holden construes *Fallen Angels* as "a densely packed suite of vignettes that have the autonomy of pop songs or stand-up comic riffs" (1997). Though this claim underestimates the film's reliance on traditional continuity devices, it nonetheless evokes the first-time viewer's impression of disjunctive and aleatory plotting. Several scenes display the autonomy Holden describes. When Killer meets an old classmate by chance, the encounter is apt to seem arbitrary at the levels of both *fabula* (a random encounter) and *syuzhet* (it is unmotivated and nonmotivating, providing no cause for subsequent action). Then there are the episodes depicting Killer's crimes. These scenes signify the assassin's empty ritual (hence the *fabula* is uninterested in identifying or individuating Killer's victims). His tasks amount to a succession of isolated killings, none of which converge on a larger objective or purpose; indeed, Killer substitutes routine for meaningful goals and purposeful action. Because they are isolated events that do not trigger subsequent action, Killer's assassinations lay bare the *syuzhet*'s episodic pattern.

Out of this episodic patterning come the tonal ruptures conventional to Hong Kong cinema. The device suggests an incoherent narration, but Wong modulates affective tone systematically. For instance, he recruits tonal contrasts so as to broadly differentiate plotlines. Whereas the first story in *Fallen Angels* is generally characterized as somber, the second story mostly displays an almost antic, surrealistic tenor. Within these broad strokes, however, are subtler deviations. The gloomy first story, for instance, is punctuated by the overtly sardonic episode introducing Killer's fatuous classmate—an episode creating a strong tonal rupture with the assassination scene that immediately precedes it. Such moments of levity are more typical of the film's second story than the first. By the same token, the riotous second story swerves onto melancholic terrain, most notably when Ho's father dies. In sum, *Fallen Angels* exhibits a greater degree of tonal coherence between its major plotlines than is commonly acknowledged. As so often in Wong's films, moreover, a feature of style or narration (in this case, tonality) is anchored in characterization. Just as the anarchic tone accompanying the second plotline befits the idiosyncratic personality of Ho and Charlie, so the downbeat mood permeating the first story matches the emotional withdrawal of Killer and Agent. Since the narration will mostly alternate between both pairs of characters, tonal fluctuations inevitably arise across the film as a whole.

Inspired by the second story's absurdity, Wong deviates from realistic causality. In such moments, the *syuzhet*'s causal links become especially tenuous. An example occurs when Ho persuades Charlie to confront her ex-lover's fiancée. The narration grants the viewer access to Ho's private thoughts: "You have to talk face to face. If that fails, you can punch him on the nose. I keep my thoughts to myself. But somehow [Charlie] appears to be able to read my mind." Inexplicably, Charlie responds to Ho's thoughts. "I think you're right. Let's go." Telepathy, therefore, provides the causal link to the ensuing sequence, in which the pair search for Blondie. In no sense is the viewer led to infer that these characters are literally mind readers. Rather, the narration generates both comedy and causality by swerving from psychological realism. At the same time, the gambit is broadly consistent with this plotline's eccentric tone and action. Ultimately, Charlie's display of telepathy calls attention to a self-conscious narration, not least because it flaunts a mode of causation not generally admissible in popular and art cinemas. Nor, I would suggest, is it permissible in the first story of *Fallen Angels*, which adheres more rigorously to standards of realism.

The film's apparently arbitrary episodes invariably harbor narrative meaning, if not causal motivation. Consider again Killer's random encounter with his obnoxious former classmate, Hoi. Wong invites us to compare the sharply different lifestyles achieved by the pair since their adolescent school days. Despite his crude personality, Hoi epitomizes bourgeois success—a city professional, he flaunts personalized business cards, plans to marry the high school beauty (Killer's unrequited sweetheart), and is featured in a *Time* magazine article. Killer, by contrast, carries only a phony business card in his wallet and a mock snapshot he passes off as a family portrait. Stressing their shared history, the episode prompts us to infer that Hoi's success was at one time also attainable by Killer. Wong presents, in other words, a counterfactual in virtual form, another forked path promising either crime and alienation, or moral conformity and social acceptance. The sequence bristles with implications: averse to decision making, Killer passively slid down the "wrong" path. Had he behaved authentically, embracing choice and responsibility, he might have found social integration and success. The main point is that this *syuzhet* episode is inconsequential only at the level of causation. Otherwise, it is thematically and narratively meaningful, situating Killer's inauthenticity within a wider network of alternative choices, missed opportunities, and possible futures.

Still, the viewer's impression of *syuzhet* digression remains strong. Subsequent episodes attenuate the plot still further, making the *fabula* seem diffuse. After the Hoi episode, the film's second reel refuses to assign Killer or Agent a local task or to establish large-scale character goals. To the viewer's knowledge, Agent and Killer have not devised future assassinations. There are no cops restlessly hunting the pair or plotting to coax them into a trap. The film's crime plot has all but dissipated. Generic schemata, often a reliable default when plots become obscure or confusing, offer the viewer little cognitive assistance here. If *Fallen Angels* initially primes us for romance between Agent and Killer, by the second reel it dissolves this narrative prospect. Romance films often posit two romantically destined protagonists separated by place or time or another external force, but seldom is the protagonists' distance self-imposed, as it is in *Fallen Angels*. (*In the Mood for Love* provides another salient example.) All the tropes of the romance genre have been discarded; indeed, our generic schemata fail us. With both romance and crime plots apparently retired, the viewer is justified in wondering what has become of the film's story. Crucially, it is at this stage in the *syuzhet*—as the story risks displacement by parametric style—that *Fallen Angels* launches its second major story. By initiating a parallel line of action at this juncture, Wong jump-starts the narrative just as its causal impetus seems spent.

Even when the first story seems vitiated, however, it does not completely disappear behind style. During its emaciated stretch of action, the *syuzhet* presents Agent draped over a jukebox in the bar. To some extent this sequence exemplifies what critics have labeled "the MTV moment," a segment given over to musical style, which prompts a pause in the narrative. (I critiqued this assumption in Chapter 2.) As Agent swoons to the jukebox tune—Laurie Anderson's

"Speak My Language"—the camera glides over her body, absorbing textures of fabric and flesh (Figure 4.2). For some critics, the story seems to stand still here not only for musical expression but for fetishistic contemplation too.[10] The MTV critic's assumption of narrative retardation (i.e., that MTV moments halt the story) finds an echo in Laura Mulvey's critique of visual pleasure. In classical Hollywood cinema, Mulvey contends, the eroticized spectacle of the female body creates "a break [in] the flow of the diegesis . . . [It] tends to work against the development of a story line, to freeze the flow of action in moments of erotic contemplation" (1975: 11). To be sure, the jukebox scene in *Fallen Angels* refuses to develop plot events; as Brunette might have it, nothing happens. Wong evidently intends for us to dwell on the scene's mood and sensuality. But this does not engender a radical break from story and character, nor does sensuous absorption arise at the expense of cognitive effort. Narrative meaning permeates the sequence, but in ways that are relatively tacit and implied.

For instance, the jukebox tune asks to be interpreted by character and theme, and not merely subsumed to the functions of sensuousness and mood setting. The song's lyric evokes both Agent's profession and existential isolation: "Now that the living outnumber the dead / I'm one of many." (That Agent herself selects this particular tune, moreover, suggests a subjective attachment to its lyrical content.) Treating the song as subjective commentary allows us to make sense of Agent's autoerotic behavior in the next scene. If we notice the solitude expressed by the lyric (and, by extension, by Agent herself), her sexual activity becomes strikingly devoid of eroticism. From this perspective, Wong undermines the jukebox scene's address to the male gaze. The strategies geared to "seduce" the viewer, therefore, are offset by our effort to interpret the song's narrative significance. Moreover, the spectator responding solely to sensuous style loses sight of character revelation. Both the tune and the scene's sensuality foreground Agent's desire for intimacy—which, as I have discussed, is a major character trait. Finally, the jukebox sequence *does* have causal effect, albeit at a tacit, interpretive level, in the ensuing autoerotic scene. In sum, the film's style-driven sequences hardly grind *fabula* progression to a halt.

What of voice-over narration, allegedly the last refuge of filmmakers reliant on postproduction plotting? To be sure, this device bolsters plot cohesion in *Fallen Angels*, but it also performs other (thematic, narrational) functions, negating the view that voice-over is simply a last-minute solution to the problem of unifying disparate, incoherent plotlines. At a narrative level, the confessional voice-over finds motivation in Killer's decision to avoid Agent. In lieu

---

10. Critic Lynda Chapple has advanced a similar claim regarding *In the Mood for Love*. The striking *qipao* worn by Su, Chapple contends, "frequently constitute a visual disruption to the narrative" (2011: 212).

of character interaction, voice-over here provides a major source of subjective access, alerting us to the protagonists' romantic inclinations. Voice-over also crystallizes the theme of authenticity. Wong marks Killer's death as poignant by reviving a foregoing stretch of voice-over dialogue: "The best thing about my profession is there's no need to make any decisions," states the assassin. "Who's to die, when, where—it's all been planned by others. I'm a lazy person. I like people to arrange things for me." Now, however, Wong extends Killer's monologue, foregrounding Killer as one more protagonist keen to break from routine. "It's been a bit different lately," Killer continues. "I want to change this habit. I don't know if it's a good decision or not, but at least it's mine." This codicil, coming in the wake of Killer's death, marks the assassin's fate as tragic, highlighting the folly of his regression into passive and inauthentic routines.

The film's polyphonic voice-overs ironically underscore the brevity of dialogue spoken within the diegesis. "Speak my language," implores Laurie Anderson—but few lines are exchanged directly between the characters. When the boisterous Hoi accosts Killer, for example, the taciturn assassin utters barely a word to his former classmate, a narrational strategy not only emphasizing Hoi's garrulous riffing but aligning Killer with the second story's mute protagonist (who himself is paired with a character—Charlie—given to constant verbal riffing) (Figure 4.3). Whereas Killer's reticence signifies a characteristic retreat from social existence, Ho's muteness conveys a bitter irony, for unlike Killer he craves social interaction and emotional intimacy.

Narrationally, moreover, Ho's voice-over can be grasped in terms of a general deviation from realism in the film's second story. Not only does the voice-over device grant Ho the power of speech, but realism is also compromised by Ho's occasional direct address to camera. Precisely because Ho is unique among the film's characters to transgress the diegetic boundary, some critics interpret Ho as a surrogate for Wong himself (Brunette 2005: 69; Stephens 1996: 18). Yet it is not necessary to presuppose a literal, autobiographical correspondence between film author and fictive agent. It is enough to understand Ho's voice-over and occasional look at the camera as instituting art-cinema norms. By means of such localized moments of self-conscious narration, the auteur cues us to broad parallels between his protagonist and his own personal vision. But to construe Ho simply as an author surrogate is to disregard the psychological change assigned to him across the film's duration. Which incarnation of Ho properly personifies Wong? The one with empathy for others or the one mired in routine, repudiating responsible action? I would argue that Ho's outlook at the climax of *Fallen Angels*, relinquishing irresponsible routines and embracing authentic interrelationships, broadly accords with Wong's worldview. For some critics *Fallen Angels* concludes on a downbeat note, positing "a chillingly desolate ending" and "a ride toward death" (Cassegard 2005: 19; Teo 2005:

91). But from the authorial perspective I have sketched, Ho's turn toward authenticity furnishes *Fallen Angels* with an irreducibly optimistic ending.

I have demonstrated that Wong's *fabula* material, *syuzhet* structures, and narrational strategies possess greater robustness and formal unity than some critical accounts have assumed. The "wispy" and "disorganized" narrative is not to be found in Wong's oeuvre. Still, it must be acknowledged that for all their strategies of cohesion, Wong's plots are not eternally fixed structures. Notoriously, the films exist in different versions. Contrasting theatrical prints may be prepared for release in different territories, as per common practice in Southeast Asia. Bordwell (2008a) has examined structural disparities within different cuts of *Days of Being Wild*, noting contrasts in plot order and preliminary exposition. More than most filmmakers, Wong lets us imagine alternative manifestations of his stories. DVD editions carry swathes of tantalizing footage excised from theatrical versions. The Kino release of *Fallen Angels* includes an extended ending in which Ho and Agent share a romantic kiss before parting ways, seemingly for good. Criterion's *In the Mood for Love* DVD carries a deleted liaison between Chow and Su. Entire plotlines and characters jettisoned from *Happy Together* emerge as deleted fragments and outtakes in *Buenos Aires Zero Degree* (1999), which documents the film's production. And alternative versions of Wong's films may yet be created. His fondness for revisiting his own work, as in the case of *Ashes of Time Redux*, augurs the possibility of past films re-emerging in fresh incarnations. Just as Wong's characters are presented with virtual alternative pathways, so Wong's spectator is invited to imagine the finished plot in myriad different forms. The films exude "a certain interactive splendor," as critic Kent Jones remarks. "Somewhere, there's an alternate universe where the character played by Stanley Kwan [*sic*] in *Happy Together* is alive and well, and Maggie Cheung and Tony Leung make love with abandon" (2001).

To a great extent, this narrative miscellany finds its origin in Wong's strategy of postproduction plotting. Wong assembles a particular *syuzhet* out of many possible *fabulas*, but innumerable alternatives are possible. In this regard, Wong is a filmmaker for the twenty-first century—an era of liminal storytelling, fan fiction, Borgesian forking paths, choose-your-own-adventure tales, DVD chapter selections, multiple versions and director's cuts, alternative endings, and so on. The film's *fabula* can be constructed for high complexity (*Ashes of Time*) or reworked for greater accessibility (*Ashes of Time Redux*). Invariably, the *syuzhet* Wong arrives at (albeit very late in the day) furnishes narrational and plot complexity, yet it subjects its difficult strategies to classical principles of construction. In other words, an aesthetic of disturbance carries the day at the levels of story and structure. Narrative comprehension is also roughened at the level of narration, as ellipticality and suppressiveness shine forth as major tendencies. I will uncover in the next chapter how such tendencies operate to complex effect in Wong's aesthetic of disturbance. And, more broadly, I will examine the significance of genre storytelling to Wong's allegedly antigeneric cinema.

5 | Frustrating Formulas
Popular Genre and
In the Mood for Love

In his study of Wong Kar-wai, Brunette posits two polarized perspectives on Wong's relationship to popular genre. In the "genre camp," he notes, are critics asserting the centrality of genre to Wong's commercial and storytelling strategies. Brunette cites Bordwell as an exponent of this perspective, adducing Bordwell's claim that "Wong's films . . . take popular norms as a point of departure" (2005: 3). A comparable view is held by cultural theorist Abbas, who argues that each of Wong's films "starts with the conventions of a popular genre—and deliberately loses its way in the genre" (1997b: 50). Against this perspective some critics posit what Brunette calls the "antigenre" view, in which genre is broadly construed as a basically inoperative element in Wong's films. Characteristic here is Chuck Stephens's assertion that Wong's "interest in formulas . . . is virtually nonexistent" (Brunette 2005: 4). Critic Tony Rayns contends that Wong is "more comfortable away from genre" (1995: 12); hence, for instance, *Ashes of Time* launches "a wholesale reinvention of the martial chivalry genre" (1994: 15).

Avoiding explicit allegiance to either perspective, Brunette's own account of Wong's generic engagement often departs from the genre adherents. His contention that Wong "begins to leave genre definitively behind" following *As Tears Go By* in 1988 indicates sympathy with the antigeneric perspective (Brunette 2005: 5). Accordingly, he echoes Rayns's assertion that *Ashes of Time* "reinvent[s the *wuxia pian*] completely" (31). Wong's best films, for Brunette, "transcend" genre conventions. They achieve a "nongeneric specialness"—which for Brunette amounts to "artistry"—that enables the filmmaker's personal auteurist expression to come to the fore (2005: 70). He comes close to identifying what I conceive as an explicit tension within Wong's films between generic formulas and authorial expression—yet I depart from Brunette in describing these films as nongeneric. Whereas Brunette implies that Wong's artistry and auteurist preoccupations emerge once genre has been subdued and transcended, I argue that these qualities emerge *through* Wong's engagement with genre. Generic norms are reworked in surprising ways, but they are not purged from Wong's films altogether. If the antigeneric and nongeneric perspectives are to hold water, a weaker version of their premises must be adopted. To insist that Wong repudiates genre is to disregard his films' often salient reworking of popular norms.

Later in this chapter I will try to demonstrate that *In the Mood for Love* anchors its narrative, stylistic, and thematic preoccupations in genre tropes and hybridity. First, however, it is necessary to reaffirm the thesis that genre holds a key place in Wong's cinema. To this end, I suggest that genre facilitates three interlinked objectives for Wong. It enables certain commercial imperatives, animates major authorial tropes, and allows the filmmaker's auteurist cinephilia to find sustained expression.

By Wong's own account, genre considerations crucially shape his films' preproduction phase. From one angle, the range of available genres finds constraints in Wong's filmmaking milieu. The road movie, for instance, is seldom evinced in Hong Kong cinema because, as local director Soi Cheang notes, "Hong Kong is so small—we just get to everywhere too soon, too quickly . . . [so] in Hong Kong it's very difficult to make a road movie" (Bettinson 2008: 221). If, as Wong has stated, *Chungking Express* is a road movie (Charity 1995: 15), it is a psychological road movie, a film mapping psychological change. It is only when Wong escapes the confines of Hong Kong—to traverse the landscapes of Buenos Aires (*Happy Together*) or the United States (*My Blueberry Nights*)—that he is able to embrace the road movie proper.

Then there is the task of raising production capital. Shrewdly alert to the local markets' successful genres, Wong entices financiers eager to capitalize on current generic trends. Thus, funding for *Ashes of Time* was acquired from Taiwan, profiting from a renewed popularity of exported martial-arts films. Additional scenes were restored for some regional territories "to make it seem more like a 'normal' *wuxia pian*" (Rayns 2008b: 8). *As Tears Go By* drew local investors keen to exploit a domestic appetite for triad films starring Andy Lau (Bordwell 2011: 171). Moreover, Wong recognized that rooting his films firmly in established genres enhanced the films' transcultural appeal. Consequently, his oeuvre is steeped in familiar generic iconography, even when this iconography seems to bear only superficially on narrative content. Wong is guileful on this point:

> it's a strategy to get the film seen. Normally the distributors here in South East Asia will ask 'Do you have action in your film?' And I can say 'Yes'. 'Do you have cops?' Of course I have a cop, but my cop is quite different. 'Do you have gangsters and gun fights?' Yes I do, but it's done differently. (Ashbrook 1997: 166)

Appropriating genre topoi thus bears fruit economically, while the topoi themselves provide raw materials for authorial experimentation.

Antigenre critics tend to misconstrue this unorthodox play with formulas as a gross eradication of genre rather than as a recasting of transcultural genre norms. But this assumption overlooks the way that Wong's generic innovations give rise to authorial preoccupations. In *2046*, the science-fiction framework motivates character doubling, with several of the film's actors portraying both futuristic agents and their twentieth-century counterparts. (Corporeally identical characters are a staple of the science fiction film—consider François Truffaut's *Fahrenheit 451* [1966] as another example allied to art cinema.) Wong's authorial emphasis on character doubling and interchangeable identities thus finds an alibi in the specific norms of a popular genre. Thanks to its fantastic armature, moreover, *2046* achieves a more direct correspondence between its two echoic plotlines than does, for instance, *Chungking Express*. In the latter film, codes of realism proper to the *policier* mandate that the two cop protagonists are embodied by distinct players; affinities between these agents are implied by rhyming motifs and actions. In *2046*, however, Wong can exploit the science-fiction genre's customary violations of realism to *explicitly* foreground the interchangeability of its characters.

The futuristic plotline in *2046*, springing subjectively from the imagination of Chow (Tony Leung Chiu-wai), establishes psychological traits as well. Chow simulates a universe in which "nothing ever changes," and gradually the viewer comes to recognize that Chow himself is resistant to change.[1] The imaginary terrain represents an idealized space wherein unpredictable and ephemeral forces are kept at bay. Chow upholsters his fictive universe with materials from his own life, imaginatively remodeling figures that populate his everyday existence and depriving them of agency. ("I made up the whole thing," he says, "but some of my experiences found their way into it.") This synthetic world enables him to control the individuals who traverse his real life and who represent potential catalysts for change. Gradually, Chow's contrived haven of similitude and omnipotence begins to seduce him away from the unsettling vicissitudes of reality. "I felt more and more at ease in my fictional world," he attests in voice-over. The film's science-fiction realm thus represents an inauthentic space, a space that at once parallels Chow's real lived existence and provides a retreat from it.[2] Furnishing a science-fiction framework enables Wong to mobilize the

---

1. It might be countered that Chow's promiscuity signifies his acceptance of change. Yet Chow's bed-hopping is itself a habitual act, a routine into which he has settled. Moreover, his promiscuity is limited to a closed set of women among whom he circulates, and thus his ostensible womanizing masks an inclination for stability and similitude. Finally, by refusing to settle with any one woman, Chow wards off the likelihood of permanent change wrought by commitment to a sole individual.

2. *2046* also recalls *Ashes of Time* in its emphasis on protagonists desperate to forget the past.

theme of inauthenticity that, as I will demonstrate later in this chapter, is so central to his authorial concerns. It is this kind of core thematic matter, as well as nuances of characterization and plot, that the antigenre position overlooks.

2046 juxtaposes two distinct genres—melodrama and science fiction—in initially disjunctive fashion. As the film progresses, however, these contrasting modes gradually cohere in each of the main plotlines. Emotion is the common link between the genres, and it becomes central to both parallel stories. Without abandoning its futuristic iconography, the science-fiction plotline settles down into an essentially melodramatic narrative invoking sentiment, romance, and thwarted desire (Figure 5.1). The melodramatic line of action reciprocally broaches what genre specialists agree is a favorite theme of science fiction: the notion of "humanness" (Neale 2000: 102–3; King and Krzywinska 2002). *2046* limns Chow's everyday existence as robotic. This analogy holds good for Chow's mechanistic tendency to foreclose his emotions and to repel the emotions of others. An assembly line of women bears witness to Chow's repudiation of emotional commitment. He values alcohol for its anesthetic effects ("It makes things easy"). His existence is also robotic in its commitment to routine—Chow is locked into an automated pattern of behavior. He traces an arc of character development that guides him toward an acceptance of emotion (he develops romantic attachments to Jingwen [Faye Wong] and Su Lizhen [Gong Li]) and change (he abandons old routines). In other words, Chow comes to accept indelibly *human* aspects of life. By organizing plot material around themes of emotion, Wong is able to harmonize two initially discordant genres. As often in Wong's films, what looks like incoherence is actually subordinated to a large-scale principle of aesthetic unity.

Claiming that Wong adopts generic frameworks is not to say that he is a slave to formula. Indeed, Wong innovates within generic contexts. His freedom within the limits of genre not only conjures an irresistibly unpredictable narrative but also assimilates into his overall aesthetic of disturbance. Disturbance here relates in part to the flouting of the viewer's expectations. *Chungking Express*, for instance, initially evokes the genre of the *policier* but subsequently introduces motifs and events that undermine any assumption of a conventional replaying of the crime thriller. Some critics have classified *Chungking Express* as a romantic comedy, which is a reasonably adequate description of the film. But romantic comedy is what the film becomes or, rather, what it reveals itself

---

The effort to eradicate memories is an act of inauthentic bad faith, a failing to which many of Wong's protagonists are prone. By the same token, the effort to memorialize the past can also constitute bad faith if the immersion in past events leads to a withdrawal from the present. For example, Chow's cadre of lovers in *2046* represents nothing but an inauthentic and impossible attempt to recreate or "clone" the idealized woman he lost, Su Lizhen (Maggie Cheung). In this respect, *2046* evokes *Vertigo* (1958)—an apt reference point, given the influence of Hitchcock on *In the Mood for Love* (discussed later in this chapter).

to be; it is not the genre that the film initially evokes. Thus, although Wong appears to abandon the *policier* genre as the film unfolds, he does not abandon *genre*—rather, he switches genre, bringing the romantic underpinnings of the film's first story more centrally into play.

If *Chungking Express* eventually discards the narrative norms of the *policier*, its initial evocation of the genre serves to sharpen character psychology. A convention (or cliché) of the *policier* is the cop protagonist whose single-minded dedication to duty isolates him from others and divests him of a personal life. As reviewers of *Chungking Express* generally noted, however, neither of the film's two cops is shown executing much police work. Devoid of this professional activity, the cops' social alienation cannot, crucially, be attributed to their thorough absorption in police matters. The source of their isolation must therefore be constituted by something other than zealous professionalism—ultimately, the film will suggest, by the characters' resistance to spontaneity and change. By initially evoking genre archetypes, Wong sets in relief the cops' more unexpected and thematically charged psychological traits.

Generic features also miscue the viewer to expect orthodox character relationships. Here *Chungking Express* primes and cues generic schemata that are ultimately misleading. As critic Susan Morrison noted of the first story's *policier* setup, "Our expectations run high; after all, he's a cop, she's a gangster; they've found each other . . . but nothing happens" (1996: 40). Moreover, both male protagonists in *Chungking Express* are linked explicitly by their social role as police officers; yet, contrary to generic expectation, the two cops are not revealed to be partners, nor indeed is it evident that they have ever met each other. The affinities and contrasts that the film establishes between these agents are evoked not by recourse to buddy formula. Rather, a comparison of the two agents plays out in more oblique fashion, through character echoes and parallels set forth across the film's successive plotlines. In this respect, *Chungking Express* departs from the storytelling norms of the *policier*. Ultimately, the film may be considered antigeneric insofar as it challenges certain generic norms; but, to the extent that *Chungking Express* engages with generic tropes and explicitly triggers generic expectations, the term "antigeneric" is inadequate and misleading.

Before turning to an analysis of *In the Mood for Love* and its generic maneuvers, I need to highlight a further impetus for Wong's generic uptake and innovation. The genre mixing of Hong Kong mainstream cinema forms an important influence, but the most significant precursors of Wong's reflexive and subversive handling of genre must surely be the European modernist auteurs, in particular those spearheading the *nouvelle vague*. Wong admires such auteur cineastes as Truffaut and Godard whose films bend popular genres to personally expressive ends. Approaching traditional genres with both affection and irreverence, the cinephile-auteur produces ostensible genre films that assault or travesty generic norms. In the case of the nouvelle vague filmmakers, and I want to argue also in the case of Wong, generic engagement enables the expression of the auteur as *cinephile*—the filmmaker announces his affection for the codes and conventions of traditional genre filmmaking. Wong has described how this implicit cinephilia influences his aesthetic choices:

> The only thing that I try to make very clear when I start a film is the genre that I want to place it in. As a kid, I grew up watching genre movies, and I was fascinated by all the different genres, such as Westerns, ghost stories, swashbucklers. . . . So I try to make each of my films in a different genre. (Tirard 2002: 197)

Genres typically fascinate the film-obsessed auteur. Hence we often find an eclectic array of genre entries in the oeuvre of such filmmakers. Like Tarantino, Truffaut, or Johnnie To, Wong is generically pluralist—his corpus of films encompasses the triad-gang drama, the martial-arts epic, the *policier*, the road movie, romance melodrama, and science fiction. Moreover, as I have noted, this kind of generic migration can also take place within a single film, as in the *Chungking Express* genre switch.

The auteur's transmutation of generic forms also attests to the pliability of genre. Undermined here is the fallacy that genre imposes rigid constraints upon artistic expression. To the contrary, as André Bazin declares, "the tradition of genres is a base of operations for creative freedom" (1985: 258). Nowhere is this more evident than in both the ludic generic maneuvers of the nouvelle vague and the free interplay of genres in popular Hong Kong cinema. Still, as I have indicated, in Wong's aesthetic of disturbance, personal expression frequently sits in tension with generic conventions. If the concept of genre evokes a homogenous taxonomy of films and directors, the concept of auteur points us toward the filmmaker's individuality and novelty.

At any rate, the main point is that genre conventions have seldom been inimical to either film art or auteur filmmakers. On the contrary, such filmmakers have typically reworked genre to artistically construct a personal worldview. If, then, the term "antigeneric" is to be usefully applied to Wong and his kin, it must be qualified to denote merely a challenge to genre norms, not a disavowal of genre altogether. A film like *Ashes of Time* is not cut from entirely new cloth; its novelty stands out precisely because of its adoption of familiar generic norms.

If Wong routinely recasts what Steve Neale calls "the rules of the genre" (1990: 47), *In the Mood for Love* appears prima facie to be an uncharacteristically conventional genre piece. Critical exegeses of the film have generally excluded questions of genre. Postmodernist and culturalist critics have tended to subsume Wong's genre uptake to the conceptual tropes of pastiche (Cameron 2007) and nostalgia (Chow 2006: 180; Teo 2001), examining the films' storytelling strategies in terms of what they might reveal about Hong Kong culture. My discussion of genre and *In the Mood for Love*, conversely, will be concerned primarily with more proximate levels of the text. As I hope to show, the film's subversion of genre, together with its complex imbrications of two generic modes, crystallizes authorial themes, renews the viewer's perception, and elicits high-order cognitive activity—thereby flouting the alleged passivity of the melodrama's (and Wong's) typical viewer.

Cries and Whispers: *In the Mood for Love*

Teo's description of *In the Mood for Love* as "a melodrama about love and romance" is characteristic of the film's critical categorization (2005: 128). To be sure, the film's overt subject matter displays the traditional features of melodrama.[3] I will demonstrate, however, that the film in fact flouts several basic conventions of the genre. Furthermore, *In the Mood for Love* adopts the "postclassical" strategy of generic hybridity—though Wong's tacit interweaving of discrete genres contradicts the more self-conscious, flagrant generic hybrids of much contemporary cinema. By undercutting key melodramatic norms and blending genres in subtle ways, Wong combines the auteur's taste for genre reworking with the cinephile's affection for distinct genres. In sum, the paradigmatic melodrama is hardly to be found in Wong's film. Later in this chapter I will examine the film's synthesis of genres, but first I must illuminate its disturbance of the prototypical melodrama. A sketch of the plot will be useful here.

In the Mood for Love begins in 1962. Two strangers, Chow Mo-wan (Tony Leung Chiu-wai) and Su Lizhen (Maggie Cheung), briefly cross paths at Mrs. Suen's boarding house in Hong Kong. Mrs. Suen leases a room to Su and her husband, while the adjacent apartment is leased to Chow and his wife. Chow and Su establish a neighborly acquaintance but soon are thrust together by a shared revelation: their spouses, they suspect, have been sleeping together. The two protagonists grow curious as to how this affair began and tentatively enact their spouses' initial overtures. Gradually, the protagonists come to acknowledge their own mutual attraction but resolve not to act further on their desire.[4]

---

3. It is perhaps evident that in using the English term "melodrama" rather than its closest equivalent in Chinese (*wenyi pian*), I mean to invoke the generic breadth of the Western term as opposed to the comparatively more circumscribed meaning denoted by the Cantonese. For elaboration on this terminological distinction, see Li (1986) and Dissanayake (1993: 3–4).

4. The film's premise here reworks the basic plot of Billy Wilder's *Avanti!* (1972), in which the protagonists (played by Jack Lemmon and Juliet Mills) adopt the routines and dining habits of their parents, the pair of whom have been carrying on a private extramarital romance. In

Nevertheless, gossip about their friendship percolates through the tenement building. Beset by rumors and aware of his nascent feelings for Su, Chow flees to Singapore. Years later, Chow travels to Cambodia and visits the ruins of Angkor Wat, where he whispers a secret into a hole in the stone.

Synoptically, *In the Mood for Love* may seem to augur a fairly typical melodrama of passion. Its story of secret liaisons, thwarted desire, and personal sacrifice is firmly embedded in the melodramatic tradition. Domestic conflict— the bedrock of the genre—is forecast by the story's marital betrayals, which prepare the way for impassioned confrontations among the central quartet of characters. And the central premise is ripe for moral didacticism and theatrical emotion, stirring in the viewer strong sympathetic emotions (pathos, sadness, admiration, and so on). However, Wong affords this melodramatic material a stylistic and narrative treatment that departs in key respects from prototypes of the genre. For instance, Wong largely banishes the spouses from the film, circumventing melodramatic conflict and exposing the adulterous figures as a kind of pretext for the main protagonists' activity.

In what other ways does *In the Mood for Love* rework the hallmarks of melodrama? Principally, the film discards the melodrama's legible and forceful expression of character emotion. If the genre is one of excess (Brooks 1995), bearing witness to the "soul-bearing histrionics" of its agents (Bordwell 1985: 70), *In the Mood for Love* favors a sustained suppression of emotion, motivated by the all-consuming conservatism of its protagonists. Moreover, the overdetermined emotions of melodrama contradict the cultural norms and display rules of the film's epoch and milieu, which regulate social behaviors according to a repressive, albeit eroding, Confucian ideology.

Often in classical Hollywood melodrama, the narrative milieu sets the protagonist's emotional display in sharp relief. In *Stella Dallas* (1937), the eponymous heroine's unpolished, lower-class "vulgarity" yields uncensored emotional outbursts; the film's omniscient narration, however, reveals that such outpourings are improper within certain social contexts. Similarly, Lana Turner's attention-grabbing actress in Douglas Sirk's *Imitation of Life* (1959)—a remake of John M. Stahl's 1934 classic—is repeatedly urged to curb her hyperbolic behavior and to "stop acting." (The melodrama's emphasis on playacting is literalized in Wong's film, which will be discussed later in this chapter.) Conversely, Su and Chow conservatively submit to the prevailing mandates of their social milieu, observing its display rules of composure, decorum, and impassivity. It is the corollary atmosphere of muted affect that prompts reviewers to remark upon the film's restraint (Howe 2001: 35; Turan 2001); as one critic writes, "*In the Mood for Love* never raises its voice . . . because it is not about

---

the process of mimicking their parents' activity, the protagonists inadvertently fall in love with each other.

passion expressed but passion concealed" (Corliss 2000: 70). By substituting excess with restraint, *In the Mood for Love* inverts the melodrama's standard emphasis on overt emotional expression.[5]

Still, *In the Mood for Love*'s affective register is not without precedent. Some critics find correspondence with Sirk's melodramas, but Sirk often delivers the sort of fraught emotional displays conventional to the genre. A better comparison is with Otto Preminger, whose *Daisy Kenyon* (1947) downplays the usual cathartic structures of classical melodrama, and with Stahl, whose *Imitation of Life* (1934) motivates its subdued atmosphere by the female protagonists' admirable dignity and self-possession. Certain low-key melodramas by Ingmar Bergman provide an antecedent from European art cinema. And a more proximate background is the Cantonese *wenyi pian*, a fictional mode broadly consonant with Western melodrama. Often depicting feudal society, the classic *wenyi pian* of the 1950s and 1960s echoed Hollywood melodramas in their narratives of self-sacrifice, patriarchal morality, and romantic or familial tragedy. Critics cite Fei Mu's Mandarin-language *Spring in a Small Town* (1948) as a close relative of *In the Mood for Love*, while Qin Jian's *Parents' Hearts* (1955) also prefigures the later film's affective "restraint." *In the Mood for Love*, then, takes its cue from a transcultural tradition of melodrama, in which the genre's enlargement of emotion is supplanted by a relatively diffuse, low-level emotional tone. As Bordwell writes, Wong "dissolves crisp emotions into vaporous moods" (2011: 179).

In traditional melodrama, the protagonist's affective state—inferably simmering at the surface—pours out into the expressive design of the diegesis. Here Wong finds an ideal context for his aesthetic principle of expressive diffusion, discussed in previous chapters. Partly as a result of character opacity, melodramas invite all features of style to express the protagonist's interior states. *In the Mood for Love* adopts this convention, as Robert Sinnerbrink notes:

> it is the recurrence of various elements such as colour palette, visual and musical motifs, gestures and expressions in performance, particular fashion

---

5. A common critical confusion in reviews of *In the Mood for Love* involves a slippage between the "conservatism" of the film itself and the "restraint" of the characters and milieu it depicts. Teo, for instance, conflates the "conservative core" of the film's narrative with the "moral restraint" of the central protagonists (2001). While the protagonists and their cotextual backdrop (that is, the diegetic environment as it is defined by a set of morals, values, and beliefs) may certainly be expressive of conservative attitudes, I think it would be misleading to suggest that the film shares an identical or even harmonious outlook with its protagonists. On the contrary, as my discussion of the film will indicate, *In the Mood for Love* adopts a quite critical stance toward its protagonists and milieu. Unlike Su and Chow (the "conservative" protagonists), those characters who flout conservative morality are neither judged *by* the film nor castigated by agents within the story.

and costume combinations, that put into play a series of subtle variations in mood throughout the film. (2012: 159)

Unlike traditional melodrama, however, the film's mise-en-scène reflects protagonists not given to outsized displays of emotion. Instead, their affective states remain firmly corseted. Thus Su wears tight-fitting cheongsams, the cramped apartment building oppressively encloses the protagonists, and an incessant rainfall delivers the pathetic fallacy, a plot device common to both Hollywood melodrama and the *wenyi pian*.[6] The downpour laments the unfulfilled romance that the protagonists themselves cannot openly mourn and presages "romantic tragedy" (Smith 2003: 129). Not incidentally, these latter two motifs—oppressive locales, ominous downpours—are iconographically associated more with film noir than with melodrama. Nevertheless, the film's mise-en-scène evokes the protagonists' ritual form of repression and self-denial, traits that will ultimately define their shared conviction to abstain from adultery.

Music, employed in melodrama principally to convey character subjectivity and cue sentimental emotions, acquires additional functions in this film. An orchestral score (composed by Shigeru Umebayashi) sacrifices dramatic key changes for a resolutely plaintive progression, and the lyrics of appropriated pop songs are exploited to provide both access to subjective states (in the manner of expressive displacement) and commentary upon story action. As Chow prepares to leave Singapore, he asks Su, "If there is an extra ticket, would you go with me?" This dialogue becomes elliptical, as Su ventures no reply. Instead the sound track is dominated by Nat King Cole's "Quizas, Quizas, Quizas," the refrain of which translates into English as "perhaps." This lyric may be grasped subjectively, as representing Su's unspoken response to Chow. But, more generally, the ambiguity conveyed by the lyric is entirely apt for the protagonists' undefined relationship and sustains the suspense around their deepening friendship.

In the Mood for Love subscribes most to melodramatic convention in its emphasis on social factors impinging on and subjugating the individual. As Robert Lang observes, the typical melodramatic agent is "acted upon" by capricious social forces outside his or her control (1989: 5). Melodramas thus confer ineffectuality upon the individual, whose autonomy is undermined by the predestined machinations of society. At first glance, this kind of melodramatic impotence is epitomized by the protagonists of *In the Mood for*

---

6. The pathetic fallacy, for instance, gains salience in Douglas Sirk's classic melodrama *There's Always Tomorrow* (1956), the plot of which is superficially echoed by *In the Mood for Love*'s tale of illicit desire. Here Clifford Groves (Fred MacMurray) falls in love with his old flame Norma Vale (Barbara Stanwyck), but his extramarital desire threatens to rend his family apart. Sirk puts the pathetic fallacy to poignant use when the protagonists resolve to stay apart, preserving the passionless "reality" of their lives.

Love. Chow and Su chafe at the constraints of the rigid social mores that prohibit their mutual desire. Both figures are posited as victims in the melodramatic mold, doomed to private suffering by prevailing social laws. Wong has described *In the Mood for Love* as being "about a certain period that has been lost" (Weitzman 1998: 46), and the milieu's condemnation of adultery emerges as one more faded anachronism of a now obsolete epoch. Indeed, by surrounding the protagonists with promiscuous and adulterous characters, Wong implies the inchoate decay of this society's stringent moral code. Vividly, the film evokes the dissolution of Confucian ethics in 1960s Hong Kong, as modernization and capitalism began to take hold.

This moral decay, which is veneered by social equilibrium, points to a societal crisis that is uncharacteristic of melodramatic fiction. As Neale writes, "melodrama does not suggest a crisis of [the legally established social] order, but a crisis within it, an 'in house' rearrangement" (1980: 22). Here *In the Mood for Love* seemingly hews to generic norm: the crisis depicted "within" the social order is the more or less nascent promiscuity that Chow and Su must confront in others and in themselves. And yet the film tacitly exceeds its generic demands to critique the milieu it presents; in other words, the crisis that the film depicts is both within and of the social order. *In the Mood for Love* thereby taps the viewer's "moral and social emotions" (Boyd 2009: 196). For the viewer is compelled to question a milieu whose regnant ideology is repressive of personal desire, forcing couples into clandestine relationships (e.g., the spouses' affair) or into an internalization and suppression of deeply felt desire (e.g., the chaste relationship between Su and Chow)—an ideological system, in sum, that is in each case compromising of authentic modes of existence.

The topos of authenticity and responsibility—a principal theme in Wong's films generally—needs some elaboration here. For Jean-Paul Sartre, the individual is authentic to the extent that he recognizes and accepts responsibility "for everything he does" (1973: 34). The authentic figure, "abandoned" to the world (and thus not the subject of an a priori metaphysical scheme), "makes himself; he is not found ready-made; he makes himself by the choice of his morality, and he cannot but choose a morality, such is the pressure of circumstances upon him" (50). The existentialist's premise of a godless universe flies in the face of melodrama's emphasis on predestination and fate. Inauthenticity, by contrast, is engendered by the individual who identifies "too much, and too easily, with the 'communal character' of his existence" (Cooper 2000: 109). Inauthentic existence, then, is evolved when individual freedom is sacrificed to prevailing social mores, eventuating in the "loss" of the self. The inauthentic self is "moulded by external influences, whether these be circumstances, moral codes, political or ecclesiastical authorities, or whatever" (Macquarrie 1973: 161–62).

In Heideggerian parlance, the individual is enveloped by the "they," the anonymous majority that seeks to vanquish personal desire and expression by coercing the individual into "being-for-others." The "they" governs social behavior and "prescribes what can and may be ventured, [keeping] watch over everything exceptional that thrusts itself to the fore" (Heidegger 1980: 165, H128). For Heidegger, ultimately, "the Self of everyday Dasein [i.e., human existence] is the *they-self* which is to be distinguish[ed] from *the authentic Self*—that is, from the Self which has been taken hold of in its own way" (1980: 167, H129, emphasis in original).

That inauthentic ways of life are prevalent among *In the Mood for Love*'s characters, along with the melancholic atmosphere permeating the film, indicates failings in the superficially reputable social order (i.e., the "they"). Putatively in a state not of mere flux but of crisis, the film's social landscape is split into two factions. There are those individuals, such as Su and Chow, who sacrifice personal contentment on the altar of socially prescribed morality; and, conversely, there are characters such as the protagonists' spouses who act on authentic desire while maintaining a veneer of social propriety.

Chow and Su are encompassed, in both the domestic and professional spheres, by examples of this latter duplicity. Aside from the infidelity of the spouses, Su observes the philandering ways of her married employer, Mr. Ho, while Chow gives ear to the sexual boasts of Ping, a promiscuous colleague.[7] If such secondary characters signify changing attitudes within the society, the protagonists set themselves apart by refusing to transgress social decorum: "we won't be like them" is the refrain they repeat with ebbing conviction.[8] In a conventional melodrama, the protagonists' moral virtue would be commended, eliciting what psychologists call "elevation"—a kind of admiration at the embodiment of high moral standards (Plantinga 2009: 183). But *In the*

7. It is possible to relate the liberalism of these secondary characters to their experience of foreign society, attitudes, and customs. The spouses, Ping, and—we may infer, given his senior position in a shipping office—Mr. Ho each make regular expeditions abroad, in contrast to Chow and Su, who are relatively parochial (a hint of their aversion to change). Moreover, Hong Kong society's impending disintegration is inferably due to cultural osmosis, the steepening infiltration of nonindigenous influences into the local sphere, thus of urban modernization and globalization. Wong indicates this influence by the presence of "foreign" appliances brought into Mrs. Suen's boarding house, for example, the neckties, handbags, and the Japanese rice cooker that delights the neighbors. Such items symbolize the significant impact that foreign influence (a "liberal" influence, to which the secondary characters are exposed) will have upon the protagonists' domestic relationships and emotional lives. To this extent, the film recalls Yasujiro Ozu's *Ohayo* (1959) with its emphasis on alien material goods (the television set, washing machine, Western-style nightgowns, and so forth) as a divisive source of pleasure and chaos.

8. This dialogue recalls Yiu-fai's rebuke to Po-wing in *Happy Together*: "I'm not like you," he insists. Later in the film, Yiu-fai retracts this remark: "I thought I was different from Po-wing," he says in voice-over, following a casual sex encounter. "[But it] turns out that lonely people are all the same."

Mood for Love denies the viewer this generic pleasure, instead foregrounding the folly of the protagonists' moral propriety. In their refusal to acknowledge society's shifting attitudes, Chow and Su eschew the knowledge that would enable them to gratify authentic desire, as well as to remain in sync with a rapidly mutating social space. Instead, the protagonists deploy moral idealism as an armature against change.

I have suggested that *In the Mood for Love* depicts a societal schism distinguishing the social conformist from the social transgressor. An ordinary melodrama would represent this schism as a Manichaean conflict. Granted, Manichaean opposites are implicit in Wong's film, which polarizes the sexual attitudes of the protagonists, on the one hand, and those of their spouses and work colleagues, on the other. Yet the secondary characters are shown to have the allegiance (if not the respect) of Su and Chow—they are the protagonists' friends, colleagues, and lovers. In the case of the spouses, moreover, their virtual absence from the film renders them unlikely antagonists. *In the Mood for Love*, then, does not posit these adulterous figures as straightforward melodramatic villains. Wong limns these secondary agents schematically, and in each case social nonconformity is marked as the character's most salient trait—that is, all of these figures are principally defined as morally and socially transgressive subjects. Moral virtue in this film is synonymous with submissiveness to the dominant ideology. And, in the transgressions of these minor characters, Su and Chow find examples to be held up for excoriation. It is thus that the protagonists differentiate themselves from their adulterous counterparts by repeatedly invoking the dualism "we" and "them."

Crucially, Chow and Su refrain from acting on their mutual desire because of the negative consequences that would befall them *as social subjects*. Su's distress at being chided by Mrs. Suen, who admonishes her for staying out late, betrays heavy feelings of social responsibility. Chow grows increasingly sensitive to the damaging effects wrought by gossip and rumor. Neither character is allowed to achieve a harmonious coexistence of private and social identities. The Kafkaesque corridors, stairways, and communal areas of the main tenement building represent sites of intersection between the protagonists' private and public selves. Mrs. Suen, the diegetic enforcer of the patriarchal ideology, delivers her lecture to Su in these apparently private living quarters (Figure 5.2). Within the film's claustrophobic enclave, individual autonomy is constantly permeated, overwhelmed, and conditioned by social doctrine.

Social melodramas tend ultimately to reward morally virtuous characters. Even in the event of the protagonist's death, affirmative standards of valor and moral fortitude carry the day. *In the Mood for Love*, however, denies its protagonists a sense of moral validation and personal triumph. It also denies the viewer the pleasurable emotion of elevation—we are granted scant satisfaction in witnessing the protagonists' virtuous display, since Wong makes it clear that such behavior finally compounds their misery. Compare the classical Hollywood melodrama, which foregrounds the value of the protagonist's sacrifice. Annie's unselfish actions in Sirk's *Imitation of Life* are pursued for the good of her light-skinned daughter, who is portrayed in the film as fundamentally sympathetic. By contrast, the title character in *Mildred Pierce* (1945) discovers that ceding her romantic ideals—as well as a stake in her restaurant franchise—is too great a sacrifice for the consequent payoff (the dubious affections of her baleful daughter). Similarly, Cary, the female protagonist in *All That Heaven Allows* (1955), gives up a romantic affair at the behest of her children but soon realizes that her sacrifice was not properly warranted—her children selfishly privilege their own happiness above all else. When one character pointedly asks Cary, "What good was your noble sacrifice?" the protagonist is persuaded to rekindle the affair.

Since *In the Mood for Love* does not provide access to the spouses—that is, to the direct beneficiaries of the protagonists' sacrifice—we are prevented from judging the merit of the sacrifice in question. Thus, the protagonists' sacrifice seems to be made in the name of certain amorphous (and socially constructed) ideals rather than for the benefit of specifically individuated figures. Furthermore, it cannot be said that the spouses are presented sympathetically, unlike the daughters in *Stella Dallas* and Sirk's *Imitation of Life*. Indeed, what little we know of the spouses—namely, their dishonesty toward the protagonists, with whom we are allied—implies that they are not deserving of the sacrifice. As *In the Mood for Love* implicitly critiques its milieu's hegemony, and, moreover, does not attempt to elicit sympathy for the spouses, it does not provide a concrete sense that the protagonists' sacrifice (that is, their decision to remain apart) contains any inherently worthwhile value. Their stoicism and sacrifice does not therefore elicit our admiration, the traditionally apt response to displays of melodramatic sacrifice.

Many melodramas, Torben Grodal points out, posit "a coupling of history and individual fate" (1997: 254). Thus, for instance, the incorporated newsreel footage of Charles de Gaulle's visit to Cambodia, while in one respect culturally specific, is not out of keeping with the norms of the genre. Nor is the extraordinary closing sequence at Angkor Wat, in which Chow performs a mythical ritual by whispering a secret into the historical ruins. Yet, in melodramatic terms, this denouement is an odd form of catharsis. Such purgation is not the corollary of an alpine emotional outburst, as we might expect in melodrama, but is at once more private, restrained, and virtually imperceptible. Chow's words are not audible on the sound track, and thus Wong's narration here flaunts its disregard for melodramatic transparency. Chow buries his unheard secret (which we nevertheless infer is the story of the protagonists' shared affection) in the ancient ruins of Angkor Wat, thereby enshrining the memory in (and as) history. In doing so, he affords the memory immortality at the same time as he marks its expiration. An intertitle prefaces this end sequence: "That era has passed. Nothing that belonged to it exists anymore." Referred to here is not only the shifting modernity of Hong Kong's cultural space but also the foreclosed private relationship shared by the protagonists. The film's catharsis, then, delivers the moment of the central relationship's simultaneous "birth" (that is, Chow's authentic acknowledgment of it) and "death" (his entombing of the memory), while the ruins of Angkor Wat serve as its symbolic burial place.

Tempting Fate: Reflectionism, Coincidence, and Chance

For much of recent history, the Hong Kong populace has negotiated turbulent and unpredictable social change. Mainland China's reunification with the territory in 1997 purportedly triggered collective anxieties pertaining to national identity, economic instability, and alleged impingements on civil liberties. Five years after the handover, Johnnie To would observe that the local Chinese "still haven't got over their historical suffering and fatalism" (Shin and Lee 2002: 38). Naturally, Hong Kong's film industry was not impervious to the city's spiritual and economic downturn. As is well known, after several years of creative and commercial prosperity, the local film market was dealt successive blows by the collapse of the East Asian economy, a growth in video piracy, and an increase in competition from rival film centers (principally Hollywood and, latterly, the South Korean cinema). In Li Cheuk-to's view, Hong Kong's prevailing "sense of doom" was shared by key personnel within the film industry, for whom the contemporary social, cultural, and industrial circumstances posed a threat to their livelihood as filmmakers (1998: 17).

Moreover, the "1997 sense of doom," as discussed in Chapter 1, was seemingly assimilated into the narrative and thematic material of the domestic commercial cinema. Triad films such as *The Longest Nite* (1998) and *Expect the Unexpected* (1998) present an irreversible determinism that thrusts characters ever closer to fated calamity. If a narrative preoccupation with doom characterized Hong Kong mainstream cinema circa 1997, the broader and less necessarily pessimistic notions of fate and predestination continued to infuse genre storytelling in the new century. Romance melodramas like *Lost in Time* (2003) and *Turn Left, Turn Right* (2003) thematize predestination at a time in Hong Kong history when the powerlessness of the local people is forcefully and recurrently underlined. During this period, the onset of Asia's economic recession, and subsequently the SARS outbreak, made salient the threat of unforeseen and deleterious circumstances—compounding, one might suppose, extant collective feelings of disempowerment. Though *Lost in Time* and *Turn Left, Turn Right* both furnish ultimately uplifting denouements, their optimistic closures belie a diegetic world in which fictive agents are overpowered by equivocal and ungovernable events. In other words, both triad film and romance melodrama, despite divergences in tone and outlook, attest to the disempowerment of the individual by nonmaterial, omnipotent, and apparently acausal phenomena.

Fate is central to *In the Mood for Love*, but the predestination theme is underpinned by Wong's authorial engagement with genre. My contention is that we can understand the film's invocation of fate without recourse to reflectionist interpretations, that is, the assumption that the filmic text mirrors and manifests real-world social anxieties. At the very least, I contend that *In the Mood for Love* does not necessarily manifest the specific anxieties most commonly invoked by critics (concerning national reunification and the Asian financial crisis). Rather the film's fatalistic undercurrent bespeaks Wong's anomalous treatment of melodrama norms, and it is by means of this treatment that authorial concerns are brought to the fore.

Melodramas are routinely studded with moments of chance and coincidence. Similarly, *In the Mood for Love*—and its protagonists—invokes metaphysical (as opposed to socially determined) fate as a means by which to account for unhappy story events. Apparently, then, Chow and Su are deprived of autonomy by a natural, as well as a societal, order. *In the Mood for Love* hints at a fate-driven diegesis. In addition to the pathetic fallacy signifying elemental forces, chance and coincidence attain narrative prominence, reinforcing the protagonists' role as victims (of fate as well as of social strictures). Rey Chow echoes this reading of *In the Mood for Love*:

> Ultimately, [Wong's] work seems to say, human relationships, even the most unforgettable ones, are only a matter of fortuitous playacting—*and perhaps not so much by human beings as by chance or fate itself* . . . [and *In the Mood for Love*'s visually stunning images] become an index to *the capricious nature of the human universe* that revolves around [the protagonists]. (2006: 183, emphasis added)

In the Mood for Love may thus be understood as a fundamentally conventional narrative involving star-crossed "lovers," whose preordained social situation prohibits personal fulfillment. Arbitrary events and social proprieties conspire to divest the protagonists of individual agency. Yet I suggest that the film subverts its apparent positioning of the protagonists as victims of fate and does so chiefly by putting into doubt the legitimacy of its narrative coincidences.

Coincidence is evoked conventionally in the opening phase of *In the Mood for Love*. Su and Chow coincidentally move into their respective apartments on the same day.[9] Character dialogue ensures that this happenstance is well marked: "What a coincidence! Moving in on the same day!" Already our generic expectations are animated—we are likely to read into these opening scenes something more than a succession of plain coincidences. Separately choosing the same day on which to move apartments, the film's romantic protagonists are, we infer, already unassailably "attuned" to each other and thus are perfectly compatible as an ideal couple. (This reading relies on the inferred presence of a predestined order of things, which teleologically governs the melodramatic universe.) Engendered by these opening scenes, then, is a set of generically informed inferences and assumptions. The rest of the film, however, invokes coincidence in a way that aims to dismantle our generic expectations.

Coincidence is next remarked upon when the protagonists obliquely acknowledge their spouses' affair. Chow wears a necktie identical to one owned by Su's husband; this item, which the protagonists believe does not retail in Hong Kong, was a gift from Chow's wife who—like Su's husband—purchased it while on a business trip abroad. A similar bit of business unravels around the identical but rare handbags owned by Su and Chow's wife. At this point, Su exclaims, "What a coincidence!" Finally, though, the protagonists' suspicion—that their spouses purchased these gifts together during a liaison on foreign soil—is quietly and mutually corroborated.

In spite of Su's exclamation, the doubling of gifts is only an apparent coincidence. A carefully motivated cause is furnished for the duplicate items—namely, the causality linking the spouses' affair, their tryst overseas, their purchasing and bestowing of gifts, and so forth. There is a sharp disparity between Su's proclamation of coincidence and the kind of coincidence identified by Mrs. Suen near the start of the film. Whereas the earlier moment of coincidence could not be attributed any discernible cause (or at least no tangible cause, if we allow that coincidences signify an invisible, transcendent phenomenon), here the coincidence is concretely rooted in causal human action. In this instance, the pronouncement of coincidence cannot be taken at face value.

Later in the film, Su learns from an acquaintance that Chow, ailing from a severe head cold, craves sesame syrup. Su prepares the snack and delivers it to him. After an ellipsis, Chow, now recovered, encounters Su in the street and greets her with the phrase "What a coincidence!" Since Chow's remark is not contradicted by wider narrative information, this present encounter may legitimately be attributed to chance. Expressing gratitude to Su for the sesame syrup, Chow tells her that he had, in his stricken state, been thirsting for just

---

9. During this sequence, which is overlaid with a comic atmosphere of pandemonium, the characters' possessions are mislaid and delivered to the wrong apartment, a foreshadowing, therefore, of the confusion of personal items—Chow's necktie, Su's handbag—that will harvest more dramatic effect later in the film.

that particular snack. Su replies, "Really? What a coincidence!" "It really was!" affirms Chow. As before, however, Su invokes coincidence disingenuously, fully aware that genuine coincidence has played no part in the actual course of events.

If we have been tracking the film's coincidences, we begin to realize that the protagonists falsely adduce coincidence for events they know to have a firm basis in causality. The phrase "What a coincidence!" is the most repeated line in the film, and yet the accuracy of the remark becomes increasingly suspect with each repetition. By the time that Su utters this phrase, it is clear that coincidence is no longer being evoked according to melodramatic convention—it signifies neither the protagonists' lack of agency nor the manifestation of an omnipotent entity. The film demystifies its most important coincidences, such that they come into focus as explicable, causal, and secular events. A key trope of melodrama is thus inverted; never the playthings of providence, the protagonists' apparent position as victims is dramatically undercut. Their circumstances are revealed to be *surmountable*, and by evaporating the shadow of deterministic fate Wong empowers these agents with the freedom of choice, belief, and action.

Thus, the cause of the protagonists' repression must reside elsewhere than in the machinations of society and fate. The answer lies in a familiar authorial theme. Like so many of Wong's protagonists, Su and Chow recoil from change. Their repression is largely of their own design, since the existence of fate can no longer be deemed the prime mover in the protagonists' inability to act. Furthermore, as I have noted, the film's conservative milieu imposes no necessary stranglehold on its inhabitants. Nowhere is this more evident than in the liberal activity of the figures surrounding the protagonists (the spouses, Mr. Ho, and Ping). Sexual freedom is attainable within the film's repressive society; it is simply that Chow and Su choose not to transgress the social laws that condemn such freedom. Oppressive social proprieties are not, then, to be held accountable for what is, in point of fact, the protagonists' willful oppression of themselves. Chow and Su are in no sense the passive victims of metaphysical or ideological forces. In other words, despite appearances to the contrary, they are not archetypal melodramatic figures.

In its articulation of a particular Chinese society, then, *In the Mood for Love* evokes and overturns the conventions of melodrama. A strongly deterministic space gives way to the agency and autonomy of its populace; and, correspondingly, the protagonists' apparent victimization is recast as conscious, active choice making—that is, their consenting capitulation to dogmatic social constraints. Wong is less concerned to denounce the film's suffocating social sphere, or even to censure the protagonists for their timorous dislike of change, than to criticize Chow and Su for living inauthentically, surrendering responsibility and truly felt desire to symbolic structures.[10] Wong here invokes the Sartrean view that, since "the situation of man [is] one of free choice, without excuse and without help, any man who takes refuge . . . by inventing [or espousing] some deterministic doctrine, is a self-deceiver" (Sartre 1973: 50). *In the Mood for Love*'s protagonists therefore exist in bad faith, for according to Sartre, in such inauthentic existence "it is from myself that I am hiding the truth" (2000: 49). Consequently, neither Su nor Chow reaches the moment of *anagnorisis* achieved by Cary at the climax of *All That Heaven Allows*, who declares, "I was so frightened, I listened to other people; I let others make my decisions."

Adopting melodramatic norms allows Wong to establish a deterministic, chance-ridden story world. *Subverting* the genre's norms enables him to mobilize authorial preoccupations. Melodramatic convention is ultimately reworked for personal expression. *In the Mood for Love* evokes a staple of the genre—coincidence—and subverts it, thereby disclosing character psychology and sharpening themes of change, responsibility, and authenticity. In the next section, I turn to another generic strategy of chief importance to *In the Mood for Love*: the practice of genre hybridity.

Crimes of Passion

In Hong Kong cinema, genre films seldom exist in pure unalloyed form. Even *As Tears Go By*, regarded by many critics as Wong's sole attempt at pure genre filmmaking, weaves a romance subplot into its main crime story. More subtly than *2046*, which juxtaposes melodrama and science fiction, *In the Mood for Love* imbricates two distinct genres. The film explicitly evokes the romance melodrama, but, just as *Chungking Express* promises the *policier* and morphs into romantic comedy, so *In the Mood for Love* reveals another generic complexion. But unlike *Chungking Express*, whose *policier* elements gradually recede, *In the Mood for Love* mixes genres more discreetly. Wong has alluded in interviews to this generic layering, suggesting that a latent genre functions beneath the film's surface melodrama. *In the Mood for Love*, he reveals, was initially conceived as an exercise in Hitchcockian suspense, with the romance story of affairs and heartache merely a pretext for a virtual detective story:

> Instead of treating [*In the Mood for Love*] as a love story, I decided to approach it like a thriller, like a suspense movie. [The protagonists] start out as victims, and then they start to investigate, to try to understand how

---

10. I should stress here that, in characterizing Su and Chow as existential subjects living in bad faith, I am not attempting to affirm Western philosophy over Eastern. Rather, my argument is that *the film itself* implicitly judges its protagonists for living inauthentically and that the fates of Su and Chow (and of the inauthentic characters in other Wong films) bear this out.

things happened. This is the way I structured this film, with very short scenes and an attempt to create constant tension. (Tirard 2002: 198)

This detective framework is discernible not only in the film's narrative structure but also, I suggest, in its mise-en-scène, iconography, and narrational point of view. A furtive detective schema consistently penetrates the film's surface, disturbing the conventions of melodrama and, most significantly, forcing us into errors of comprehension.

As Wong indicates, *In the Mood for Love* can be understood as a virtual detective story, depicting the protagonists' investigation into a secret infidelity. While the spouses' surreptitious affair constitutes the narrative "crime," the protagonists' postmortem of the affair represents the narrative "investigation." In invoking the structure of a detective narrative, Wong also activates the moral dimension of the detective universe. If the protagonists' playacting is analogous to an investigation, the spouses' affair acquires the moral status of a crime. (I am not arguing that Wong confers this perspective on the spouses, only that it is the view shared by the protagonists.) It is their own simplistic morality that Chow and Su must confront when they become conscious of their own illicit emotions, a revelation that occurs as they reenact their spouses' coquetry.[11] This reenactment literalizes a cliché of the detective genre, that of retracing the criminal's movements (or reenacting the crime).

Generic schemata allow the poetician to expose familiar detective tropes and to ascribe generic motivation to apparently unconventional, antigeneric story action. Consider again the protagonists' role play. Far from a detached reenactment, the investigation leads Su and Chow to identify with the extramarital desire they simulate.[12] Echoed here is a detective fiction trope whereby detective and criminal become closely associated. This results in a blurring of morality—the polarities of good and evil are collapsed, and the detective's moral identity threatens to be absorbed by the criminal's (and vice versa). Against the film's *overt* melodramatic template, this role-play trajectory appears idiosyncratic, even antigeneric. But by drawing upon the film's *tacit* detective schema we begin to discover quite traditional generic maneuvers. In this instance, then, storytelling is not antigeneric; rather, it cleaves to a generic paradigm that the film on the whole keeps hidden.

---

11. In their assumption of alternative identities, *In the Mood for Love*'s protagonists recall Faye's flirtation with the stewardess's identity in *Chungking Express*. Unlike Su and Chow, however, Faye resists the temptation to inauthentically immerse herself in her romantic rival's identity. Instead she pursues an authentic course of action by acknowledging and fulfilling desires of her own, experiencing life in California.

12. A kind of ambiguous double relationship is implied in the protagonists' mutual attraction: Has Su fallen in love with Chow or with the character he incarnates (which is, paradoxically, Su's own husband)? Is Chow attracted to Su or merely to his wife's "copy"?

Tacit detective elements are brought palpably to the fore by the film's scenographic design. Noir iconography invades the mise-en-scène—ringing telephones and doorbells remain discomfortingly unanswered (as in Preminger's noir-melodrama *Daisy Kenyon*), cigarettes are obsessively smoked and furnish a ubiquitous marker of anxiety,[13] and at night a perpetual torrent engulfs the lamp-lined streets. An otherwise latent detective schema here parades on the film's surface, cuing the viewer to search for other detective elements in the film.

Aside from story action and iconography, these detective elements radiate from the film's narrational point of view. It is here that the film most consistently subverts conventional melodramatic storytelling. Bordwell argues that a melodrama's narration is characterized by communicativeness and omniscience (1985: 70–73). A melodrama will construct knowledge hierarchies that bestow epistemic authority upon the viewer. For Edward Branigan, hierarchies of knowledge allow us to "evaluate whether the spectator knows more than (>), the same as (=), or less than (<) a particular character at a particular time" (1992: 75–76). Melodramas predominantly cleave to the following pattern: S > C, where S denotes the spectator and C denotes the diegetic characters. In conventional melodrama, the narration creates a "disparity of knowledge" structured to situate the spectator on the top tier of the epistemic hierarchy. Consequently, the melodrama's narrative is presented with maximum transparency, mobilizing mainstays of the genre such as legibility of action and dramatic irony.

By contrast, the detective film contrives a mode of narration governed by opacity, repressiveness, and retardation. Omniscience and transparency are jettisoned. Even the investigation stage of the narrative is characterized by some degree of uncommunicativeness. In accordance with its narrative emphasis on concealment and mystery, the detective film harnesses its narration to the restriction of the viewer's knowledge. In Branigan's terms, the spectator and the protagonist tend to occupy the same strata in the hierarchy of knowledge (S = C), though sometimes the spectator will know even less than the detective (S < C).

In the Mood for Love's investigation is communicated with detective-style repressiveness. It is not until the third reel that we are alerted unequivocally to the protagonists' suspicion of their spouses. By this stage the film has strongly

---

13. In Wong's film, as in noir, cigarettes and smoking may imply duplicity and obscurity. But *In the Mood for Love* lends this generic motif an ironic spike. The omnipresence of lit cigarettes underscores the protagonists' chasteness, so obvious is the lack of a postcoital situation in which a cigarette may be shared. Inverting noir's causal association of smoking and sex, cigarettes in Wong's film are ineffectual preludes to sex, the film staging an elaborate but infertile game of foreplay. Chow and Su are perpetually in the mood for love, but they do not—as far as we are aware—actually *make* love.

hinted at marital discord (Chow's wife invariably works late; Su's husband takes frequent and protracted trips abroad). But the narration is extremely reticent in revealing both the spouses' affair and the protagonists' suspicion of it. Only when Chow first broaches the infidelity with Su is the viewer brought into knowledge of the crime and its incipient investigation. True to detective tradition, *In the Mood for Love* does not allow us "access to the detective's inferences until he or she voices them" (Bordwell 1985: 67).

Revelation of the spouses' affair invites the viewer to re-examine earlier plot action. Although *In the Mood for Love* will concentrate our attention on present and future action involving the protagonists, narrational ploys such as this prompt us to reappraise scenes whose proper context the narration has suppressed. For example, we must retroactively assign a dual motive to a conversation between Su and Chow's wife. Such scenes are to be construed no longer as neighborly encounters but as phases in an investigation. We might assume, then, that the film adheres to the kind of temporal flexibility that Tzvetan Todorov finds central to detective fiction (1977: 42–52). But contra Todorov, the retrospection cued by *In the Mood for Love*'s narration does not encourage us to reconstruct the *crime* (the spouses' activity) so much as guide our attention to an earlier stage of the protagonists' *investigation*—thereby buttressing our assumption that the spouses are not the center of story interest.

Wong also employs the repressiveness of detective narration to make story events ambiguous. This is especially evident in the scenes of role play, which often begin in medias res and which present ambiguous cues to the performative nature of the protagonists' interaction. Scenes of this kind initiate fluctuating hypotheses: Are the protagonists conversing as themselves or as the spouses they impersonate? The viewer must keep both possibilities in play while awaiting unambiguous cues to clarify the actual state of events. Once it has established the protagonists' penchant for performance, the narration can meddle with our assumptions. It may, for instance, force us to recast ostensible role-play action as authentic dialogue between the protagonists—or vice versa. Occasionally, Wong appends a role-play scene to a "straight," nonsimulated exchange between Chow and Su, so that we mistakenly infer a continuation of natural character interaction. *In the Mood for Love* thereby exploits ground-shifting tactics to render the veracity of character action uncertain.

In the Mood for Love flaunts a narration that is restricted as well as repressive. Unlike melodramatic narration, which provides omniscient access to a cross section of characters, the narration here is mostly restricted to the trajectory of one or both of the protagonists. The narration briefly deviates from this intrinsic norm at an early stage in the film, before the viewer is made aware of the spouses' affair. Here our spatiotemporal attachment to the protagonists is momentarily broken to grant us oblique access to the two spouses.[14] Following an exchange with Su, Chow's wife (whose visual legibility is obscured by distant, out-of-focus, and back-to-camera compositions) is heard to say to an offscreen male figure, "It was your wife." The narration then cuts abrasively to new action.

The scene's narration is *at once* communicative and repressive. Character dialogue is fairly communicative, cuing the viewer to infer an illicit relationship between the spouses. Yet both the brevity of the moment and its oblique visual treatment disorient and quite probably distract the viewer from the dialogue's import, causing us to miss or misconstrue essential story information. We may, for example, be unclear as to the identity of the man and the woman in the scene, particularly since the imagery does not present them legibly. (Su's husband is not shown even in oblique fashion; and in typical noir style, a large object—in this case, a lamp—ominously dominates the foreground of one shot, allowing Wong's penchant for facial masking to come forth and obstruct our view of Mrs. Chow.) This oblique visual treatment of the spouses prevails throughout *In the Mood for Love*. Insofar as they are corporeally present in the film at all, the spouses are invariably obfuscated by repressive framings or by obtrusive objects in the mise-en-scène. The narration's uncommunicative presentation of these characters further sharpens our assumption that they are marginal to the film's interests. Still, the prospect of the spouses emerging more prominently into the action is not extinguished—the narration refuses to conclusively foil our expectation of melodramatic conflict.

But what is achieved by shrouding the spouses in obscurity? Most significantly, I would argue, the physical void represented by the spouses means that these agents are more effectively supplanted—in the mind of the viewer—by the protagonists who simulate their activity. For the viewer, then, the adulterous couple becomes synonymous with, and thus inseparable from, the main protagonists.

A fallout of this conflation is that character individuation becomes difficult to execute. Stylistically, *In the Mood for Love* exacerbates this effect, furnishing visual compositions that sometimes encourage a confusion of its two pairs of characters. Two contiguous shots in particular are worth highlighting. In the first shot, a woman stands in the shower, sobbing. We see the woman through her mirror reflection; she is turned away from the camera, which frames her obliquely from a high angle. Furthermore, the dimly lit, out-of-focus image serves to weaken our visual hold on the woman. The second shot frames a man's hand in close-up, tapping on the door. As the image fades to black, the

---

14. The term "spatiotemporal attachment" comes from Murray Smith (1995). Smith's term "concerns the way in which the narration restricts itself to the actions of a single character, or moves freely among the spatio-temporal paths of two or more characters" (83).

sequence comes to an end. Narrational point of view is hardly melodramatic, or communicative, here. Who are the figures in these shots? Is the woman in the shower Su or Chow's wife? Does the hand at the door belong to Chow or Su's husband? A repressive detective narration retards and lays bare character individuation: because we have not been granted an adequate purchase on the spouses' physical appearance and because of the narration's repressiveness, we are unable to individuate the characters with confidence. Consequently, in an important sense, the central protagonists become indistinguishable from the spouses. According to Wong, "at first I wanted to have all four characters in the film played by Maggie [Cheung] and Tony [Leung], both the wife and Mrs. Chan, and the husband and Mr. Chow" (Brunette 2005:130).[15]

This putative interchangeability is also connoted by the gifts from abroad that the spouses present their partners. In a searching conversation (noted above), Chow hints that Su's handbag is strikingly similar to the one owned by his wife; Su observes that her husband owns a necktie precisely the same as the one worn by Chow. This sartorial duplication thus creates more correspondence between the protagonists and their adulterous doubles: Chow and Mr. Chan wear identical ties and Su and Mrs. Chow shoulder similar handbags. Wong provides the payoff for all this doubling later in the film. By exploiting our awareness of these sartorial likenesses, he undermines our already tentative grasp of story action.

Consider the scene in which Su rehearses a confrontation with her husband. It begins with characteristic repressiveness. Exposition of the narrative space, and of the characters within the space, is eschewed in favor of a single long take, which frames Su clearly in medium shot. Crucially, the narration does not provide facial access to the man that Su addresses (who, though visible in the foreground of the frame, is turned away from the camera). Once more we are denied adequate knowledge of the narrative context, and thus we are not sufficiently au courant to realize that Su's "confrontation" is merely a performance and that the man she addresses is not her husband but Chow. That Su confronts the obliquely positioned man about an infidelity reinforces our assumption that the man is Su's husband.

Moreover, the repressiveness of the composition, together with our belief that Chow and Mr. Chan are physically alike (i.e., they are attired similarly), coaxes us into a mistaken inference. The composition also sustains the pattern of obscurely rendering the man we assume to be Su's husband (out of focus, turned from camera, and cropped by the frame edge), thus further encouraging us to form the incorrect inference (Figure 5.3). At last, we might suppose, the

---

15. That Wong would occasionally enlist Maggie Cheung and Tony Leung to act as off-camera stand-ins for the husband and wife would seem to confirm that Su and Chow are meant to *embody* for us their respective counterparts.

film brings to fruition our generic expectation of marital conflict. It is not until the narration supplies the reverse shot of Chow that our error is revealed. At this point, Wong forces us to revise our understanding of the narrative situation, the characters' relationships, and the authenticity of the emotion expressed by Su. This scene's repressive detective narration generates several inferential possibilities among which the spectator oscillates. The fact that the narration has misled us previously does not prevent us from succumbing once more to its deceptive maneuvers, and we must attempt to determine the epistemic status of the action.

The narrative communicativeness of the cut to Chow's face, while canceling out one hypothesis, triggers new ones. We must now speculate that Su is confronting Chow with respect to an offscreen affair of which she suspects him. This hypothesis engenders several further conjectures, none of which the spectator can corroborate at this stage in the narrative. If Chow is having an affair, why is Su distressed? Is her distress an expression of sympathy for Chow's wife? Is Su upset that she herself is not the object of Chow's affections? Or have Chow and Su been engaged in a romance unbeknownst to the viewer, to which Chow has now been unfaithful? The narration's ellipticality encourages us to fill in missing action by inferring a greater development in the protagonists' relationship than we have witnessed. Finally, the spectator—still reeling from the narration's deceptive tactic—must balance these theories against a broader hypothesis: namely, that the protagonists' activity is merely the latest stage in their ongoing, obsessive rehearsal. Our comprehension of the scene is thus constantly in flux. Repeatedly we are forced to revise our assumptions and to imagine what has occurred during the film's elided periods. Moreover, the film's generic shape shifting comes palpably into play in this sequence: what at first appears to be a situation conventional to the melodrama—a scene of domestic conflict—is revealed to be something rather more unusual and complex. The scene's apparent melodramatic content, then, is disarrayed by a detective narration that is both reticent and misleading.

I have argued that *In the Mood for Love* puts in tension the "rules of the genre" and authorial expression. At the film's coda, genre elements recede to allow the auteur to come forward. Prefaced by an intertitle confirming the extinction of the story's main epoch ("That era has passed. Nothing that belonged to it exists anymore"), the final scene plays out amid the ruins of the Angkor Wat temple. In sharp contrast to the stifling Hong Kong locale, this vast and austere terrain suggests a landscape burned clean of moral and ideological constraints. Genre elements have been vanquished too. Granted, the film's pattern of repressive narration is sustained at the coda—Chow's whispered words are tantalizingly inaudible. But aside from narrational mode, nothing in the sequence evokes the detective film or the melodrama. In effect, the film here sheds its genre armature to lay bare the hand of the auteur. The Manichaean genre tropes that traditionally provide narrative closure are supplanted by a self-consciously ambiguous, "art-film" ending. (Still, this scene cannot properly be called antigeneric, since art cinema is itself a mode replete with norms of style and story.) Disdaining formulaic closure, *In the Mood for Love* concludes on a plaintive note of nonresolution, the protagonists' fate irreducibly in their own hands . . . as it was all along.

In adopting genre as a schema by which to articulate personal preoccupations, Wong deforms generic norms and roughens habituated responses to familiar patterns, thereby repudiating the passive spectatorship associated with melodrama. As I have shown, *In the Mood for Love* poses advanced perceptual and cognitive challenges to its viewer, complicating narrative comprehension. The "false bottoms" of the film's role-play sequences, for instance, preclude the viewing passivity so often attributed to both traditional melodrama and Wong's cinema. At the same time, the film rejects the melodrama's bathos and sentimentality, resisting the use of standard emotion triggers and favoring a diffuse emotional atmosphere over explicit emotional manipulation. Moreover, if the protagonists display the passive resignation traditional to the genre, they nevertheless avoid the overwrought emotional paroxysms expected from such films. Li has claimed that Wong's films "deal with primary emotions" (2002), but *In the Mood for Love*, like all Wong's films, goes beyond the portrayal and elicitation of basic, primary emotions and animates instead the "higher" emotions—complex and compound affective states that are no less strong or saturated. Indeed, I might argue that the film's restrained emotional atmosphere heightens the poignancy of the protagonists' suffering. Melodramatic flamboyance is further tempered by the film's detective elements, which place stress on reticence, restrictedness, and repressive narration. Yoking the detective genre to melodrama befits a filmmaker with a cinephile's appreciation of genre. And by tacitly blending these discrete genres, *In the Mood for Love* preserves the formal unity characterizing all aspects of Wong's cinema.

6 | Appropriations, Reflections, and Future Directions

The foregoing analysis of Wong's work has demonstrated his artistic ingenuity and accomplishment. In the following section, I examine Wong's most
recent feature-length film, *The Grandmaster* (2013), from the perspective of
the parameters and contexts that have structured this book so far: musical
and visual style, story and narration, and popular genre. *The Grandmaster* has
become Wong's biggest commercial success to date, igniting claims that Wong
has entirely abandoned his "local" sensibility and the complex storytelling style
for which he is renowned. Detractors argue that *The Grandmaster* testifies
to Wong's turn (or regression) to popular genre and an international mode
of address. Indeed, several critical reviews describe this film as an atypical or
anomalous entry in Wong's authorial oeuvre. Yet *The Grandmaster* embodies
and extends many of the stylistic, narrative, and thematic features identified in
the preceding chapters, no matter the film's "anomalous" global popularity and
impressive box office success (it grossed $45,270,000 in the PRC market alone).
The Grandmaster's aesthetic strategies attest to Wong's continued endurance as
an innovative and artistically relevant filmmaker in world cinema.

As Bordwell (1981, 1988, 2005) has shown, a director's importance and
fecundity can be further highlighted by examining the uses his or her work gives
rise to. In what ways has Wong's cinema been appropriated? This study has
placed particular stress on the viewing effects engendered by Wong's films; but
what of the films' wider artistic and social effects, effects that Wong might not
have intended or foreseen? In this concluding chapter, I go on to sketch Wong's
influence on contemporary world cinema. In summarizing the book's main
concerns, I also discuss how one particular film—*Happy Together*—has been
appropriated by queer scholarship and thus has yielded broad social effects. I
take this opportunity to hypothesize some of the ways that a poetics of cinema
can illuminate the kinds of culturalist inquiries pursued by queer theorists.
Finally, I briefly sketch potential pathways for Wong's future productions.

The Grandmaster

Foshan, China, 1936. Southern martial artists nominate Ip Man (Tony Leung Chiu-wai), an affluent kung-fu exponent, to represent the region against northeastern opponent Gong Yutian (Qingxiang Wang). Ip Man wins the duel, provoking the ire of Gong's daughter, Gong Er (Zhang Ziyi) (Figure 6.1). Anxious to restore family honor, Gong Er exhorts Ip Man to fight her, and she defeats the southerner by means of the obscure "Sixty-Four Hands" technique. Subsequently, Ip Man and Gong Er forge a tentative friendship. When the Sino-Japanese War divests Ip Man of family and fortune, he joins an exodus to Hong Kong. Also resident in Hong Kong is the Razor (Chang Chen), a defected Kuomintang agent and kung-fu adept. Ip Man begins teaching at a martial-arts school and longs to see Gong Er—and the Sixty-Four Hands technique—once more. In China, meanwhile, Gong Er seeks revenge against renegade disciple Ma San (Zhang Jin) for killing her father.[1]

Amassing huge revenues domestically, *The Grandmaster* demonstrated both the popular and the prestige value of the Ip Man brand. The Ip Man cult—itself launched on the cult of Bruce Lee—coalesced in the post-1997 era, as China sought greater economic integration with Hong Kong. The Chinese film industry embraced the figure of Ip Man for ideological and political reasons. During this period, the Ip Man legend projects an ideologically cogent (if anachronistic) symbol of a unified China.[2] Straddling Foshan (Mainland China) and Hong Kong, Ip Man's biographical legend situates him as an inter-mediate figure, not so much a Mainlander or a Hong Konger as a holistic Chinese subject. Ip Man's historical epoch also finds felicitous contemporary resonance. The ferment of the Sino-Japanese War intensified cultural unity among ethnic Chinese, and millions of Mainlanders (Ip Man included) took refuge in Hong Kong. As Wong notes, "This is the first time that martial artists from different parts of China united under one flag to defend the country" (Rohter 2014). In reconstructing this history, *The Grandmaster*—appositely a Hong Kong–China coproduction—evokes contemporary Chinese Communist Party rhetoric toward a unified nation-state. In addition, the Shanghai-born Wong downplayed China's cultural divisions in promotional interviews for the film (see for example Tsui 2013). Yet neither Wong nor *The Grandmaster* should be seen as an avatar of conservative Chinese Communist Party propa-ganda. Rather, Wong molds the Ip Man legend to his own authorial concerns and tacitly pierces the nascent mythos.

---

1. This synopsis and the discussion that follows relate to the Hong Kong / Mainland Chinese version of *The Grandmaster*. The film was reworked for release in overseas territories.
2. Hence the strident nationalism found in Wilson Yip's *Ip Man* (2008) and *Ip Man 2* (2010).

The Grandmaster evinces the formal rigor typical of Wong's films. Plot action obeys a reel-by-reel logic, revealing the organizational hand of editor William Chang. Pledged to organic unity, Wong and Chang marshal vagrant plotlines and characters—the legacy of Wong's high shooting ratio—into coherent order. Intertitles parsing the action betray the practice of postproduction plotting, but they impose structural logic on the multiple plot strands. Not that *The Grandmaster* is formally pedestrian. Mobilizing an authorial program of aesthetic disturbance, Wong roughens formal conventions. *The Grandmaster* is solidly built, but occasional non sequiturs—most notably, the Razor's action line—risk deforming the integrity of the whole.[3] Genre norms get roughened too. Granted, *The Grandmaster* animates key tropes of the martial-arts film: revenge, betrayal, high-stakes wagers, and the overarching Manichaeism ingredient to the genre (Ip Man is irreducibly benevolent; Ma San irredeemably treacherous). But Wong subjects these and other genre tropes to imaginative revision, as when the anticipated climactic fight sequence—which, in traditional kung fu plots, fills one or more reels—gives way to the kind of pensive coda associated with art cinema (not to mention Wong's own elliptical epilogues in, for example, *Days of Being Wild* and *In the Mood for Love*). Wong's film meshes popular and art traditions, and the strategy refreshes generic formula.

The Grandmaster flaunts genre elements, but at its center is an art-film protagonist. Initial scenes establish Ip Man's essential passivity—he does not act but is acted upon, does not choose but is chosen. Contra genre norms, he is inclined to neither revenge nor hubris. Insofar as Ip Man makes an active choice, it is to *not* act, recalling the negative goals conceived by *In the Mood for Love*'s protagonists ("We won't be like them"). When, for instance, Gong Er beckons Ip Man to the North, the kung-fu master holds fast in Foshan. So much inaction makes for an atypical kung-fu genre hero. More specifically, Wong creates a personalized variant of the Ip Man legend. In other words, the auteur's strategy of disturbance recasts Ip Man as an archetypal Wong protagonist—hesitant, impassive, and averse to purposeful action.

As always in Wong, however, the protagonist must change. Attesting to *The Grandmaster*'s structural finesse, the film's principal characters (Ip Man and Gong Er) trace a crisscross arc of psychological change. At the film's start Ip Man pursues no purposeful goal of his own. But, plunged into poverty by the Sino-Japanese War and forced into exile, he begins to act decisively and conceives goals (as when he actively seeks knowledge of the Sixty-Four Hands method). A refugee stripped of family and home, Ip Man can now only

---

3. Daring to confound comprehension, this plotline draws resonance less from causal construction than from its parallels with other plot episodes. Echoic action posits the Razor as Ip Man's doppelgänger. Wong subjects rhyming sequences to subtle variation, as when the Razor's comparatively bloody rain-drenched fight—echoing Ip Man's opening skirmish—emphasizes the ruthless brutality of the Kuomintang regime.

"advance" purposively, his psychological growth triggered by emotional loss. Gong Er maps an opposite arc of change. Implacably goal-driven almost from the start ("I can only advance," she declares, "I can't stop."), Gong Er satisfies her compulsion to mete out retribution to Ma San. Yet, with vengeance sated, her father murdered, and her romantic prospects stymied by a sacred pledge, Gong Er sinks into stagnation. Such diametric trajectories reveal a filigreed plot construction, but they also italicize an authorial topos of untenable romance. Cast upon divergent albeit intersecting paths, the protagonists come forward as a fundamentally incompatible romantic couple. As such, they assimilate neatly to Wong's gallery of mismatched lovers.

Most tacitly, Wong yokes the Ip Man legend to a signature theme of authenticity. Just as the protagonists of *In the Mood for Love* and *Fallen Angels* deny personal responsibility, so *The Grandmaster*'s heroine inauthentically ascribes personal choice to metaphysical fate. Gong Er attributes her own melodramatic sacrifice—relinquishing personal fulfillment (marriage, motherhood) for the sake of filial loyalty—to a putative cue from the afterlife. Likewise, Ip Man finds recourse to providence when Gong Er declares her love for him: "What we have is simply fate," he avers, prevaricating over his feelings. *The Grandmaster* evokes Chinese milieus steeped in superstition: Confucian martial artists summon arcane pretexts (such as "the will of heaven") as substitutes for personal choice and action. In *The Grandmaster*, as throughout his oeuvre, Wong exposes the protagonists' inauthentic behavior, lamenting a too-convenient impulse to sacrifice personal desire on the altar of social propriety and metaphysical fate.

In sum, Wong both roughens the Ip Man legend and assimilates it to his authorial program. Crucially, Wong's Ip Man is not flawless. When, during the Japanese occupation, Ip Man accepts enemy supplies for his malnourished family, the film hints at a compromised integrity. Moreover, whereas Ip Man is a monogamous husband in Wilson Yip's *Ip Man* (2008), he flirts with adulterous desire in *The Grandmaster*. And yet Wong does not wholly skewer the Ip Man legend. Indeed, he exploits art cinema norms—chiefly the device of subjective opacity—to equivocate on Ip Man's own illicit desire. Whereas Gong Er explicitly professes romantic love, Ip Man remains emotionally reticent. Even Ip Man's voice-over narration, potentially a device granting subjective access, reveals nothing of his desire for Gong Er. By ambiguating Ip Man's affection for Gong Er, Wong preserves the image of a mythically superior grandmaster unyielding in decency, loyalty, and honor. And by roughening the legend, *The Grandmaster* provides a glimpse of the fallible human being now enshrined as myth.[4]

---

4. *The Grandmaster* bears comparison with Steven Spielberg's contemporaneous *Lincoln* (2012), a film similarly centered on a historical figure mythologized by popular culture. Like Wong's

Wong accentuates the drama by means of a musical sound track rich in period detail and epic romanticism. Preexisting Mandarin oldies combine with William Chang's meticulous set and costume design to conjure a sense of historical period. An orchestral music score, specially composed by Nathaniel Méchaly and Shigeru Umebayashi, confers a romantic tenor upon the encounters (and nonencounters) between Ip Man and Gong Er, which is particularly important since their relationship is at times opaque and ambiguous (the string-led theme, for instance, marks their long-distance exchange of missives as tender and heartfelt). As so often, Wong seizes the music track as a conduit for cinephiliac expression: the symphonic score on occasion quotes Ennio Morricone's main theme for *Once upon a Time in America* (1984) directed by Sergio Leone, the latter an enduring source of influence and intertextuality for Wong (recall the Leonesque elements in *Ashes of Time*). Here the allusion is apt to connote both the ambition and ambience of epic filmmaking and to evoke "a kung fu world which existed before the PRC was founded" (Zhang 2013).

At the visual level, *The Grandmaster* provoked the charges of "self-indulgence" (Robey 2013) and "insubstantial style" (Rayns 2013: 77) targeted at Wong's previous films. Yet its visual schemas both constitute signature choices and mesh with narrative themes. Periodically flaring the lens animates the disturb-and-refresh schema, expressionistically accenting Gong Er's desperate bid for vengeance. Cutaways to water droplets, twists of cigarette smoke, and splintered icicles serve not only as rhythmic punctuation but as expressive displacement, offsetting the emotional reticence of Ip Man and the Razor. In addition, a host of visual trademarks—step printing, edge framings, jump cuts, back-to-camera staging, refracted imagery, and visual motifs of clocks and trains—asserts Wong's authorial control, shattering the premise that Christopher Doyle is the chief source of Wong's aesthetic program. (Philippe Le Sourd was *The Grandmaster*'s cinematographer.) As well, the film teems with intraoeuvre allusions: a close-up of a pen hovering hesitantly over a sheet of paper (*2046*), a close view of a puddle reflection yielding an upside-down locale (*Happy Together*), a medium shot juxtaposing the midground protagonist against accelerated foreground and background planes (*Chungking Express*), a protagonist whispering into a crevice (*In the Mood for Love*), the male hero massaging his lover's legs (*Chungking Express*), and so on. (The metaphor linking Ip Man to a bird is but one of the film's nonvisual allusions, recalling Yuddy in *Days of Being Wild*.) Though in some ways less oblique

film, *Lincoln* is less a cradle-to-the-grave biopic than an examination of the mythical protagonist *within a particular epoch*, depicting the change wrought upon him by the times and vice versa. *Lincoln* and *The Grandmaster* both employ the metaphor of the flame (in Ip Man's case, the "torch" of Wing Chun and moral excellence passed forward to subsequent generations) and ruminate on the specific era and how the mythic hero fits into it.

than Wong's previous films,[5] *The Grandmaster*'s visual narration—as with its large-scale form and themes—is entirely subsumable to the author's oeuvre; hence, it is far from anomalous and atypical.

Ostensibly parametric devices manifest narrative themes. One flagrant image presents Ip Man ascending steps at the height of the Japanese invasion, but his semblance of progress is undone by the composition's acutely canted angle. Such compositions, tipping the camera on its side, resonate with the thematic emphasis on horizontality established at the film's start. Beginning in medias res, *The Grandmaster* sets up this theme in its precredits sequence. Kung fu, says Ip Man to an unidentified figure, boils down to "two words: horizontal, vertical. Make a mistake—horizontal. Stay standing and you win." At the climax, the formal symmetry typically favored by Wong Kar-wai and William Chang is mobilized. Postproduction plotting facilitates this structural finesse, as Ip Man asserts in voice-over, "It all comes down to two words. Horizontal. Vertical." By the film's end, Ip Man has endured and—in relation to kung fu, if not his romantic and familial life—triumphed; by his own terms, he winds up in a vertical position. By this logic, the horizontality of the camera signifies a moment of profound disequilibrium, apt for the sudden incursion by Japanese forces into Shanghai.

Finally, *The Grandmaster* endows visual motifs with cohesive purpose. The film's various "family" snapshots, for instance, bind temporally and spatially distinct plotlines together, and they are particularly effective in suggesting how—in wartime and its aftermath—the nuclear family is displaced by make-shift families comprising strangers bonded by common goals (e.g., nationalistic fervor [the Japanese army] or the pursuit of physical excellence [the Wing Chun classmates]) (Figure 6.2). Similarly, the button motif braids together various plot phases but goes further to represent a meaningful item for both Ip Man and Gong Er. For Ip Man, the button, taken from a luxurious fur coat purchased during this period of affluence, is a vestige of a prosperous existence now lost—a prosperity that was both financial and personal (e.g., Ip's domestic contentment, before his family was obliterated during the Sino-Japanese War). Starting over in Hong Kong, Ip pins the button to a wall (as a reminder of his past happiness) in lieu of the family portrait destroyed during the Japanese onslaught. Still later, Ip transfers the token to Gong Er, and the motif assumes new significance. This memento of Ip's marriage comes to represent Gong Er's romantic hope and desire (for Ip). It is thus significant that Gong Er returns the button to Ip Man at their final encounter, in effect relinquishing her chance for

---

5. *The Grandmaster*'s combat scenes, choreographed by Yuen Woo-ping, are necessarily more legible than those in *Ashes of Time*. Martial arts equals precision, Ip Man tells Gong Er, and the film's duels are staged and shot principally to underscore this principle. Hence every strike and counterstrike, deftly calibrated by the martial-arts heroes, is laid bare by Wong's visual narration.

romantic fulfillment. It is a gesture echoed earlier in *The Grandmaster*, when Gong Er returns her engagement ring to her fiancé. Both scenes mark the end of a romantic relationship for Gong Er (albeit a tacit and suppressed romance in Ip's case), and both relationships are terminated by Gong Er's own actions. The migratory button motif serves at once to evoke Ip Man's belated desire for change (he surrenders the last vestige of an irrecoverable past) and to convey Gong Er's inauthenticity (she repudiates the gift of Ip's memento and, by extension, Ip himself).

Intertextual Appropriation: Beyond Parody

The Grandmaster found acclaim not only in Asian territories but in the North American market, where it was distributed by the Weinstein Company as a Martin Scorsese Presentation. Wong's reputation as a cinematic stylist has, at least in the West, been bolstered by the patronage of esteemed masters of film style such as Scorsese and Tarantino. Indeed, one mark of Wong's importance as a world cinema director is the stylistic influence he has exerted upon international filmmaking since the 1990s. I take *Chungking Express* and *In the Mood for Love* to be the landmark films, each prompting a string of parodies, homages, and rip-offs. If *In the Mood for Love* has been co-opted and transformed most visibly in Western cinemas, the influence of *Chungking Express* has been felt most keenly in Asian cinema.[6] In both contexts, filmmakers have appropriated Wong's hallmarks of style and story for different ends. Some films limit Wong's influence to localized devices or isolated scenes; others elevate his authorial traits to large-scale principles of design. Still others have assimilated features of Wong's style to their own authorial aesthetic. A far from exhaustive sample of such films includes South Korea's *All About My Wife* (2012), Mainland China's *Suzhou River* (2000) and *Keep Cool* (1997), and Hong Kong's *The Blade* (1995), *Made in Hong Kong* (1997), *Viva Erotica* (1996), *Ballistic Kiss* (1998), *Butterfly* (2004), *Beyond Our Ken* (2004), and *First Love: Litter on the Breeze* (1997).[7]

Local directors repurposed Wong's devices for outrageous parody. Wong Jing's *Whatever You Want* (1994) and *Those Were the Days* (1997) are typical cases, aping the juxtaposed action speeds of *Chungking Express* and *Ashes*

---

6. A notable exception is Andrea Arnold's social-realist drama *Fish Tank* (2009), which pays homage to *Chungking Express* by employing the song "California Dreamin'" repetitively on the sound track (as a symptom of the female protagonist's self-absorption and yearning for escape) and by adopting a trope whereby the young woman secretly trespasses in the male protagonist's home.

7. In Taiwan, the 1990s films of Tsai Ming-liang—including *Vive l'amour* (1994), *The River* (1997), and *The Hole* (1998)—entered an intriguing dialogue with Wong's cinema, adopting and transforming some of Wong's thematic and visual motifs.

of Time. Similarly, Blackie Ko's *Days of Being Dumb* (1993) travesties the step-printed chase-and-fight scenes of *As Tears Go By* and *Days of Being Wild*, veering toward antic humor; director Ko also plunders the latter films' stars, Tony Leung Chiu-wai and Jacky Cheung, for this triad spoof. In *From Beijing with Love* (1994), Stephen Chow references a famous image from *Chungking Express*, again by means of juxtaposed rates of motion; later, Chow recasts the coda of *Days of Being Wild* as an elaborate exercise in self-grooming, his suave double agent primping himself with blow-dryer and curling iron. Wong has even been complicit in lampooning his own work, producing send-ups directed by Jet Tone's Jeff Lau. *The Eagle-Shooting Heroes* (1993), filmed concurrently with *Ashes of Time*, throws the latter's star-laden cast into a splashy, exuberant costume farce. Lau's *A Chinese Odyssey 2002* (2002) imitates the credits sequence of *In the Mood for Love* before quoting a *wuxia* clash from *Ashes of Time*, riffing on Cop 223's monologues from *Chungking Express* and wringing gags from *Days of Being Wild*.

If so much local appropriation pushed Wong toward fresh stylistic departures, his reworked style—embodied initially by *In the Mood for Love*—soon became fodder for other filmmakers. In Hong Kong, Freddy Wong's *The Drunkard* (2010), culled from the same literary source as *In the Mood for Love*, pastiches the visual design of Wong's film almost to the point of plagiarism. Appropriation often took the form of pastiche and parody, but sometimes directors took Wong's films as a point of departure. For instance, Sofia Coppola's *Lost in Translation* (2003) incorporates tropes from *In the Mood for Love* but absorbs its homage into personal preoccupations. Like Chow and Su, Coppola's protagonists flirt with infidelity; at the climax, an inaudible whisper recalls the coda of Wong's film. But Wong's theme of lonely people adrift in a teeming metropolis finds fresh expression in Tokyo. Further, Coppola exacerbates her protagonists' isolation by making them American exiles plunged into an alien culture. If *Happy Together* furnishes a similar conceit, it highlights its protagonists' cultural anomie less pointedly than does Coppola's film. Not so much a source of pastiche or homage, *In the Mood for Love* provides a kernel for Coppola's thematic and visual examination of cultural alienation.[8]

More overtly derivative is Xavier Dolan's *Les amours imaginaires* [*Heartbeats*] (2010). Stylistic debts to *In the Mood for Love* abound in Dolan's film, which depicts a love triangle among Marie, her best friend, Francis, and the young man they fall for, Nicolas. A string-led rendition of 1960s tune

8. Famously, Sofia Coppola acknowledged Wong's influence while accepting her Academy Award for *Lost in Translation*. Other US examples of Wong's influence include Spike Jonze's *Adaptation* (2002) and David O. Russell's *Silver Linings Playbook* (2012). Jonze's shots of time-lapse traffic accompanied by the Turtles' "Happy Together" hark back to Wong's 1997 gay drama, while Russell follows *Lost in Translation* in adopting the "unheard whisper" device.

"Bang Bang" comprises an overt leitmotif, accompanying decelerated imagery of photogenic players—an irresistible evocation of the Nat King Cole ballads in Wong's film; back-to-camera framings, shots of midsections, and slow motion sequences accentuate the female protagonist's pinned-back hair and form-fitting dress, recalling the sensual figure of Maggie Cheung; cigarettes and smoking come forward as prevalent motifs and, as in Wong's film, ironically underscore the protagonists' sexual frustration; and the protagonists' every gesture and movement is romanticized by close-ups and languid tracking shots. For all its stylistic borrowings, however, Dolan's film assigns fresh functions to Wong's devices. Dolan pastiches only the sensuous dimension of *In the Mood for Love*, eschewing the perceptual obstacles scattered throughout Wong's film.[9] Moreover, Dolan's romance triangle wrings different expressive qualities from Wong's sensuous visual strategies. Here sensuous and perspicuous facial close-ups capture not only repressed desire but also suppressed jealousy and resentment simmering between the love rivals. Dramaturgically, too, *Heartbeats* swerves from a recurrent Wong trope. Purged of their desire for Nicolas, Marie and Francis rebuild their friendship—until Louis Garrel seductively enters the drama at the climax. Unlike most of Wong's characters, Dolan's protagonists fail to break their cycle of self-destructive behavior.[10]

In the Mood for Love finds another heir in Abbas Kiarostami's *Certified Copy* (2010). Two unhappily married strangers meet in Tuscany and pretend to be husband and wife. As the pair wend their way through the foreign landscape, *Certified Copy* hints at other progenitors—chiefly Roberto Rossellini's *Voyage to Italy* (1954) and Richard Linklater's *Before Sunrise* (1995) and *Before Sunset* (2004). But the echoes of *In the Mood for Love* are undeniable. Unhappy with their lot, Kiarostami's protagonists, Elle and James, adopt a façade of marriage, simulating the role of spouses. In effect, they embody each other's actual spouse, as at times occurs in Wong's film. As their simulation intensifies, the distinction between make-believe and genuine romantic desire grows fuzzy—are the protagonists falling in love for real? Like *Lost in Translation*, moreover, *Certified Copy* transforms *In the Mood for Love*'s muffled whisper motif. And Kiarostami's trademark fondness for offscreen space dovetails with the scenographic design of *In the Mood for Love*, not least when mirrors and other reflective materials activate hidden areas of space. Finally, the male protagonist is a writer, like Chow. In Kiarostami's hands, those elements reminiscent of *In the Mood for Love* are not simply appropriated but

9. Ironically, Dolan's partial pastiche of Wong's style prompted critics to gripe that "'Heartbeats' is . . . a classic example of style over substance" (Nelson 2010)—a complaint often directed at Wong's own work.

10. Xavier Dolan's *Tom at the Farm* (2013), though less stylistically indebted to Wong than *Heartbeats*, extends the Canadian director's allusions to Wong's films (in this case, *Happy Together*).

recast and defined anew: Kiarostami yokes the role-play conceit to thematic material not explicitly developed in Wong's film. In the opening sequence, the male protagonist pontificates on the subject of his new book—the value of imitation artworks relative to originals. He tells his audience, "The copy itself has worth, in that it leads us to the original and in this way certifies its value. And I think this approach is not only valid in art. I was particularly pleased when a reader recently told me that he found in my work an invitation to self-inquiry, to a better understanding of the self."[11] This stretch of dialogue is significant, for it motivates the protagonists' simulated activity later in the plot—their "copy" of wedlock has value of its own and leads the participants to self-realization. (The same is true, one might say, of Chow and Su.) More generally, Kiarostami elaborates Wong's role-play contrivance through the explicit theme of authenticity and artifice (of both art and human relationships). Like all good artists, Kiarostami transforms existing tropes into new forms of expression; and, like all good artworks, *In the Mood for Love* provides filmmakers with a fertile source of expression and ingenuity.

Social Appropriation: The Poetics of Culture

Appropriation of Wong goes beyond the uptake of other filmmakers. Wong's films are "used" in various ways by different audiences and for different ends. Throughout this book I have tried to suggest that Wong's films cue viewers to predictable responses, but this is not to place the text in deterministic relation to the viewer. As Bordwell points out, "By constructing the phenomenal film, the filmmakers control very strongly, though not absolutely, the viewer's perception of it" (2008b: 50). The viewer may respond in ways that do not match the filmmaker's intentions, extrapolating beyond particular cues or subjecting the work to willfully "perverse" readings. Scholarship, too, appropriates films according to particular research agendas. Wong's *Happy Together*, for instance, has been appropriated by scholars working within a particular strand of cultural studies: queer theory. Analyses of *Happy Together* such as those written by Chris Berry (2000), Audrey Yue (2000), David L. Eng (2010), and Marc Siegel (2001) represent illuminating interventions that encourage us to perceive Wong's film in fresh ways.

All film analysis is driven by research questions that shape the critic's priorities; the film under scrutiny is at the mercy of the analyst's agenda. Throughout this book, on the one hand, I have treated Wong's films from a broadly aesthetic angle, no doubt at the expense of other issues. Abbas, on the

---

11. One could argue, given *Certified Copy*'s close kinship with the precursors mentioned, that Kiarostami's emphasis on art and imitation carries a reflexive thrust, but I would want to resist this conjecture.

other hand, professes to "use [Wong's films] to pursue a particular theme" of cultural disappearance (1997b: 1). The critics cited above appropriate *Happy Together* not to examine its reworking of genre conventions or its strategies of character engagement. Rather they appropriate the film according to quite another agenda, inquiring into the film's representation of gay sexuality, and centering on a cluster of problems: Is *Happy Together* a queer film? How queer is it? How is its queerness constituted? Is the film homophobic? Approaching *Happy Together* from a particular standpoint inevitably marginalizes certain aspects of the film, but it can shed valuable light on other aspects. Studies of culture and aesthetics can usefully function side by side, just as top-down and bottom-up theory can work in concert. Top-down analysis should not simply be a matter of schema application but should be an opportunity to test and, if necessary, revise the schema. Treating a theory as a corrigible set of propositions open to revision enriches both the theory and the grasp of the films it illuminates.

The queer theorists' research questions are not out of bounds to the poetician. A poetics of *Happy Together* might probe the issues of queerness and homophobia along several dimensions. At the level of the work, one might examine how the film's characters are depicted. Are the characters reducible to their sexuality? How does the narrative develop the protagonists' traits, actions, and goals? Fueling the homophobic thesis, one might note that the central gay relationship is presented as frequently volatile and physically abusive. Further, the film affirms Yiu-fai's platonic friendship with Chang, suggesting that it is more stable and durable than his homosexual relationship with Po-wing. However, one would need to acknowledge the scenes of genuine warmth, humor, and tenderness between the gay couple. Apart from narrative development and characterization, the poetician would examine how audiovisual style, large-scale form, narration, and so on, conspire to ideological effect. Of course, to explore the questions adopted by Berry et al., the analyst needs conceptual definitions of queerness and homophobia. These concepts are not immanent within the film. But, again, a priori schemas should be tested against the artwork and revised accordingly. Research questions might be further enlightened by constructing a historical poetics of *Happy Together*. What historical norms of gay cinema does *Happy Together* adopt, recast, or discard? Are these norms transculturally shared? Surveying the 1990s Asian queer cinema and its US counterpart might highlight (for instance) dominant narrative tropes against which to evaluate *Happy Together*. Wong's plot avoids that era's gay film trope of HIV/AIDS, illness, and death (*Philadelphia* [1993], *Longtime Companion* [1990], *Safe* [1995]); of caricature and feminization (*All's Well, Ends Well* [1992], *A Queer Story* [1997], *Farewell My Concubine* [1993]); and of trivializing camp. Nor does it reinforce popular cinema's depiction of gays as dangerously psychotic (*Full Contact* [1992], *American Beauty* [1999]). Irrespective of whatever cultural theory or social evidence one might bring to *Happy Together*, the discussion is always rooted in close analysis of the film and its backgrounds. No less than cultural theories, poetics analysis is essential to confronting that initial cluster of problems posed by queer theorists: Is *Happy Together* a queer film? Is it homophobic?

Reflections and Directions

The poetics of Hong Kong cinema I defend here—drawing upon the work of David Bordwell, Kristin Thompson, the Russian formalists, André Bazin, Rudolf Arnheim, and others—seems to me crucial to a better understanding of Hong Kong movies. Beyond this, a poetics of Hong Kong cinema can potentially illuminate Hollywood movies. A comparative study of transcultural norms, such as that advocated by Bordwell, can shed light on various national and regional filmmaking traditions. It can also reveal the choice situation of Hong Kong directors operating within different institutional and historical contexts. Further, the poetics approach can highlight the ways that Hong Kong directors, by recasting and innovating schemas, push filmic conventions in fresh directions. That is, it can lead to a greater knowledge of the medium and its possibilities. By extension, the poetics approach leads to greater discoveries about the viewer. For instance, it might suggest how distinctive filmmaking traditions (e.g., Hong Kong action cinema) sharpen specific viewing skills—skills that may be distinctive to Hong Kong cinema or transculturally shared with other filmmaking traditions. I have also tried to demonstrate the methodological virtues of a film poetics. The book's film analyses employ an inductive method, starting from the bottom up. Consequently, the generalized principles I postulate, such as expressive displacement, motivated sensuousness, and an aesthetic of disturbance, emerge not from predetermined grand theories but from close analysis of the works' aesthetic qualities. An objector might counter that by relying on neoformalist concepts (such as roughened form and the dominant) I have mapped preexisting concepts onto Wong's films—exactly the method I caution against. But these concepts are heuristic tools; the critic cannot know in advance how they are constituted within the work, what they might reveal about the work, or how they contribute to the work's meanings. They are means by which to extrapolate principles and norms shaping the work, principles that are not known to the analyst beforehand. In a given film, roughened form may pertain only to an isolated segment or device. But, by approaching Wong's films inductively, I have suggested that roughened form—or what I have called "disturbance"—is less an occasional device than a constructive principle; perhaps even the "dominant" of Wong's cinema.

Indeed, I have argued that in Wong's cinema an aesthetic of disturbance permeates all features of story and style—musical and visual style, narrative structure, narration, and genre. Disturbance also characterizes the viewer's perception, comprehension, and emotional response. In addition, I have suggested that this aesthetic springs largely from Wong's distinctive working habits and mode of production. The aesthetically avant-garde tendency within Wong's work is subordinated, I have argued, to the traditional principles of the well-made story. In a way, this means that Wong is a conservative filmmaker, but this is not to deny the difficulties posed by his work or the innovations it has engendered. At a more abstract level, my postulation of an aesthetic of disturbance—and other arguments about Wong's cinema that I have set forth—arises in response to a set of questions framing this book. What principles of story and style govern Wong's cinema? How do the films generate complex effects? How do they extend, revise, or conform to pertinent traditions of cinema? What is the role and significance of sensuousness in Wong's work? To what extent can the films be subsumed to parametric form? Can they be characterized according to established genre frameworks? How can the films' affective tone and emotional effects be characterized?

In addressing these questions, I have found it necessary to counter or qualify standard descriptions of Wong's cinema. Thus, throughout the book I have tried to redress claims such as the following: *Happy Together* displays "a striking mannerist style in search of content" (Rosenbaum 1998). Call this the aesthete perspective. The previous chapters have sought to disclaim the premise that Wong's films are primarily sensuous, wholly stylistic, superficial, and devoid of ideas. Nor, I have argued, do they seduce the viewer into passive dream states. Likewise, I have qualified the postmodernist perspective, which portrays Wong's films as fragmented, nostalgic, prone to pastiche, and radically new. And I have nuanced the allegorist perspective, challenging the assumption that Wong's films are best understood as 1997 allegories and, moreover, that this allegory forms the basis of their artistic and cultural value. I have not denied that at least some of Wong's films allegorize the 1997 handover. Nor have I argued for poetics to supplant culturalist approaches. Indeed, I believe that culturalism and poetics can be joined together, just as I believe that bottom-up and top-down analysis constitutes complementary analytical practices.

What of Wong today? Critical and audience reaction to *The Grandmaster* suggests that he provided a successful payoff to the tantalizing one sheets and coy teaser trailers that sustained a patient, enthusiastic audience through the film's years of gestation. In the wake of *The Grandmaster*'s acclaim, Wong prevaricated in interviews about his next film production. Perpetually, it seems, Wong's career has always been caught in a swirl of mooted projects and uncharted directions. There are the mythical unmade films, intriguing enterprises that may never reach fruition. Most tantalizing among these is *The Lady from Shanghai*, an aborted romantic thriller set in the 1930s (purportedly not related to Orson Welles' 1947 noir). It was budgeted at $30 million to facilitate both the film's international stars (Nicole Kidman and Gong Li) and its extensive location shooting in Russia, Shanghai, and New York (Frater 2006; Lim 2006). The film's preproduction goes back at least to 2003, but the project had fizzled by 2008.

Aside from his own films, Wong remains a discerning producer of other directors' work. Under the auspices of Jet Tone, he has produced films mainly for pan-Asian markets and the Chinese diaspora (e.g., *Miao Miao* [2008]). As a producer he is equally savvy about the international market. During the long gestation of *The Lady from Shanghai*, Wong and Jet Tone strategically issued the film's sleek teaser poster at the 2006 Berlin Film Festival, reviving audience interest. Today, the international market remains paramount for Wong's own films, which target at least as much a Western cognoscenti as a pan-Asian audience. For instance, *Ashes of Time Redux*, like many Wong films (particularly since the mid-1990s), was intended less for the local Hong Kong market than for international distribution on the festival circuit. As Wong stated in 2001, "Our films are no longer bound by the local markets. With the decline of the Asian economy, we must discover new ways of financing movies and new audiences" (Beals 2001: 68).

Since then, Hong Kong directors have turned increasingly to Mainland China for cofinancing and greater market share. The rise in Chinese coproductions coincided with the 1997 reunification, and it surged as the local territory negotiated video piracy, the Asian economic crisis, the SARS epidemic, the dominance of Hollywood product, and the exodus of local talent to the United States. Another major stimulus was the Close Economic Partnership Arrangement, signed in 2003, which exempted Hong Kong movies from the PRC's quota restrictions, granting local movies exhibition in the lucrative Chinese market. Coproduction regulations were also relaxed, removing strictures that had previously disadvantaged the Hong Kong party (see Bordwell 2011: 194). Under these circumstances, the Hong Kong–China coproduction model represents an enticing option for local directors. Chinese coproductions spread risk, provide greater market access, furnish access to extensive infrastructure and studio facilities, offer more options for location shooting, and generally boost production values (see Bettinson 2012: 6–10). The PRC's "blackout" policy, periodically allowing domestic films to dominate China's box office by suspending Hollywood imports, provides a further strong incentive to Hong Kong directors. Yet China coproductions can exact severe costs. Most impedimental is PRC censorship, an opaque and capricious system militating against types of content popular with Hong Kong audiences (e.g., ghost stories, outré violence, morally corrupt heroes). Authority figures (police officers, doctors, teachers) are not to be criticized; criminals should not be glorified; politically sensitive issues must be avoided. Some Hong Kong directors, seeking to preempt Mainland censors, exercise self-censorship at the risk of sanitizing their own work (9). Further, the rise in Chinese coproductions augurs the decline of Cantonese-language cinema, jeopardizing popular local traditions such as *mo-lei-tau* comedy. In short, Hong Kong–China joint ventures imperil both local cultural traditions and free creative expression.

It is hard to imagine Wong accepting such constraints. Though his films are often partially financed by Mainland studios, and *The Grandmaster* is a PRC coproduction, Wong has mostly sought production allies outside the state system. Logically, given Wong's reliance on Western markets, he gravitates toward European partners, particularly from France. But he also favors a pan-Asian model of production, assembling investors, cast, crew, and locations from different Asian territories. Of course, these coproduction models impose constraints of their own (for instance, financiers often favor their own market and expect the filmmaker to cater to that territory's tastes and demands). In any case, as Andrew Sarris once wrote, "no artist is ever completely free, and art does not necessarily thrive as it becomes less constrained" (1962: 65). Like all directors reared in Hong Kong's popular cinema, Wong knows how to create art under stringent conditions. Artistically speaking, however, his is a cinema without compromise. His oeuvre testifies to a consistency of vision. Themes braided throughout his films, such as the fallacy of self-deception, articulate an authorial worldview. And a dedication to favorite compositional principles governs his oeuvre. Committed to popular appeals, Wong constructs his films as richly sensuous experiences. He also constructs them as difficult experiences, pressing the limits both of filmic form and of the viewer's perception. These twin impulses—so central to Wong's artistic sensibility—produce a poetics of cinema at once intellectually keen and profoundly affecting.

Bibliography

Abbas, Ackbar. 1997a. "The Erotics of Disappointment." In *Wong Kar-wai*, edited by Daniele Riviere, 39–81. Paris: Editions Dis Voir.

———. 1997b. *Hong Kong: Culture and the Politics of Disappearance*. Minneapolis and London: University of Minnesota Press.

———. 2001. "(H)Edge City: A Response to 'Becoming (Postcolonial) Hong Kong.'" *Cultural Studies* 15 (3/4): 621–26.

Ashbrook, John (ed.). 1997. *The Crime Time Filmbook*. Hertfordshire: No Exit Press.

Bazin, André. 1985. "On the *Politique des Auteurs*." In *Cahiers du Cinéma: The 1950s; Neo-Realism, Hollywood, New Wave*, edited by Jim Hillier, 248–59. Cambridge, MA: Harvard University Press.

Beals, Gregory. 2001. "It's Nostalgia in the Future." *Newsweek* (May 21), 68.

Berry, Chris. 2000. "Happy Alone?" *Journal of Homosexuality* 39 (3–4): 187–200.

Berry, Chris, and Mary Ann Farquhar. 1994. "Post-Socialist Strategies: An Analysis of *Yellow Earth* and *Black Cannon Incident*." In *Cinematic Landscapes: Observations on the Visual Arts and Cinema of China and Japan*, edited by Linda C. Ehrlich and David Desser, 84–100. Austin: University of Texas Press.

Bettinson, Gary (ed.). 2008. "New Blood: An Interview with Soi Cheang." *Journal of Chinese Cinemas* 2 (3): 211–24.

——— (ed.). 2012. *Directory of World Cinema: China*. Bristol and Chicago: Intellect Press.

———. 2013. "The Sounds of Hong Kong Cinema: Johnnie To, Milkyway Image, and the Sound Track." *Jump Cut: A Review of Contemporary Media*, no. 55. http://www.ejumpcut.org/currentissue/BettinsonToAudio/index.html. Retrieved March 7, 2014.

——— (ed.). 2014. *Directory of World Cinema: China 2*. Bristol and Chicago: Intellect Press.

Betz, Mark. 2010. "Beyond Europe: On Parametric Transcendence." In *Global Art Cinema: New Theories and Histories*, edited by Rosalind Galt and Karl Schoonover, 31–47. Oxford and New York: Oxford University Press.

Biancorosso, Giorgio. 2010. "Global Music/Local Cinema: Two Wong Kar-wai Pop Compilations." In *Hong Kong Culture: Word and Image*, edited by Kam Louie, 229–46. Hong Kong: Hong Kong University Press.

Binns, Alexander. 2008. "Desiring the Diegesis: Music and Self-Seduction in the Films of Wong Kar-wai." In *CineMusic? Constructing the Film Score*, edited by

David Cooper, Christopher Fox, and Ian Sapiro, 127–40. Newcastle upon Tyne: Cambridge Scholars Publishing.

Blake, Nancy. 2003. "'We Won't Be Like Them': Repetition Compulsion in Wong Kar-wai's *In the Mood for Love.*" *Communication Review* 6 (4): 341–56.

Bordwell, David. 1981. *The Films of Carl-Theodor Dreyer.* Berkeley, Los Angeles, London: University of California Press.

———. 1985. *Narration in the Fiction Film.* London: Routledge.

———. 1988. *Ozu and the Poetics of Cinema.* Princeton, NJ: Princeton University Press.

———. 1989. *Making Meaning: Inference and Rhetoric in the Interpretation of Cinema.* Cambridge, MA, and London: Harvard University Press.

———. 2000. *Planet Hong Kong: Popular Cinema and the Art of Entertainment* (1st edition). Cambridge, MA; London: Harvard University Press.

———. 2001. "Transcultural Spaces: Toward a Poetics of Chinese Film." *Post Script* 20 (2/3): 9–24.

———. 2005. *The Cinema of Eisenstein.* New York and London: Routledge.

———. 2007. "Bergman, Antonioni, and the Stubborn Stylists." *Observations on Film Art: David Bordwell's Website on Cinema* (August 11). http://www.davidbordwell.net/blog/2007/08/11/bergman-antonioni-and-the-stubborn-stylists/ Retrieved August 3, 2012.

———. 2008a. "Years of Being Obscure." *Observations on Film Art: David Bordwell's Website on Cinema* (June 24). http://www.davidbordwell.net/blog/2008/06/24/years-of-being-obscure/. Retrieved April 8, 2012.

———. 2008b. *Poetics of Cinema.* New York and London: Routledge.

———. 2011. *Planet Hong Kong: Popular Cinema and the Art of Entertainment* (2nd edition). Madison, WI: Irvington Way Institute Press.

Bosley, Rachael K. 2001. "Infidelity in the Far East." *American Cinematographer* 8: (2) (February): 22–30.

Boyd, Brian. 2009. *On the Origin of Stories: Evolution, Cognition, and Fiction.* Cambridge, MA; London: Belknap Press / Harvard University Press.

Branigan, Edward. 1992. *Narrative Comprehension and Film.* London: Routledge.

Brooke, Michael. 2008. "My Blueberry Nights" (review). *Sight & Sound* (March), 74.

Brooks, Peter. 1995. *The Melodramatic Imagination: Balzac, Henry James, Melodrama, and the Mode of Excess.* New Haven, CT: Yale University Press.

Brooks, Xan. 2007. "Cannes Opens with a Dud: The New Wong Kar-wai." *Guardian Film Blog.* http://www.guardian.co.uk/film/filmblog/2007/may/16/cannesopens withyetanother. Retrieved August 3, 2012.

Brunette, Peter. 2005. *Wong Kar-wai.* Urbana and Chicago: University of Illinois Press.

Cameron, Allan. 2007. "Trajectories of Identification: Travel and Global Culture in the Films of Wong Kar-wai." *Jump Cut: A Review of Contemporary Media*, no. 49 (Spring). http://www.ejumpcut.org/archive/jc49.2007/wongKarWai/

Campbell, Joseph, and Bill Moyers. 1988. *The Power of Myth*, edited by Betty Sue Flowers. New York: Bantam Doubleday.

Carroll, Noël. 1996. "Prospects for Film Theory: A Personal Assessment." In *Post-Theory: Reconstructing Film Studies*, edited by David Bordwell and Noël Carroll, 37–68. Madison: University of Wisconsin Press.

Cassegard, Carl. 2005. "Ghosts, Angels, and Repetition in the Films of Wong Kar-wai." *Film International* 16 (4): 10–23.

Chan, Natalia Sui Hung. 2000. "Rewriting History: Hong Kong Nostalgia Cinema and Its Social Practice." In *The Cinema of Hong Kong: History, Arts, Identity*, edited by Po Shek Fu and David Desser, 252–72. Cambridge: Cambridge University Press.

Chan, Stephen Ching-kiu. 2001. "Figures of Hope and the Filmic Imaginary of Jianghu in Contemporary Hong Kong Cinema." *Cultural Studies* 15 (3/4): 486–514.

Chang, Justin. 2007. "*Blueberry* Holds No Language Barrier." *Variety* (May 16). http://www.varietyasiaonline.com/index2.php?option=com_context&task=view&id=1. Retrieved June 21, 2007.

Chapple, Lynda. 2011. "Memory, Nostalgia and the Feminine: *In the Mood for Love* and Those *Qipaos*." In *Millennial Cinema: Memory in Global Film*, edited by Amresh Sinha and Terence McSweeney, 209–21. London and New York: Wallflower Press.

Charity, Tom. 1995. "Hong Kong Phewy." *Time Out* 1306 (August 30–September 6): 14–15.

Chatman, Seymour. 1990. *Coming to Terms: The Rhetoric of Narrative in Fiction Film*. Ithaca, NY; London: Cornell University Press.

Chaudhuri, Shohini. 2005. *Contemporary World Cinema: Europe, the Middle East, East Asia, South Asia*. Edinburgh: Edinburgh University Press.

Cheng, Scarlet. 2000. "Ahfei Zheng Zhuan / Days of Being Wild." In *International Dictionary of Films and Filmmakers: Films* (4th edition), edited by Tom Pendergast and Sara Pendergast, 18–20. Detroit and London: St. James Press.

Chion, Michel. 1994. *Audio-Vision: Sound on Screen*. Translated by Claudia Gorbman. New York: Columbia University Press.

Chow, Rey. 1999. "Nostalgia of the New Wave: Structure in Wong Kar-wai's *Happy Together*." *Camera Obscura* 42:31–47.

———. 2006. "Sentimental Returns: On the Uses of the Everyday in the Recent Films of Zhang Yimou and Wong Kar-wai." In *Reading Chinese Transnationalisms: Society, Literature, Film*, edited by Maria N. Ng and Philip Holden, 173–87. Hong Kong: Hong Kong University Press.

Cocteau, Jean, and André Fraigneau. 1972. *Cocteau on the Film: Conversations with Jean Cocteau*. Translated by Vera Traill. New York: Dover Publications.

Collier, Joelle. 1999. "A Repetition Compulsion: Discontinuity Editing, Classical Chinese Aesthetics, and Hong Kong's Culture of Disappearance." *Asian Cinema* 10 (2) (Spring/Summer), 67–79.

Cook, Pam. 1979/1980. "Star Signs." *Screen* 20 (3/4) (Winter): 80–88.

———. 2005. *Screening the Past: Memory and Nostalgia in Cinema*. London and New York: Routledge.

Cooper, David E. 2000. *Existentialism: A Reconstruction* (2nd edition). Oxford: Basil Blackwell.

Corless, Kieron, and Chris Darke. 2007. *Inside the World's Cannes Premier Film Festival*. London: Faber and Faber.

Corliss, Mary. 2000. "Murder on the Riviera." *Film Comment* 36 (4) (July/August): 67–70.

Davis, Bob. 2005. "A Time-Traveling Romance." *American Cinematographer* 86 (9) (September): 26–29.

de Carvalho, L. M. M. 2008. "Memories of Sound and Light: Musical Discourse in the Films of Wong Kar-wai." *Journal of Chinese Cinemas* 2 (3): 197–210.

Dissanayake, Wimal (ed.). 1993. *Melodrama and Asian Cinema*. Cambridge: Cambridge University Press.

———. 2003. *Wong Kar-wai's Ashes of Time*. Hong Kong: Hong Kong University Press.

Douchet, Jean. 1998. "The French New Wave: Its Influence and Decline." *Cineaste* 24 (1): 16–18.

Doyle, Christopher. 2003. *There Is a Crack in Everything*. Hong Kong: Scout Gallery.

Doyle, Christopher, and Tony Rayns. 1998. "Don't Try for Me, Argentina." *Projections 8: Film-makers on Film-making*, edited by John Boorman and Walter Donahue, 155–82. London and Boston: Faber.

Dyer, Richard. 1993. *The Matter of Images: Essays on Representation*. London: Routledge.

Eisenstein, Sergei. 1986. *The Film Sense*. London: Faber and Faber.

Ekman, Paul (ed.). 1982. *Emotion in the Human Face*. Cambridge, New York, Paris: Cambridge University Press.

Elley, Derek. 1997. "Happy Together" (review). *Variety* (May 19–25): 50.

Eng, David L. 2010. *The Feeling of Kinship: Queer Liberalism and the Racialization of Intimacy*. Duke University Press.

Fonoroff, Paul. 1999. *At the Hong Kong Movies: 600 Reviews from 1988 Till the Handover*. Hong Kong and New York: Odyssey Publications.

Forde, Leon. 2000. "Close Up on Wong Kar-wai." *Screen International* (November 10): 23.

Frater, Patrick. 2006. "Cannes Can't Go Wong." *Variety* (February 12). http://www.variety.com/article/VR1117937983?refCatId=2139. Retrieved September 25, 2012.

Garwood, Ian. 2000. "Must You Remember This? Orchestrating the 'Standard' Pop Song in *Sleepless in Seattle*." *Screen* 41 (3) (Autumn): 282–98.

Greenhalgh, Cathy. 2005. "How Cinematography Creates Meaning in *Happy Together* (Wong Kar-wai, 1997)." In *Style and Meaning: Studies in the Detailed Analysis of Film*, edited by John Gibbs and Douglas Pye, 195–213. Manchester: Manchester University Press.

Grodal, Torben. 1997. *Moving Pictures: A New Theory of Film Genres, Feelings, and Cognition*. Oxford: Clarendon Press.

———. 2009. *Embodied Visions: Evolution, Emotion, Culture, and Film*. New York: Oxford University Press.

Grossman, Andrew. 2000. "The Rise of Homosexuality and the Dawn of Communism in Hong Kong Film: 1993–1998." In *Queer Asian Cinema: Shadows in the Shade*, edited by Andrew Grossman, 149–86. New York, London, Oxford: Harrington Park Press.

Hampton, Howard. 1996. "Blur as Genre." *Artforum* 34 (7) (March): 90–93.

Heidegger, Martin. 1980. *Being and Time*. Translated by John Macquarrie and Edward Robinson. Oxford: Basil Blackwell.

Hewett, Ivan. 1997. "High Noon in Hong Kong." *BBC Music Magazine* 5 (9) (May): 28–31.

Holden, Stephen. 1997. "Film Festival Review; Better a Broken Heart Than Shot in the Heart." *New York Times* (October 7). http://movies.nytimes.com/movie/review?res=9D0CE2D8113DF934A35753C1A961958260&pagewanted=print. Retrieved September 25, 2012.

Howe, Desson. 2001. "A Smoldering 'Mood for Love.'" *Washington Post* 18 (18) (February 26–March 4): 35.

Hu, Brian. 2006. "The KTV Aesthetic: Popular Music Culture and Contemporary Hong Kong Cinema." *Screen* 47 (4) (Winter): 407–24.

Hunter, Stephen. 2005. "Wong Kar-wai's *2046*: What's Love Got to Do with It?" *Washington Post* (September 9). http://www.washingtonpost.com/wp-dyn/content/article/2005/09/08/AR2005090801902.html. Retrieved August 3, 2012.

Jeong, Seung-hoon. 2012. "The Surface of the Object: Quasi-Interfaces and Immanent Visuality." In *Deleuze and Film*, edited by David Martin-Jones and William Brown, 210–26. Edinburgh: Edinburgh University Press.

Jones, Kent. 2001. "Of Love and the City: Wong Kar-wai's *In the Mood for Love*." *Film Comment*. http://www.filmcomment.com/article/of-love-and-the-city-wong-kar-wais-in-the-mood-for-love. Retrieved September 25, 2012.

Kauffmann, Stanley. 2005. "Varieties of Love" (*Eros* review). *New Republic* (May 2 and 9), 24–25.

Kei, Sek. 1997. "Hong Kong Cinema from June 4 to 1997." In *Fifty Years of Electric Shadows*, edited by Law Kar, 120–25. Hong Kong: Urban Council of Hong Kong.

Kei, Shu. 1991. "Notes on Hong Kong Cinema 1990." In *The 15th Hong Kong International Festival*, 130–32. Hong Kong: Urban Council.

Kelly, Christopher. 1999. "The Unbearable Lightness of Gay Movies." *Film Comment* 35 (2) (March/April): 16–25.

King, Geoff, and Tanya Krzywinska. 2002. *Science Fiction Cinema: From Outerspace to Cyberspace*. London: Wallflower Press.

Krutnik, Frank. 1998. "Love Lies: Romantic Fabrication in Contemporary Romantic Comedy." In *Terms of Endearment: Hollywood Romantic Comedy of the 1980s and 1990s*, edited by Peter William Evans and Celestino Deleyto, 15–36. Edinburgh: Edinburgh University Press.

Lang, Robert. 1989. *American Film Melodrama: Griffith, Vidor, Minnelli*. Princeton, NJ: Princeton University Press.

Leahy, James. 1995. "The Children of Godard and 90s TV." *Vertigo* 1 (5) (Autumn/Winter): 42–48.

Lee, Bono (ed.). 2004. *William Chang, Art Director*. Hong Kong: Hong Kong International Film Festival Society.

Leung, Ping-Kwan. 2000. "Urban Cinema and the Cultural Identity of Hong Kong." In *The Cinema of Hong Kong: History, Arts, Identity*, edited by Poshek Fu and David Desser, 227–51. Cambridge: Cambridge University Press.

Li Cheuk-to (ed.). 1986. *Cantonese Melodrama 1950–1969*. Hong Kong: Urban Council.

———. 1995. "The Polarization of Art and the Marketplace." In *The 19th Hong Kong International Film Festival*, 27–32. Hong Kong: Urban Council.

———. 1998. "The 1997 Mentality in 1997 Films." In *Hong Kong Panorama 97–98*, 17–19. Hong Kong: Provisional Urban Council.

———. 2002. "In the Mood for Love." Criterion Collection website. http://www.criterion.com/current/posts/197-in-the-mood-for-love. Retrieved August 3, 2012.

Lim, Dennis. 2006. "The Master of Time: Wong Kar-wai in America." *New York Times* (November 19). http://www.nytimes.com/2006/11/19/movies/19lim.html?pagewanted=all. Retrieved September 25, 2012.

Lippe, Richard. 1998. "Gay Movies, East and West: *In & Out / Happy Together*." *CineAction* 45 (February): 52–59.

Ma, Jean. 2010. *Melancholy Drift: Marking Time in Chinese Cinema*. Hong Kong: Hong Kong University Press.

Macquarrie, John. 1973. *Existentialism*. London: Penguin.

Marchetti, Gina. 2000. "Buying American, Consuming Hong Kong: Cultural Commerce, Fantasies of Identity, and the Cinema." In *The Cinema of Hong Kong: History, Arts, Identity*, edited by Poshek Fu and David Desser, 289–313. Cambridge: Cambridge University Press.

Martinez, David. 1997. "Chasing the Metaphysical Express: Music in the Films of Wong Kar-wai." In *Wong Kar-wai*, edited by Daniele Riviere, 29–38. Paris: Editions Dis Voir.

Maslin, Janet. 1994. "Mocking MTV Style and Paying Homage to It." *New York Times* (September 26). http://www.nytimes.com/1994/09/26/movies/film-review-mocking-mtv-style-and-paying-homage-to-it.html. Retrieved September 25, 2012.

McCarthy, Todd. 2000. "Cannes Unspools More Style Than Content." *Variety* (May 26). http://variety.com/2000/voices/columns/cannes-unspools-more-style-than-content-1117822109/. Retrieved August 3, 2012.

McElhaney, Joe. 2004. "The Object and the Face: *Notorious*, Bergman and the Close-up." In *Hitchcock: Past and Future*, edited by Richard William Allen and Sam Ishii-Gonzales, 64–84. London: Routledge.

McGrath, Declan. 2001. *Screencraft: Editing and Post-Production*, 157–63. Boston and Oxford: Focal Press.

Morrison, Susan. 1995. "*La Haine, Fallen Angels*, and Some Thoughts on Scorsese's Children." *CineAction* (December): 44–50.

———. 1996. "John Woo, Wong Kar-wai, and Me: An Ethnographic Mediation." *CineAction* 36 (September): 37–41.

Mulvey, Laura. 1975. "Visual Pleasure and Narrative Cinema." *Screen* 16 (3) (Autumn): 6–18.

Neale, Steve. 1980. *Genre*. London: BFI.

———. 1990. "Questions of Genre." *Screen* 31 (1) (Spring): 45–66.

———. 2000. *Genre and Hollywood*. London: Routledge.

Needham, Gary. 2006. "The Postcolonial Hong Kong Cinema." In *Asian Cinemas: A Reader & Guide*, edited by Dimitris Eleftheriotis and Gary Needham, 62–71. Edinburgh: Edinburgh University Press.

Nelson, Rob. 2010. *Heartbeats* [*Les amours imaginaires*] (review). *Variety* (May 16) http://www.variety.com/review/VE1117942778/. Retrieved November 5, 2012.

Plantinga, Carl. 2009. *Moving Viewers: American Film and the Spectator's Experience*. Berkeley, Los Angeles, London: University of California Press.

Polan, Dana. 2001. "The Cinema of Wong Kar-wai—a Writing Game," compiled by Fiona A. Villella. *Senses of Cinema* 13 (April 10). http://sensesofcinema.com/2001/wong-kar-wai/wong-symposium/

Rayns, Tony. 1994. "Chaos and Anger." *Sight & Sound* 4 (10) (October): 12–15.

———. 1995. "Poet of Time." *Sight & Sound* 5 (9) (September): 12–17.

———. 2000. "Charisma Express." *Sight & Sound* 10 (1) (January): 34–36.

———. 2008a. "The American Way." *Sight & Sound* 20 (3) (March): 32–34.

———. 2008b. "Ashes to Ashes." *Sight & Sound* 20 (10) (October): 8.

———. 2013. "In Search of the Auteur." *Sight & Sound* 23 (6) (June): 76–77.

Rivette, Jacques. 1985. "The Age of *Metteurs en Scène.*" In *Cahiers du Cinéma: The 1950s—Neo-Realism, Hollywood, New Wave,* edited by Jim Hillier, 275–79. Cambridge, MA: Harvard University Press.

Robey, Tim. 2013. "Berlin Film Festival 2013: *The Grandmaster*" (review). *Telegraph* (8 February). http://www.telegraph.co.uk/culture/film/filmreviews/9857639/Berlin-Film-Festival-2013-The-Grandmaster-review.html. Retrieved March 13, 2014.

Robinson, Luke. 2006. "Wong Kar-wai's Sensuous Histories." In *Consuming China: Approaches to Cultural Change in Contemporary China,* edited by Kevin Latham, Stuart Thompson, and Jakob Klein, 190–207. London and New York: Routledge.

Rohdie, Sam. 1997. "The Independence of Form." *Pix* 2 (January): 116–25.

———. 1999. "Wong Kar-wei, l'auteur." *Iris* 28 (Autumn): 107–21.

Rohter, Larry. 2014. "Wong Kar-wai on *The Grandmaster.*" *New York Times* (January 10). http://carpetbagger.blogs.nytimes.com/2014/01/10/wong-kar-wai-on-the-grand master/?_php=true&_type=blogs&_r=0. Retrieved March 12, 2014.

Romney, Jonathan. 2005. "*2046*" (review) *Independent / ABC* (January 16): 17.

Romney, Jonathan, and Adrian Wooton (eds). 1995. *Celluloid Jukebox: Popular Music and the Movies since the 50s.* London: BFI.

Rosenbaum, Jonathan. 1998. "Cult Confusion (Happy Together)." *Chicago Reader* (January 22). http://www.chicagoreader.com/chicago/cult-confusion/Content?oid =895367. Retrieved November 5, 2012.

Rushton, Richard. 2012. *Cinema after Deleuze.* London and New York: Continuum.

Sailer, Steve. 2005. "*2046*" (review). *American Conservative* (September 12). http://www.isteve.com/Film_2046.htm. Retrieved August 3, 2012.

Sarris, Andrew. 1962. "Toward a Theory of Film History" (extract). In *Theories of Authorship: A Reader,* edited by John Caughie, 65–66. London and New York: Routledge.

Sartre, Jean-Paul. 1973. *Existentialism and Humanism.* London: Methuen.

———. 2000. *Being and Nothingness: An Essay in Phenomenonological Ontology.* Translated by Hazel E. Barnes, London: Routledge.

Scott, A. O. 2008. "On the Road, with Melancholia and a Hankering for Pie and Ice Cream." *New York Times* (April 4). http://movies.nytimes.com/2008/04/04/ movies/04blue.html. Retrieved August 3, 2012.

Shin, Thomas, and Bono Lee. 2002. "On-Edge Filming and Big Name Casting: Johnnie To's *Fulltime Killer* and *Running Out of Time 2.*" In *Hong Kong Panorama 2001– 2002,* edited by Bono Lee, 37–40. Hong Kong: Hong Kong Arts Development Council.

Shumway, David R. 1999. "Rock' n' Roll Sound Tracks and the Production of Nostalgia." *Cinema Journal* 38 (2) (Winter): 36–51.

Siegel, Marc. 2001. "The Intimate Spaces of Wong Kar-wai." In *At Full Speed: Hong Kong Cinema in a Borderless World,* edited by Esther C. M. Yau, 277–94. London and Minneapolis: University of Minnesota Press.

Sinnerbrink, Robert. 2012. "*Stimmung*: Exploring the Aesthetics of Mood." *Screen* 53 (2) (Summer): 148–63.

Smith, Greg M. 2003. *Film Structure and the Emotion System.* Cambridge: Cambridge University Press.

Smith, Jeff. 1998. *The Sounds of Commerce: Marketing Popular Film.* New York: Columbia University Press.

———. 1999. "Movie Music as Moving Music: Emotion, Cognition, and the Film Score." In *Passionate Views: Film, Cognition, and Emotion*, edited by Carl Plantinga and Greg M. Smith, 146–67. Baltimore and London: John Hopkins University Press.

Smith, Murray. 1995. *Engaging Characters: Fiction, Emotion, and the Cinema.* Oxford: Clarendon Press.

———. 2001. "Parallel Lines." In *American Independent Cinema: A Sight and Sound Reader*, edited by Jim Hillier, 155–61. London: BFI.

Stephens, Chuck. 1996. "Time Pieces: Wong Kar-wai and the Persistence of Memory." *Film Comment* 32 (1) (January/February): 12–18.

Sternberg, Meir. 1978. *Expositional Modes and Temporal Ordering in Fiction.* Bloomington and Indianapolis: Indiana University Press.

Stokes, Lisa Odham. 2002. "Being There and Gone: Wong Kar-wai's *In the Mood for Love* as a Pure Mood Poem." *Tamkang Review* 32 (2) (Winter): 127–49.

Stringer, Julian. 2002. "Wong Kar-wai." In *Fifty Contemporary Filmmakers*, edited by Yvonne Tasker, 395–403. London and New York: Routledge.

Tambling, Jeremy. 2003. *Wong Kar-wai's "Happy Together."* Hong Kong: Hong Kong University Press.

Tan, Ed. S. 1996. *Emotion and the Structure of Narrative Film: Film as an Emotion Machine.* Mahwah, NJ: Lawrence Erlbaum.

Taubin, Amy. 2005. "The Long Goodbye." *Film Comment* (July–August), 26–29.

———. 2008. "*Chungking Express*: Electric Youth." Criterion Collection website. http://www.criterion.com/current/posts/766-chungking-express-electric-youth. Retrieved September 25, 2012.

Teo, Stephen. 2000. "Local and Global Identity: Whither Hong Kong Cinema? *Senses of Cinema* 7 (June). http://sensesofcinema.com/2000/7/asian-cinema/hongkong/. Retrieved March 25, 2012.

———. 2001. "Wong Kar-wai's *In the Mood for Love*: Like a Ritual in Transfigured Time." *Senses of Cinema* 13 (April–May). http://www.sensesofcinema.com/contents/01/13/mood.html. Retrieved March 25, 2012.

———. 2005. *Wong Kar-wai.* London: BFI.

Thompson, Kristin. 1988. *Breaking the Glass Armor: Neoformalist Film Analysis.* Princeton, NJ: Princeton University Press.

Thomson, David. 2010. "Wong Kar-wai." In *The New Biographical Dictionary of Film* (5th edition), 1053. New York: Little, Brown.

Tirard, Laurent. 2002. *Moviemakers' Master Class: Private Lessons from the World's Foremost Directors.* New York and London: Faber and Faber.

Tobias, Scott. 2001. "Interview: Wong Kar-wai." *A.V. Club* (February 28). http://www.avclub.com/articles/wong-karwai,13700/. Retrieved August 3, 2012.

Todorov, Tzvetan. 1969. "Structural Analysis of Narrative." *Novel* (Fall): 70–76.

———. 1977. *The Poetics of Prose.* Translated by Richard Howard, Oxford: Basil Blackwell.

Tong, Janice. 2008. "*Chungking Express*: Time and Its Displacements." In *Chinese Films in Focus II*, edited by Chris Berry, 64–72. Basingstoke, England; New York: BFI/Palgrave Macmillan.

Toop, David. 2005. "Falling into Coma: Wong Kar-wai and Massive Attack." In *Pop Fiction: The Song in Cinema*, edited by Steve Lannin and Matthew Caley, 156–61. Bristol and Chicago: Intellect.

Tsui, Clarence. 2013. "Wong Kar-wai on *The Grandmaster*," *Hollywood Reporter* (February 7). http://www.hollywoodreporter.com/news/berlin-2013-wong-kar-wai-418839. Retrieved July 8, 2013.

Tsui, Curtis K. 1995. Subjective Culture and History: The Ethnographic Cinema of Wong Kar-wai." *Asian Cinema* (Winter): 93–124.

Turan, Kenneth. 2001. "In Thrall to a Romantic Spell." *Los Angeles Times* (February 2). http://articles.latimes.com/2001/feb/02/entertainment/ca-20316. Retrieved August 3, 2012.

Udden, James. 2000. "Hou Hsiao-hsien and the Poetics of History." *Cinema Scope* 3 (Spring): 48–51.

———. 2006. "The Stubborn Persistence of Wong Kar-wai." *Post Script* 25 (2): 67–79.

Ventura, Elbert. 2005. "Pop Sensibility." *New Republic* (February 2). http://www.tnr.com/docprint.mhtml?i=online&s=ventura020205. Retrieved September 13, 2012.

Vernallis, Carol. 2001. "The Kindest Cut: Functions and Meanings of Music Video Editing." *Screen* 42 (1) (Spring): 21–48.

Weitzman, Elizabeth. 1998. "Wong Kar-wai: The Director Who Knows All about Falling for the Wrong People." *Interview* 28 (2) (February): 46.

Williams, Tennessee. 1961. *Orpheus Descending*. Middlesex: Penguin.

———. 1987. *The Roman Spring of Mrs Stone*. London: Grafton Books.

Wilson, Flannery. 2009. "Viewing Sinophone Cinema through a French Theoretical Lens: Wong Kar-wai's *In the Mood for Love* and *2046* and Deleuze's *Cinema*." *Modern Chinese Literature and Culture* 21 (1): 141–73.

Wong Kar-wai. 2007. "A Short Note from WKW." *My Blueberry Nights: Music from the Motion Picture*. CD sound track liner notes. Studio Canal / Block 2 Music.

Yau, Esther C. M. 2001. *At Full Speed: Hong Kong Cinema in a Borderless World*. London and Minneapolis: University of Minnesota Press.

Yau, Ka-fai. 2001. "3rdness: Filming, Changing, Thinking Hong Kong." *Positions: East Asia Cultural Critique* 9 (3): 535–57.

Yeh, Emilie. 1999. "A Life of Its Own: Musical Discourses in Wong Kar-wai's Films." *Post Script* 19 (1) (Fall): 120–36.

Yeh, Yueh-yu. 2001. "Politics and Poetics of Hou Hsiao-hsien's Films." *Post Script* 20 (2/3): 61–76.

Yoke, Kong Kam. 2000. "Tony Leung Chiu-wai: Playing the Role, Living the Part." *Cinemaya* 49: 29–34.

Yue, Audrey. 2000. "What's So Queer about *Happy Together*? A.k.a. Queer (N) Asian: Interface, Community, Belonging." *Inter-Asia Cultural Studies* 1 (2): 251–64.

———. 2008. "*In the Mood for Love*: Intersections of Hong Kong Modernity." In *Chinese Films in Focus II*, edited by Chris Berry, 144–52. Basingstoke, England; New York: BFI/Palgrave Macmillan.

Zhang, Rui. 2013. "Wong Kar-wai's Lost Kung Fu World." *China.org.cn* (January 12). http://www.china.org.cn/arts/2013–01/12/content_27667754.htm. Retrieved March 12, 2014.

Index